DIVISION OFFICER'S GUIDE

A Handbook for Junior Officers and Petty Officers
of the U.S. Navy and the U.S. Coast Guard—
Afloat, in the Air, under the Sea, Ashore

DIVISION OFFICER'S GUIDE

Tenth Edition

By CDR James Stavridis, USN

Naval Institute Press
Annapolis, Maryland

© 1995, 1989, 1982, 1976, 1972, 1962, 1959, 1957, 1952 by the United States Naval Institute, Annapolis, Maryland

Library of Congress Cataloging-in-Publication Data

Stavridis, James.
    Division officer's guide / by James Stavridis.—10th ed. p.   cm.
    Rev. ed. of: Division officer's guide / by John V. Noel, Jr. and James
Stavridis. 9th ed. 1989.
    Includes bibliographical references (p.   ) and index.
    ISBN 1-55750-163-7 (alk. paper)
    1. United States. Navy—Officers' handbooks.   2. United States. Navy—Petty
officers' handbooks.   3. United States. Coast Guard—Officers' handbooks.
4. United States. Coast Guard—Non-commissioned officers' handbooks.
I. Noel, John Vavasour, 1912–   Division officer's guide.   II. Title.
V133.N6   1995
359'.00973—dc20   95-14860

Printed in the United States of America on acid-free paper ∞

9 8 7 6 5 4 3 2   02 01 00 99 98

To the officers, chiefs, and sailors of the Fleet,
with respect and admiration

The division officer is the core of the Navy's spirit.

Admiral Arleigh Burke, U.S. Navy
Chief of Naval Operations, 1955–61

Contents

Appendixes

Foreword to the
First Edition

Division Officer's Guide has been written for the benefit of division officers, who constitute the foundation upon which a ship's organization is built. Division officers are close to their men; they organize, train, and direct them according to the fundamental precepts of the Naval Service and with due regard for their individual development and personal needs.

This book is not a detailed study of each task to be performed by a division officer, but more a summary of what must be accomplished on board ship in the management of a strong, effective unit of men and women. Junior officers will find here many of the lessons usually learned only through long years of experience.

L. T. DuBose
Vice Admiral, U.S. Navy
(Chief of Naval Personnel, 1951–53)

Preface to the Tenth Edition

As Admiral Arleigh Burke said over forty years ago, "the division officer is the core of the Navy's spirit." Every day, the division officers of the Navy and Coast Guard, both afloat and ashore, stand before their sailors and set the tone that will characterize that day. They provide the day-to-day guidance, leadership, and direction for the efforts of the entire Navy and Coast Guard. Division officers are at the very heart of all that is accomplished on the figurative and literal deck plates of the sea services.

Despite the critical importance of all that they do, division officers are often very young men and women undertaking their first job after receiving their commissions. This tenth edition of the *Division Officer's Guide* will provide them with basic lessons of leadership, organization, administration, and training. It offers much useful information on counseling techniques, the conduct of inspections, maintenance responsibilities, and preparation of correspondence. It concludes with some useful thoughts on career planning.

All of these are challenging subjects and are not learned exclusively from reading books. Much of the division officer's job will be learned on the deck plates, from other more experienced officers in the wardroom or ready room, from chief petty officers, and often from sailors in the division. Almost all of what is offered in this tenth edition is itself the product of experience at sea, a great deal of it learned from three great captains for whom I was fortunate to serve—Captain R. F. Gaylord, USN (Ret); Rear Admiral T. C. Lockhart, USN (Ret); and Captain L. E. Eddingfield, USN. I have also been fortunate to have the love and support of my wife, Laura, herself a Navy junior and a great source of ideas and inspiration throughout my days at sea.

Originally written in 1952 by Captain John V. Noel, Jr., the *Division Officer's Guide* was last revised in 1989. Much has changed in those years, and the challenges today's division officers face are far different in some ways—and very much the same in others—from those Admiral Burke spoke of four decades ago. The Cold War has passed to history, women serve superbly in almost all of our ships at sea, technology has changed virtually every aspect of naval operations—the Navy and Coast Guard are far different in so many ways. Yet a great constant remains—the direct impact that the division officer has on sailors each day. It is a challenge worth living up to in the fullest sense, and I hope the *Division Officer's Guide* will be helpful to the outstanding men and women undertaking the great adventure of life as a junior officer in the Navy and Coast Guard. They are indeed the core of our spirit, and the hope of our future as well.

DIVISION OFFICER'S GUIDE

1 /Introduction

Leading sailors is an art, not a science.—*Admiral Arleigh Burke*

The *Division Officer's Guide* helps division officers learn and apply those principles of leadership necessary for the successful management of the men and women for whom they are responsible—their division. It aids them in instilling in these sailors obedience, confidence, respect, and loyal cooperation—qualities without which successful naval leadership cannot be accomplished. Leadership is an art whose practice, as the result of experience, is based on certain principles and attitudes rather than on abstract or inspirational concepts. In times past this art has been learned and the attitudes acquired by means of a long apprenticeship at sea under experienced, seasoned officers, assisted by experienced senior petty officers.

But the expansion of our Navy, the introduction of sophisticated modern equipment, and the requirements of heavy operating schedules have forced junior officers into positions of immediate responsibility with no time for apprenticeship. Leadership is more important than ever in our smaller, higher-quality, heavily tasked Navy and Coast Guard.

Leadership

According to General Order 21 (as first issued) leadership is defined as "the art of accomplishing the Navy's mission through people." It is the sum of those qualities of intellect, human understanding, and moral character that enable a person to inspire and manage a group of other people successfully. Effective leadership, therefore, is based on personal example, good management practices, and moral responsibility. It should be worthwhile to enlarge a bit on this concept.

The first component mentioned above is personal example.

Your subordinates will reflect your sincerity, enthusiasm, smart appearance, military behavior, technical competence, and coolness and courage under stress. To be an effective leader you must look and act like one; in your own way, of course, after your own fashion. Above all, you must look and behave like a professional and show obvious pride in your job.

The second major component of leadership is effective management. Leaders, like musicians, surgeons, and scientists, do not spring forth full grown as masters of their art. They serve an apprenticeship during which they practice the disciplines of their profession. Management, common to almost all fields of human endeavor, is one of these disciplines.

This is a book on a particular kind of management, the management of a group known in the Navy as a *division*. To manage means "to bring about; to succeed in accomplishing; to take charge or take care of; to dominate or to influence; to handle, to direct, to govern; to control in action or in use." All of these meanings are relevant to the term *management* as it will be used in this book. *In learning to manage, you will take the first step in learning to lead.*

Third, but by no means the least important aspect of leadership, is moral responsibility. This may sound like an abstraction to you, but it's quite simple. The difference between Hitler and Churchill was not only their methods but also their motives. Irresponsible leadership threatens, bluffs, deceives, and oppresses; morally responsible leadership guides firmly and honestly, with every possible regard for human dignity. Both may obtain similar short-term results. Your division spaces could be brought up to excellent condition by threatening to punish every sailor if these results were not obtained. But in the long run, your people would let you down, and none would be encouraged to reenlist.

The basic unit in the Navy has always been the division. As long as the seagoing Navy was composed only of ships, there were no units other than the division; now there are personnel in aircraft squadrons, submarines, construction battalions, underwater demolition teams, air crews, and in departments of shore stations whose organization may differ slightly in detail or in terminology from the traditional division. For convenience, however, in this book the term *division* is used in a comprehensive sense to include *all* comparable basic units in the Navy. Similarly, while this guide will be addressed to a typical division officer afloat, it is also applicable, in all but a few details, to all officers and petty officers, male and female, whether afloat, in the air, or ashore, who deal directly with enlisted men and women.

In writing for *all* officers, it is recognized that many readers are noncareer or reserve officers whose eventual careers will be far removed from naval administration. However, few people, at some point in their business or professional lives, can escape the need for knowing the fundamentals of human management. Organizing a group of men and women or obtaining productive effort from an organization already in operation are experiences that almost all of you who read these pages will have, whether or not you make the Navy your career. In almost every field of human endeavor, those who are most successful are those who can coordinate the efforts of their associates and motivate the work of their subordinates. Unless you become a writer or a research scientist, or follow some similar highly individualistic pursuit, you will, in some degree, in or out of the Navy, be an organizer and a leader. Thus, the skills and the self-confidence that you will gain by learning to be an efficient division officer or petty officer will be of immense advantage to you even if you leave the service.

A division may consist of twenty specialists in a small ship or several hundred sailors in the E division of a large aircraft carrier. A division may be composed of highly trained and skilled technicians or may be made up largely of inexperienced seamen. Whatever the size, importance, or composition of a division, its supervision is a responsibility of the utmost importance. It cannot be run by remote control.

A division officer is one regularly assigned by the commanding officer to command a division of the ship's organization. Division officers are responsible to, and, in general, act as assistants to, the department heads.

Division officers have always been recognized as major links in the long chain of naval command. They operate at the core of the Navy spirit. They must understand the mission of their ship or unit, and at the same time concentrate on a great many specific details regarding their division. They perform their duties on a level at which they must produce immediate results. No vague directives can be written by them for subordinates to work out the details. They must be capable and skilled in their profession, as well as approachable, in order to encourage the confidence of their sailors. Division officers must complete large amounts of paperwork, yet must find time for daily supervision of, and personal contact with, their people. *It is this supervision and guidance that must be recognized as your most important duty.* Men and women are obviously by far the most important factors in the success of any cooperative effort; it must be to your sailors that you devote the greater part of your time and attention. In small ships, the division officer may also be head of a department; this gives him or her additional responsibilities and work.

The division officer, the assistant or junior division officer, and that key person, the leading division chief petty officer, are the leaders who really make or break an organization. They are in direct, daily contact with the sailors. In carrying out the policies of the commanding officer, as amplified by the executive officer and the department heads, division leaders set the pace and tone of their units. Either their understanding, ability, and enthusiasm produce smart, able, and efficient crews, or their lack of these qualities results in sloppy, poorly disciplined units. Just as a division is only as efficient as the sum of the efforts of the people in it, so a ship can be only as good as the sum of its divisions.

Purpose of the *Division Officer's Guide*

The *Division Officer's Guide* is not a complete manual for naval officers. It does not include all the information and all the directives that are found in standard official publications. It is designed as a companion volume to the well-known *Watch Officer's Guide,* which assists young officers in standing efficient deck watches at sea and in port, and to *The Naval Aviation Guide,* which provides guidance for young pilots and naval flight officers in their duties pertaining solely to aviation. The *Division Officer's Guide,* in a similar manner, will assist the younger officer and petty officer in discharging the remainder of their responsibilities in the administration of their subordinates and their preparation for combat. This book is applicable to all officers on board ship, in aircraft squadrons, or ashore. It presents material not readily found elsewhere, material that applies specifically to the management of a division. The *Division Officer's Guide* can be especially useful in helping you to meet your Personnel Qualification Standard (PQS), since it covers most of the subjects with which you must be familiar.

While Coast Guard, aviation, and submarine officers, as well as officers ashore, have their special problems in running their divisions, the differences from a surface ship situation are matters of terms and details, not of policy or principle. Although the environment is different, the basic human problems are the same. Where major points of special application do exist, such as an aircraft squadron embarked in a carrier, the matter is covered in detail.

A Division Officer's Day in Port

For the benefit of those who have not yet been assigned to sea duty, there follows a description of a normal day for a typical division officer. Let us assume you have been assigned as communications officer aboard an *Arleigh Burke*–class destroyer. Your immediate supervisor is a senior lieutenant, the operations officer, and your division is part of the Operations Department.

Breakfast is served in the wardroom from 0630 until 0730, and you turn out early enough to finish eating by 0700. You do so for two reasons. First, there is not enough room to seat all officers at once; second, by finishing at 0700 you give yourself sufficient time before Quarters to organize your day and read your message traffic, which you will pick up at Radio Central.

Planning and flexibility are the real keys of effective management on board ship. The Plan of the Day, the Plan of the Week (which is published on Friday for the following week), your message traffic, yesterday's notebook page, and the word that comes out at Quarters are the ingredients of your day's work. Although everything seems to be laid out for you, flexibility will be needed as you reorder your priorities to accommodate the ever-changing demands of shipboard life.

Quarters is normally held at 0740. Officer's Call is held at 0730. At Officer's Call, the executive officer will put out any hot word and instructions for the day. You will then proceed to your division's quarters location, where you can discuss business with your chief and the leading petty officers and refine your plans for the day. At 0740, the leading first class petty officer calls a formal roll. The chief gives you the muster sheet and makes his or her report.

At Quarters, you see your division to pass on the word. Your chief has read the Plan of the Day to the division, and they are waiting for your announcements and an inspection of their uniforms and personal appearance. It is important, if at all practical, that you speak to all of your subordinates each day. Whether it is to stress an item in the Plan of the Day, to make an announcement brought from Officer's Call, or just to comment on some item of interest to the entire division, it is to your benefit to stand in front of the entire division and reinforce the fact that you are their division officer. Quarters is generally the only time you will get to do this, and this is really what Quarters is all about. A muster of the crew can be held on station and often is. Quarters is the major instrument for establishing the vitally important communications between leaders and their subordinates. After you make your announcements, have the chief dismiss the division.

At this point, as the crew members proceed to their working spaces, you will gather your senior petty officers, receive any special-request chits, discuss them if need be, and agree on the work for the first hour of the morning. You will then take the special-request chits directly to the department head for action; if you hand-carry them, he or she will act on them right away. Special-request chits are very important to the persons who submit them; even if they seem trivial, you should respect the importance placed on them. Prompt action, even if negative, lets the persons know their desires were considered and decided upon, not simply ignored as insignificant. If at all possible, special-request chits should be processed within two working days at the most.

As soon as you have taken care of the special-request chits, head for your division spaces. Your presence gets things going and shows you are interested in the progress of the work. You need not stay long, but you should be seen there. This will also give you an opportunity to check the material condition of your spaces. Time in port is maintenance-intensive and requires your close involvement. It is an ideal time to check on work in progress, verify requisitions for replacement parts submitted for approval by your people, and conduct spot checks on completed preventive maintenance.

After you have determined that the day's work is on track, you should drop by the departmental office to clear your incoming basket of paperwork. The simplest way to handle paperwork is to take each item and act on it. Quite often there will be some research required, or consultation with your technicians, or other action such as drafting a letter for the department head. You will spend between one and two hours on a typical day's paperwork, after which you might stop by the wardroom for a cup of coffee, and 'then go back to your spaces, to spend an hour or so with your division.

Work will begin shortly after 0800. By 0900, the crew should be completely involved in its work (preparation for some jobs could make work slow in starting). The hour from 0900 to 1000 is the best time for individualized instruction and on-the-job training or field day and maintenance work. You should try to be available to your petty officers as they direct the sailors, and you should directly supervise some evolutions. By 1030, your department head may have generated some more projects for you. You will spend the hour before 1130 lunch most effectively by working on these new tasks.

Eat a light lunch and try to work out at least three times per week as required by Navy physical readiness standards. Set an example to your division in this regard! Lunch hour is a great time to work out.

The day resumes at 1300, and, again, you head for your spaces. The afternoon is the best time for team training, since group activity is easier to get moving than individual work in the afternoon, particularly after lunch.

Team training will typically last until 1530, after which you begin to wrap up the day. It's time for a cleanup, stowage of equipment or classified material, tools, paintbrushes, etc. By 1600 your personnel will be heading for the compartment to prepare for liberty. You will make another pickup of your message traffic, and then your paperwork, just before liberty call. You will examine your projects; if they are going to pile up, you will have some "after hours homework," typically about an hour's worth, after which you'll probably hit the beach for liberty yourself.

The preceding routine is more accurately described as that of an ideal day rather than a typical day. In the course of the many days you will spend as a division officer, there will be few "ideal" or "typical" days—things are always going fast and furious on a ship or submarine, or in a squadron. Your department head will change his or her mind about priorities, the executive officer will put out a new policy, there will be a crisis when a sailor in your division decides she or he isn't being treated fairly, your chief will come to you with a thousand different problems and questions—all are part of the excitement and challenge of serving as a division officer.

Winston Churchill, a great leader as a junior officer, wrote in his memoirs of the early years of his career, *My Early Years: A Roving Commission:*

> When I look back upon those early days, I cannot but return my sincere thanks to the high gods for the gift of existence. All the days were good and each day better than the other. Ups and downs, risks and journeys, but always the sense of motion, and the illusion of hope. Come on now all you young people all over the world. You have not an hour to lose. You must take your place in Life's fighting line. Twenty to twenty five! There are the years! Don't be content with things as they are. Don't take No for an answer. Never submit to failure. You will make all kinds of

mistakes; but as long as you are generous and true and also fierce, you cannot hurt the world!

Into each of your days will fall a few mistakes, some happy victories, and the chance to make a great deal of difference in the lives of your sailors. Seize the day and let your enthusiasm and enjoyment of your job show—you *will* succeed!

2/Leadership

> Perhaps the most important characteristic of all for a person in any profession is integrity. In the Navy, integrity is absolutely essential or the person fails and the service fails.—
> *Admiral Arleigh Burke*

The essence of your job as a division officer is leadership. You must begin every day with the fundamental goal of motivating your people to the very highest levels of performance. This can be a very daunting task to a young man or woman coming out of a junior officer training program, and there seemingly are few specific rules and guidelines concerning your role as a Navy leader. Fortunately, the Navy provides some very solid preparation and training in the art and science of leadership. In this chapter, some of the fundamental principles of leadership—which truly is both an art *and* a science—will be discussed.

You should consider the ideas presented here, listen and observe those who have been on board the ship or in the squadron longer than you—whether fellow officer, chief, or petty officer— and gradually develop your own personal approach to leadership. There is no *single* path to effective leadership, no perfect technique that will work in every situation. You must adapt your style and approach to your own personality, to the individuals you are trying to lead, to the command atmosphere in which you are working, and finally to the short- and long-range missions of your command. Above all, *be yourself*—develop a style of leadership that works *for you* and constantly seek to improve your ability to motivate the outstanding young men and women assigned to your division!

Core Values

At the very heart of the leadership challenge is communicating the core values of the naval service. Much of good leadership is grounded in three simple words: *Honor, Commitment,* and *Courage*

—the naval service's core values. All that you do in your day-to- day role as a leader should reflect these core values, and each is enshrined in the oath of office taken by all officers and sailors of the sea services.

Honor: The first words of the oath are "I will bear true faith and allegiance." This means that all members of the sea services should conduct themselves in the highest ethical manner in all relationships with peers, superiors, and subordinates. This is particularly applicable to you, the division officer, as a leader and role model. Be honest and truthful in all your dealings with everyone. Be particularly willing to make honest recommendations up the chain of command, and always speak loyally and enthusiastically about the Navy—even when you are feeling a little down yourself. Abide by an uncompromising code of integrity, and particularly avoid even the slightest appearance of inappropriate behavior. Remember, your honor is the most important thing you possess.

Commitment: A second key part of the oath is, "I will obey the orders." As a naval leader, you must not only obey orders, but demonstrate loyalty up and down the chain of command, and constantly show respect for all people working for you without regard for race, religion, or gender. Each individual must be treated with the very highest levels of dignity. You must be committed to positive change and constant improvement; to working together as a team player on your ship or submarine, or in your squadron; and to the highest degree of moral character, technical excellence, quality, and competence.

Courage: The final section of the oath is, "I will support and defend." All division officers must have and show courage—it is as simple as that. Courage is important to a leader both as a physical quality in the face of challenging situations and as a moral attribute in the day-to-day operation of an organization. It takes courage to lead a division into combat and courage to try to change old ways of doing business. Courage is required to deliver bad news to the captain and to admit that one has made a mistake. In many ways, all that you do as a division officer, in both war and peace, will turn on your ability to convey courage as a leader.

Navy Objectives

Just as you must be able to convey the Navy core values to your people, you should understand the fundamental objectives of the Navy and be able to explain them. This doesn't mean that you should give lectures on U.S. foreign policy or the Navy's role in global geopolitics; but in normal conversation and discussion about your ship, submarine, or squadron, you should be able to provide a sense of purpose and mission—that is all part of a leader's role.

The stated mission of the Navy is to "be organized, trained, and equipped primarily for prompt and sustained combat incident to operations at sea." To that end, the Navy's capabilities must provide a global strategic reach, fully integrated with the other services; contribute to strategic deterrence; provide peacetime presence overseas; respond to regional crises; and be prepared both to counter a global threat and to successfully contain regional disturbances.

The United States is a maritime nation, and our country will continue to depend on the oceans of the world for security, trade, and access to allies and friends. The Navy will be required to preserve freedom of the seas, protect our nation's shores, and serve as an instrument of U.S. foreign policy.

With the end of the Cold War, new threats and problems are emerging. Proliferation of high-technology weapons of mass destruction, regional instability, competition for scarce resources, ethnic disputes, religious conflicts, and other manifestations of a less-ordered global scene are coming to dominate the international landscape. The Navy's role in all of this remains to operate and maintain the best Navy in the world, with the finest aircraft, ships, submarines, and weapons.

As indicated in the Navy's fundamental strategic document, . . . *From the Sea,* our role is to participate in joint operations to project power from the sea, provide sustained forward presence, and effectively assist in containing crisis in regional settings. The direction of the Navy and Marine Corps team is to provide the nation with naval expeditionary forces, shaped for joint operations, operating forward from the sea, tailored for national needs. As a division officer, you should be very familiar with the Navy's strategy, "... *From the Sea*," and similar documents.

Principles of Naval Leadership

While all leadership challenges are different—based on the personnel involved, command atmosphere, and mission of a given unit—there are some enduring principles of naval leadership that each division officer should think about, incorporate into his or her leadership philosophy, and refer to occasionally.

Know your job. This first and simplest principle of leadership is, in many ways, the most difficult to execute. It requires that a division officer understand the authority and responsibility conferred upon naval officers; know and act in accordance with Navy rules, regulations, and policies; clearly understand Navy and command mission; and be technically and tactically competent. These are not simple challenges, and they require a great deal of formal and informal study from even the best and brightest division officer.

You have to pay attention during pipeline training; keep your notes; and refer back to them. You must study technical manuals and strive to be a technical expert on your assigned gear. When your department head asks a question and you don't know the answer, know where to find it and get back to your boss quickly with the answer. Talk to your chiefs and technicians—they can help you learn more all the time.

Know yourself. Even the most complete knowledge of the job is *in*complete without a matching knowledge of your own capabilities and limitations. Seek to identify your own strengths and weaknesses and gradually improve yourself in areas of weakness. And don't be too hard on yourself, either as a leader or as a division officer—everyone makes mistakes. Maintain a sense of humor, especially about yourself!

Know and take care of your subordinates. This is simple—put the welfare of the men and women for whom you are accountable before your own welfare. Take time to learn about everyone in your division, represent their interests up the chain of command, be sensitive to their backgrounds and cultures, and be a good counselor to them. Always take time to talk to the people who work for you, listen to what they say, and seek to improve them and their situation—and you won't go far wrong as a leader. You should know where all your people live, if they are married, if they have children, and what their career goals and aspirations are. Take pride in knowing all about your people—it will help you a great deal in all that you do.

Set a positive example. Be upbeat and enthusiastic all the time, no matter how difficult things become. You set an example every minute you are before your subordinates, and they will look to you constantly for cues on how to respond to all the situations they face. You must be consistent, strong, and take pride in your organization. Never talk down the Navy, your ship or squadron, or anyone else in your command. And it is equally necessary to maintain a sharp military appearance, demonstrate a high level of energy, and conduct yourself in accordance with Navy core values of honor, commitment, and courage.

Remember: How the day goes in your division will be largely a reflection of the attitude and appearance you show at Quarters every morning. Understand that you can't afford the luxury of being tired, sloppy, or demoralized at morning Quarters. You set the tone!

Project a clear vision and communicate effectively. Your command should have a clearly articulated command vision; if it doesn't, develop one for your division and chop it through your chain of command to make sure you are on the right track. Communication means talking, writing memos, posting signs and cartoons, and perhaps developing a simple newsletter. Get your message out—be proactive and have a plan! Make sure you have a divisional bulletin board where you post your plan, the command plan, and any information you are trying to get out. Always be thinking of how you can get the word out: formally—Quarters, memos, bulletin board, newsletter; or informally—by walking around and talking to your people.

Direct, motivate, and develop subordinates. For starters, provide your subordinates with clear, unambiguous tasks—this will give them a sense of responsibility. Challenge them with a task and let them take it on in *their* way. If they need more guidance and direction, it will become clear quickly, so long as you have created a climate of teamwork and cooperation in your division in which people aren't afraid to communicate and ask questions. You must hold people accountable, but use mistakes as a means to constructively improve performance. Be friendly, cheerful, and positive, as a rule—don't let your emotions get away with you, especially when correcting a subordinate's efforts.

In a couple of well-known phrases, "remove barriers" and "create trust."

Demonstrate effective management skills. Get organized! You need to set clear divisional goals and objectives, conduct long- and short-term planning, organize action plans to reach those goals, and optimize use of personnel and material resources. To do this, you should gather data concerning issues and problems before making decisions about them; combine experience, knowledge, and common sense in making decisions; and expeditiously address and resolve conflicts. Manage time well by doing the following simple things:

• Set goals and prioritize them

• Make a daily "to do" list and ACT on it; "A" for most important, "B" for medium, and "C" for less important

• Constantly ask yourself, "what is the best use of my time right now?"

• Handle each paper only once

• DO IT NOW!

Also, use the Navy Leader Planning Guide or a planning book of some kind to keep track of each day, what the priorities are, and how you are meeting them. Be organized, and expect the same of all your people.

Build effective teams. This is the best long-term contribution you can make to your division. People work better on teams. You must encourage and reward effective teamwork, promote a positive team image, and implement a process that fully indoctrinates new team members and gets them involved in your team concept as soon as they check into the division. Sit down with your division chiefs and leading petty officers and formally discuss how to set up teams within your division to take on tough tasks and standing requirements. You will be amazed at the results!

Leadership Competencies

A competency is simply an area of skill. In order to be a good leader and division officer, you will need competencies in at least five key areas. There are others that are specific to your individual job and situation, but these are a starting point.

1. *Communication.* Nothing is more important. You must develop your skills in speaking and writing every day. Through practice and study, you can improve in all communication skills. An excellent resource for written communication is Shenk's *Guide to Naval Writing* published by the U.S. Naval Institute. As far as verbal communication goes, here are a few things to keep in mind:

   • When in front of your division, speak up. Sound confident and sure of yourself. Know your message before you start talking.

   • It is perfectly acceptable to speak from notes, perhaps from a small notebook, to refresh yourself on your message.

   • Make eye contact with members of your audience. Let your eyes travel around the group.

   • When speaking one-on-one, be polite and respect other opinions. Give the other person a chance to respond with ideas and thoughts. Don't get into a transmit-only mode of doing business.

2. *Supervision.* This is the control, direction, evaluation, and coordination of the efforts of your subordinates. The best form of supervision is walking around through your spaces, seeing what your people are doing, and ensuring quality is fundamental in every process in which your division is involved.

3. *Teaching and counseling.* You will spend a great deal of time mak-

ing sure your subordinates learn about every aspect of their job, life in the naval service, and—to some degree—how to improve themselves as citizens and people. Take a pragmatic problem-solving tack rather than a philosophical advisory approach. Sometimes you will need to refer a situation to your department head, the chaplain, or a service agency if it is beyond your ability to handle.

4. *Team development.* You must develop bonds among all in your division so that they function as a team. Organizing your teams around tasks and challenges will foster spirit and hard work, and pay dividends in the long run. Each division is different in this area, so seek advice from your department head and discuss your approach with your chief and senior petty officers.

5. *Personal competencies.* Some of the other personal skill groups that apply for a division officer include technical and tactical proficiency—either air or seamanship, for example; decision making, which will become more complex the longer you are in the Navy; planning, which must be clear and detail oriented; computer literacy, which is absolutely necessary in today's sea services; and professional ethics—such as loyalty to the nation, navy, and command; devotion to your duty; and the highest standard of personal integrity.

A Code for Naval Leaders

A few basic truisms about our code of naval leadership are worth bearing in mind. These are gathered from the *Navy Policy Book:*

• *Leadership is the essence of our profession.* It is the ability to inspire people and make them feel confident that they can do the job no matter how tough it gets. Leadership provides direction, sets priorities, and upholds standards.

• *People are the Navy's most valuable asset.* The same statement holds true for you as a division officer—your people are by far your most valuable asset, no matter how expensive the machines and systems entrusted to your care. A corollary to this is the fundamental concept that we must retain our quality people. Each person in your division has been extensively trained and prepared for his or her job—each represents an investment by our nation in its security. A positive atmosphere in your division will aid you in retaining your valuable people.

• *Provide recognition to deserving people.* When people do well, be sure they are rewarded, both informally by your personal comments and reactions, and formally through letters of appreciation and commendation, and medal nominations. Our people work incredibly hard, both at sea and ashore. Awards and other recognition mean a great deal to the sailors in your division and will help create a positive command atmosphere.

• *Listen to your people.* Cooperation and teamwork are vital for readiness and accomplishing the mission, so encourage open communication up and down the chain of command within your division. Involve your subordinates in all aspects of planning, decision making, and problem solving—although remember you are in charge and must be decisive when the chips are down.

• *Accept change and plan for uncertainty.* There is an old saying that you must always have a "Plan B." This means that even when everything has been carefully planned, the nature of naval operations is such that something will change or go wrong; you must therefore be ready with a backup plan. Don't become frustrated or upset—try to think through the crisis and come up with a solution, working with your division and your chain of command.

Division Excellence

Division officers, in their role as leaders of the division, should think about key areas for excellence. Generally, a good division excels in five areas: planning, maintaining standards, communicating, esprit de corps, and training.

1. *Planning.* A one-year outlook is essential for your division. It ought to incorporate training, advancement, and improvement of each member of the division. It should lay out key goals for the year and include a sense of the ship's schedule.
2. *Maintaining standards.* The key here is keeping a steady strain. If you wait until just before an inspection to enforce standards,

you will fail. Keep pressing forward all the time and require your people to maintain a reasonable, achievable level of performance across the board.

3. *Communicating.* Nothing is more important. A good leader constantly thinks about how to get the word out and keep people informed, while simultaneously listening to news coming up from the chain of command from the members of the division. Use every means at your disposal to disperse information and, even more important, be a good listener!

4. *Esprit de corps.* Try to develop in your people a sense of pride about everything they are associated with—your division, the entire command, and the Navy. Many of them will not have had the experience of being on a winning team—make sure they understand what a privilege it is to be part of a great group like your division.

5. *Training.* This is a major part of the leadership challenge you will face. You will succeed as a leader if your people look forward to training, believe they are undergoing realistic and meaningful training, and understand the purpose for each type of training you put them through. Training will be discussed in more detail later.

Total Quality Leadership

Since the early 1990s, the Navy has been investing a great deal of time, money, and effort into implementing Total Quality Leadership (TQL). It is the application of quantitative methods to assess and improve materials, services, and processes of the organization as well as to meet the needs of the end user, both inside and outside of the Navy, now and in the future.

TQL is a top-down approach to managing work and leading people that has quality as its focus. Quality is defined by the user or customer of the organization's products and services. What this means in a practical sense is that customer needs drive the design and continuous improvement of processes and systems affecting those products and services. In other words, the needs of our sailors and their families drive the systems that support them. It is the job of our leadership to ensure that the weapons, ammunition, training, transport, health care, housing, and all other goods and services applied to sailors are of predictable high quality, are of sufficient quantity, and are available on time.

TQL is an approach to leading and managing that is based on an understanding of how all systems of work and people blend together to meet mission requirements. We know from experience that as quality improves, operational readiness also improves, productivity increases, and costs decline benefiting the user and, ultimately, the American taxpayer.

While a complete discussion of TQL is far beyond the scope of this book, every division officer should be aware of the basic tenets outlined above and the following fourteen points of TQL. These are adapted from W. Edwards Deming's fourteen points and appear in the *Navy Leader Planning Guide*.

1. *Create and publish for all employees a statement of the aims and purposes of the command, department, division, or other organizational component.* The leaders of these organizations must demonstrate constantly their commitment to this statement. Two things to bear in mind are: a long-term strategic approach is required—quality cannot be merely an intermittent priority. Leaders must be committed to people and jobs.

2. *Adopt a new philosophy.* Everyone, especially top leadership, must learn the new philosophy. The Navy cannot afford to accept previously acceptable levels of delay, defective material, and/or defective workmanship.

3. *Understand the purpose of inspection.* Inspections must support the improvement of process and reduction of cost. Even 100 percent inspection does not assure quality. The problem is in the process, not the product, so managers need to provide tools and delegate action to appropriate levels. In simplest terms, the role of inspection is process improvement.

4. *End the practice of awarding business on the basis of price tag alone.*

Instead, minimize total cost. Lowest bid has no meaning without some measure of quality. Remember, low-quality materials and services are unacceptable.

5. *Improve constantly and forever the system of production and service.* Data and measurement are necessary, and quality is a changing target—therefore continuous improvement is related to innovation. As a division officer, you should always look for ways to improve the process through innovation!

6. *Institute training.* Job training never stops.

7. *Teach and institute leadership.* The fundamental goal of leadership is to help people do a better job, to coach and counsel sailors, not to judge them, and to seek improvements and change. Change requires leadership.

8. *Drive out fear.* The most fundamental job of division officers is create trust—create a climate for innovation, help shipmates acquire new knowledge, and waste no time being afraid.

9. *Optimize toward the aims and purposes of the company and the efforts of teams, groups, and staff areas.* Understand the customer-supplier concept, establish cross-functional teams, and promote vertical and horizontal communication.

10. *Eliminate exhortations for the workforce.* Slogans do not help people do the job better. Most problems are not due to people, but to the system itself.

11. *Eliminate numerical quotas for production; and eliminate management by objective.* Instead, learn the process and how to improve it. Leaders need to focus on constant improvement, not quotas that impede quality and remove pride of workmanship.

12. *Remove barriers that rob people of pride of workmanship.*

13. *Encourage education and self-improvement for everyone.* Cross-training and retraining in new technologies and skills keep all your sailors fresh. Innovation comes from active minds, and an active mind is one that is constantly challenged.

14. *Take action to accomplish the transformation.* Leaders will agree to carry out the new philosophy, establish a critical mass, and allow everyone to take part.

Here is a good TQL thought to close on, from over two hundred years ago. George Washington observed at his second inaugural address: "One of the difficulties in bringing about change in an organization is that you must do so through persons who have been most successful in that organization, no matter how faulty the system or organization is. To such persons, you see, it is the best of all possible organizations, because look who was selected by it and look who succeeded most within it. Yet these are the very people through whom we must bring about improvements."

A Final Thought

The essence of leadership is making people better. In most cases, people will sense what your expectations are and meet them. If you believe in your people, support them, and challenge them, they will almost always rise to the occasion and perform superbly. On the other hand, if you are suspicious, quick to criticize, and unsupportive, they will frequently perform poorly. Believe in your people, let them know you trust them, listen to them, be biased toward change and improvement, and you will shine as a Navy leader. In a phrase, people will almost always be what you expect them to be.

3/Organization

> There must be a common purpose or there can be no
> success.
> —*Admiral Arleigh Burke*

Importance of Organization

An officer or a petty officer should be concerned with organization
in any job. In taking over new duties or in seeking to improve the
efficiency of the unit, an officer in the Navy should learn early that
the best way to start doing the job is to examine the organization.
Even assuming that you have no authority to change it, it is important to understand your organization thoroughly. In addition to
providing the obvious framework that distinguishes a division from
an unorganized group of sailors, organization provides the members of a group with a strong sense of unity. Knowing how your division is organized is the first step in taking charge of it. If you happen to be a department head on a small ship, organization is even
more important. In this chapter, as in the rest of the book, the
words *division* and *department* usually can be used interchangeably.

Basic Principles

One of the meanings of *organize* is, "to prepare for the transaction
of business." That is a good way to look at your division or department. Are you well organized to accomplish the business of daily
living, of training, and of fighting? We are not concerned with abstract theories here. A number of well-established principles should
be observed in the organization of any unit. After going over these
principles briefly, illustrating each one in terms of a naval situation, we will describe the specific duties of a division officer. Examine the following ideas in relation to your job. This examination
should result in a good understanding of your organization.

Organization can be defined objectively and without reference to persons or individuals. Note that a ship's Battle Bill contains no names; it is a list of duties. The process of organizing con-

sists of determining what activities are necessary for any particular major purpose or mission, and then arranging the corresponding duties in a pattern that permits the efficient flow of responsibility and authority through the individuals subsequently assigned.

The very first principle of organization is that *every job given your division, every duty for which your division is responsible, must be assigned to one or more of your people.* Let us assume that the Special Sea Detail Bill assigns the telephone talker on the bridge as part of your division's responsibilities. It is not only necessary to assign, by name, someone for this job, it is also essential to give some petty officer the responsibility of instructing the talker. Replacing the talker with a trained person in the event of an absence or transfer is another consideration.

Where, you may ask, are the duties and responsibilities assigned to my division listed? The answer is: in your *Ship's Organization and Regulations Manual* (including the Battle Bill). Check through all the bills methodically, searching for the obscure assignments that may be effective only on rare occasions, but that must be made and kept up-to-date. For example, your ship may operate for months in clear weather without having to station fog lookouts, but when the occasion arises, and the word is passed, the lookouts must be posted instantly. You will be held responsible if your division is supposed to provide fog lookouts and they fail to appear because assignments have not been made or are not up-to-date.

The second principle is that *all the responsibilities assigned to your subordinates must be clear-cut and fully understood by them.* Each of the duties and functions for which your division is responsible must be clearly assigned to one of your hands. If the job is a big one, he or she will need help, of course; but one person should be responsible. For example, if your division is required to assign a signalman to the duty motor whaleboat, you must make certain that a qualified signalman in each watch and section is instructed to be in the boat when it is called away.

Each piece of machinery or equipment for which your division is responsible must be assigned to someone who *knows* that the upkeep and maintenance of that particular item is *his* or *her* responsibility. Within the Planned Maintenance System (PMS) (see chapter 9) each piece of equipment is assigned to an individual. In addition, "responsibility cards" are posted in each space or compartment to denote divisional responsibility for the upkeep and maintenance of that space.

A third principle of organization is that *no specific responsibility should be assigned to more than one person.* Closing certain watertight doors, for instance, should not be left to a group of compartment cleaners who happen to work in that area. One person should be given the responsibility and should check the doors each time closures are made and sign the DC closure log. Others may, of course, do the actual closing, but that one person should be responsible. You may not consider it necessary in all cases to follow this precept; some duties may seem so obvious that there appears no need to spell out the specific responsibility. But beware of falling for this easy rationalization; the person you trusted may be transferred or may be sick. Suddenly you find a job not done, and all your inquiries are met with excuses and evasions, because no one, in fact, was assigned that responsibility. For example, when sweepers are piped after working hours in port, it may be normal procedure for the duty petty officer to see that your spaces are swept down. Unless the responsibility for this detail is made known *in writing* to the division petty officers of each section, a petty officer new to your division may fail to ensure that a sweep down has been performed. The subsequent inquiry (after a reminder from the officer of the deck, let us say) will only embarrass you further, because the new petty officer can say with perfect logic that he or she did not know what his or her responsibilities were.

A fourth basic principle is that *each member of the organization, from top to bottom, should know to whom he or she reports and who reports to her or him.* In other words, who is in charge of whom, and when? Circumstances often require unusual arrangements, but the important point is that all personnel should know their responsibilities and the limits of their authority. It is also important that, insofar as possible, no one has more than one boss for a particular task. This is another precept that appears obvious, but few naval units are completely free from confusion on the lower levels of supervision in regard to who reports to whom. If a deck division is not carefully organized down to the last seaman, a mild form of chaos can occur on the lowest levels.

A fifth principle is one that is frequently violated: *responsibility must be matched by authority and accountability.* If you hold your gun captain responsible for the efficiency of her gun crew, then give her freedom to assign and drill her personnel. Let her recommend drill schedules, for example, and take her recommendations into consideration in assignment of the annual marks. Insofar as possible, let her consider the crew her own. Permit her to endorse or reject special requests. If she can only supervise the work and has no power to give rewards or show dissatisfaction, then her authority is being hampered unnecessarily. It should be clear that the petty officer is accountable for the success or failure of her people.

A sixth basic principle is *do not have too many persons report to one leader.* The number of people who can be administered properly by one supervisor is known to students of organization as the "span of control." This number varies, of course, with the nature and complexity of the work. Let us suppose that you have a large division and one outstanding chief petty officer. You can place this chief directly in charge of your entire division or you can divide it into three parts with a responsible petty officer in charge of each section. The petty officers would report to the chief. The latter arrangement would conform to Navy usage and would be the best arrangement in a division because the petty officers, while not as experienced as the chief, could handle their own sections. The chief then could concentrate on the more important matters and not waste time or talent on small details, and his or her responsibilities would not exceed his or her optimum span of control.

It is a common organizational failing in deck divisions that include specialists, such as gunner's mates, to concentrate all the seamen into one or two large groups and then expect one or two harassed boatswain's mates to look after and supervise all of them.

Petty officers naturally want to specialize in order to develop skills useful in their naval and perhaps postnaval careers. Being human, they are not averse to neglecting their military responsibilities at the same time. A division officer must use *all* the petty officers in the division, including the specialists. One petty officer cannot properly control more than 12 or 15 people when responsible for their appearance at inspection, their work assignments, and all the many other details of their day-to-day supervision.

Another important principle of organization is to *exercise control on your proper level* and not get lost in a maze of trivialities that belong to a lower echelon. Unless you take the trouble to make certain that your petty officers know their jobs, and then leave them alone to do them, you will never be free of the thousand and one minor details that can prevent you from doing your real work of supervision. You must delegate the details to your assistants in order to leave time for the planning, overall supervision, and inspection that no one but you can do.

This does not relieve you as the division officer of the responsibility for the personal appearance of your sailors. Therefore, it is important for you to spot-check your people. Take the time to talk with them individually. You must also allow time to check important maintenance items, such as the alignment of your radars. It is a question of selecting the most important tasks to do yourself, and delegating the others to your assistants.

By delegating duties and authority to the lowest competent level, you will free yourself for your own training and qualifications. Delegating also helps you grade your petty officers in working under limited supervision. Always remember, however, that authority can be delegated, but the responsibility for getting the work done quickly and well remains with you!

A final principle of organization is to *divide the work load fairly among your subordinates*. Often the easy way to get something done is to give it to your most efficient assistant. This common practice of piling the work on the strongest back can have two most unprofitable results. First, it encourages the less-productive sailors to do and learn nothing, because very little is demanded of them.

Second, uneven distribution of the work load generates almost indispensable subordinates whose detachment will temporarily wreck your unit. Make certain that all officers and petty officers carry their share of the load to avoid penalizing the most competent. The additional effort involved usually pays off in the long run.

The chances are that you will find an organization already set up and working when you take over. Don't be too hasty to change things, even if you have the authority and even if some of the above principles seem to be violated. Few human relations problems can be solved according to strict rules. Circumstances and personalities may lead to logical exceptions. But knowing the principles can often result in a greater understanding of an existing organization and should lead to well-considered changes, if circumstances so require.

Basic Directives

Standard Organization and Regulations of the U.S. Navy (OPNAVINST 3120.32 series) issued by the Office of the Chief of Naval Operations, is the basic source for material relating to the organization of naval units. This publication is the guide for type commanders who originate a standard organization manual for their own type of unit. Each unit, in turn, either adopts the standard organization manual or makes relatively minor changes in it, as may be required by nonstandard equipment, a shortage of personnel, or changes in equipment or armament. In all these basic commands (ships, stations, facilities, and aviation squadrons), the personnel are organized in divisions. Their division officers are all governed by the applicable portions of OPNAVINST 3120.32 quoted in this guide.

This instruction contains a description of the duties, responsibilities, and authority of the division officer. The guidance included is general in nature and applies to a division officer and his or her assistants in all types of units.

Commandant Instruction M5400.7 series is the Coast Guard organization manual. Shipboard organization and regulations can be found in the CG-260 series, commonly called the O and R manual. The CG-300 is the shipboard regulations manual. *Standard Organization and Regulations of the U.S. Navy* OPNAVINST 3120.32 series is provided to some classes of cutters as an unofficial guide and is most useful. For shipboard organization and regulations, be sure that you use the manual specified for your unit. Chapter 3 of *Coast Guard Regulations* specifically details the duties of division officers.

Ship's Organization and Regulations Manual

A ship's organization is made up of two parts: the administrative organization (described in the following pages) and the battle organization set forth in the Battle Bill. The Ship Manning Document (SMD) or Squadron Manning Document (SQMD) can serve as the Battle Bill. Note that it lists stations, not names. It is based on the ship's equipment and the armament to be manned, together with the personnel assigned to the ship.

The organizational manning of a unit is developed as the result of analyzing and tabulating the work load involved with all facets of operating and maintaining a fully ready unit and translating that work load into manpower requirements.

A division officer is not concerned with developing a Battle Bill, but is required to conform to it when making out the Watch, Quarter, and Station Bill. Another feature of the Battle Bill is that it lists the stations to be manned, not only at General Quarters, but also during the various conditions when fewer than all hands are required. Definitions of Condition Watches I through V are found in OPNAVINST 3120.32. It should also be noted that the Battle Bill indicates in most cases the duties to be performed at each station, as well as the succession to command in the event of casualties.

Administrative Organization

A comparison of the administrative organization and the battle organization indicates that the division of personnel in administrative departments closely approximates that found in the major battle components. However, to meet the requirements of sound organization principles, the administrative organization structure must allow for the carrying out of certain functions which have no place in battle. In the day-to-day routine, the needs of training and maintenance are emphasized, and certain support measures are necessary for administrative reasons.— *Standard Organization and Regulations of the U.S. Navy.*

The first major subdivision of the ship's organization manual is administrative (see in chaps. 1, 2, and 3 of OPNAVINST 3120.32 series). This includes the ship's organization charts down to the division level. Functional guides for each key officer are also included.

The second subdivision of the ship's organization is the watch organization, described in chapter 4. Both the underway and in-port watch arrangements are specified.

A third major aspect of a ship's organization is the organizational bills—administrative, operational, and emergency. Chapter 6 of OPNAVINST 3120.32 contains standard unit bills to be used either as they are written or as guides to assist type and unit commanders in formulating bills for their units. A "bill" is naval terminology for a written procedure to meet a need (as for berthing) or an emergency (such as fire). A bill is a directive that lists the tasks to be performed, the material needed, and who is to take the prescribed action. Note that none of these bills contain names. Personnel requirements are indicated by division, rate, and rating; the division officer translates these into specific personnel when he or she makes out the Watch, Quarter, and Station Bill for his or her division. The Berthing and Locker Bill assigns living compartments and lockers. The Cleaning, Preservation, and Maintenance Bill assigns to departments responsibility for spaces, machinery, and equipment. The Personnel Assignment Bill assigns officers and enlisted personnel to billets within the ship's organization.

These are all examples of administrative bills. Operational

bills are developed to establish standard procedures for conducting recurring shipboard evolutions. The Replenishment Bill describes the stations to be manned and the duties to be performed during underway replenishment. The Special Sea and Anchor Bill assigns personnel to stations and duties when the ship is being handled in restricted waters. There are others, such as the Rescue and Assistance Bill and the Heavy Weather Bill. Emergency bills are written to provide for the proper shipboard response to emergencies that may occur, such as collision, grounding, or man overboard.

The Shipboard Nontactical ADP Program (SNAP III) computer system allows for the automated maintenance of all administrative, organizational, and emergency bills outlined in OPNAVINST 3120.32 series as well as those additional bills that may be required by unit commanders. Once the initial unit bills and assignments have been created, division officers can easily update, review, and print a variety of reports relating to any or all of the unit's bills and/or assignments contained within the computer's database. Additionally, the SNAP III system is flexible enough to allow division officers to create special-purpose reports of their own design.

Basic Definitions

This is a good place to pause for some basic definitions. A *billet number* is merely a device for assigning personnel. While sailors come and go, a billet number remains fixed and can thus be used to designate a bunk, a locker, a rate, and any number of special duties and details on various administrative and emergency bills. The first letter or digit represents the division, the second digit is the watch section, and the last two digits show the position within the watch section. Billet 2-301, for example, may be listed for the petty officer in charge of the third section of the second division. A particular bunk and locker in the division compartment can be tagged with that number. Billet numbers may not always be convenient to use in assigning personnel; each ship determines whether or not to use them, depending on circumstances. As a division officer, you should know how to use billet numbers if the ship's policy requires them. Most ships do not use billet numbers.

The primary unit of a ship's company for purposes of liberty, watch standing, messing, and berthing is the *section*. The number of sections within the division may vary, and will depend on the number of watch sections within the individual unit. Each section includes adequate ratings and numbers to staff all required stations in emergency bills. During normal peacetime in-port conditions, a ship is generally required to keep a minimum of one-fifth of her crew on board in a duty status. Her underway watch bill will normally provide for three or four sections, depending upon the number and qualifications of personnel assigned. The ship's divisions will be organized into sections that allow an easy transition from in-port to underway status, and billet numbers are assigned accordingly.

A *rating* is a Navy occupation such as a boatswain's mate (BM) or a gunner's mate (GM). A *rate* is a combination of a rating and a paygrade. For example, a GM who is an E-5 is a GM2. There are three types of ratings: a *general rating* is a broad occupational field such as gunner's mate (GM). A *service rating* is a subdivision of certain general ratings created by defining a specific area of qualification such as a gunner's mate guns (GMG) or a gunner's mate missiles (GMM). An *emergency rating* is only identified during wartime. An example is information security specialist (ESK).

Special watches will be established for particular evolutions, such as an anchor watch, engineering light-off watch, or unusual weather or ship operations requirements. Of particular importance is the establishment of an adequate watch organization to maintain safety.

Ship's Regulations

Usually bound with the *Ship's Organization and Regulations Manual,* and contained within chapter 5 of OPNAVINST 3120.32 series, are the ship's regulations. These should be made known to all your subordinates. A recommended method is to maintain in your living spaces, shops, and offices, wherever your people congregate, a special binder in which are inserted copies of the ship's regulations, as well as the ship's Watch Bill; Cleaning, Preservation, and Maintenance Bill; and any other parts of the *Ship's Organization and Regulations Manual* that are of direct concern to your people. Division officers and leading petty officers should have similar binders for daily use and consultation. In addition, pages from OPNAVINST 3120.32 series containing extracts from Navy regulations can be ordered through the Supply Department in poster size for display in berthing compartments and crew's lounges.

Organization of a Typical Division

There are certain similarities between almost all divisions, whether they are on ships, squadrons, or submarines. The following paragraphs point out some of the key players and their relationships, and discuss how most divisions are organized to do business.

Division Officer

The chart (fig. 3-1) shows the most basic divisional organization, and at the top is the division officer. Key responsibilities of this officer are:

• Be responsible for the conduct of subordinates. Don't forget this key aspect of your job as a division officer—you are ultimately responsible for the conduct and performance of the people in your division, just like the captain is for the entire ship. Don't make excuses or blame problems on your people—recognize *you* are responsible!

• Keep informed of the capabilities and needs of each subordinate; and maintain the efficiency, morale, and welfare of the division. Think consciously every day: "What can I do to make this division run better? How can I make things better for my people?"

• Report to the executive officer, via the department head, on all issues, concerns, plans, and problems within the division. Don't hold back—your chain of command needs to know what is going

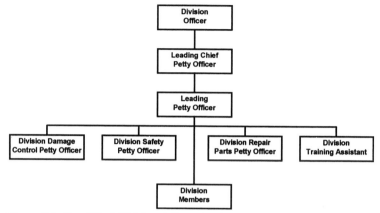

Figure 3-1. Simplified Divisional Organization

on. See your department head at least two times a day, and certainly once in the morning and once before you both leave in the evening.

• Personally supervise and frequently tour spaces and observe personnel, ensuring that spaces, equipment, and supplies assigned to the division are satisfactorily maintained. Get in all your spaces each day, if at all possible, and always look your people over in the morning. Pick one space a day and take a detailed look at safety, cleanliness, damage control, and readiness. Likewise, each day try to focus on one person in your division in terms of such things as advancement, career concerns, and appearance.

• Report any equipment casualties immediately, via the department head and executive officer, to the commanding officer. If something is down, let the chain of command know right away!

• Administer safety, Personnel Qualification System (PQS), Planned Maintenance System (PMS), security, and other important programs. Pick a program each week and ensure that your division is ready. Ask the ship expert (such as the ship's PQS coordinator) to give you a hand until you are familiar with each program you are responsible for in the division.

• Assign personnel to watches and duties as required. Your chiefs and leading petty officers will send these up the chain of command. Look at them hard and don't just blindly accept what comes up.

• Schedule and conduct training, including indoctrination of new personnel, preparation for advancement in rating, and team training. Again, question what is sent up—is it the best you can provide your people?

• Initiate and turn in enlisted performance evaluations on time or early! Take the time to do these right. A good reference is Shenk's *Guide to Naval Writing*.

• Forward requests for leave, liberty, and special privileges with recommendations. Always send chits up within 24 hours, and never, never procrastinate on a chit. Sometimes you need more information, but if so, let both the person who submitted the chit and the chain of command know you are holding it to gather more info and give them the day you expect to forward it. That chit is critically important to the man or woman who submitted it—treat it with respect and get an answer as quickly as you can.

• Conduct periodic musters, inspections, and exercises. Take them seriously and let the chain of command know the results.

• Cooperate with other division officers in the department, and recommend improvements to the department head.

• Supervise the performance of work centers in the division, through the leading chief and petty officers.

Leading Chief Petty Officer

Your chief is the most important person in your years as a division officer. He or she will be the cornerstone of everything you are trying to accomplish as a division officer, and is a person you can talk to candidly and frankly about how things are going, what you are trying to accomplish, and how your people are performing. You and the chief should talk constantly throughout the day, starting with a quick discussion each morning of the day's events. You should also catch up in the late afternoon before knock-off. Tell your chief what the department head is looking for; together the two of you are the top management and leadership team for your division.

The chief's responsibilities include:

• Assist the division officer in preparing watch and liberty lists

• Assist in assigning personnel in cleaning stations, and supervise assigned petty officers in their cleaning duties

• Prepare, for submission to the division officer, requisitions required to maintain allowances

• Assist in training and PQS qualification of division personnel

• Under the supervision of the division officer, assign tasks and generally supervise the division section leaders

• Supervise the division damage control petty officer in his or her duties

• Perform other duties as assigned

Leading Petty Officer

Each division should have, in addition to a leading chief, a leading petty officer (LPO). He or she is generally the senior E6 in the division and represents a key link between you, the chief, and the personnel in the division. It is important that the LPO be honest, straightforward, and respected by the people in the division. The LPO is also often the work center supervisor. Duties of the LPO include:

• Support the chief and division officer in the implementation of all command, department, and division policies

• Keep the chain of command informed of all personnel and material concerns of the division; advance all special request chits and leave requests immediately with recommendations

• Be trained in 3M systems, with a working knowledge of all provisions of the 3M manual

• Screen and sign all 3M documents, prepare schedules, boards, and follow up on all 3M feedback reports

• Provide 3M training and instruction, supervise the accomplishment of PMS and Maintenance Data System (MDS), and disseminate all changes to the system applicable to the division

Division Damage Control Petty Officer

In most divisions, the maintenance of damage control equipment and the training of personnel in damage control is entrusted to a relatively senior petty officer. This individual should be carefully selected for maturity, respect, and knowledge of damage control. The DCPO's duties include:

• Know all phases of the ship's damage control organization and procedures

• Assist in instructing division personnel in damage control, fire-fighting, and nuclear-biological-chemical (NBC) defense procedures

• Ensure preparation and maintenance of damage control checklists for the division's spaces

• Supervise setting of specified material conditions within division spaces and make reports as required

• Do all damage-control (DC) PMS for the division carefully, fully, and honestly; report to the division officer all discrepancies or problems

Division Safety Petty Officer

Another key member of your divisional leadership team is the safety petty officer:

• Complete all safety PQS, serve as a member of the ship's safety council, report on safety issues to both the division officer and the ship's safety officer

• Ensure that all members of the division work on their safety PQS, receive safety training, and are safety conscious

• Inspect the division's spaces weekly and ensure that no safety discrepancies exist

Divisional Training Assistant

One of the key missions of each division is training. To organize, conduct, and review training, you need an assistant who is motivated and dedicated to training.

Divisional training assistant (DTA) duties include:

• Assist the division officer in planning, developing, and coordinating the division training program within departmental and unit training objectives

• Develop monthly division training schedules, and obtain the training space and material to support these schedules

• Train instructors within the division

• Supervise preparation of training materials, and review curricula, courses, and lesson plans prepared within the division

• Obtain, maintain possession of, and issue training aids and devices

• Observe instruction given at drills, on watch, on stations, and in classrooms

• Maintain training records and prepare required reports

• Keep personnel informed of PQS and training progress, using graphs, charts, and visual means

• Initiate requisitions for division training supplies and materials, supervise the administration of PQS, schedule people for schools, ensure that they arrive on time, and consult with the departmental training coordinator on training issues

Repair Parts Petty Officer (RPPO)

The RPPO is the supply expert within the division. He or she is in charge of ordering spare parts, coordinating with the supply department, keeping both repair and routine spare parts and supplies available to the division, and keeping the division officer appraised on supply matters. The RPPO should also receive training from the supply department in supply procedures. As the division officer, you should make sure that the RPPO is fully trained and "up to speed" on supply issues, particularly ordering, turn-in of used parts, and record keeping. The best way to do so is to coordinate with the supply department and be sure they are providing sufficient training for your RPPO.

Division in the Spotlight

Many ships have a "division in the spotlight" program in which various aspects of the division's organization, maintenance, training, and structure are reviewed by the command on a quarterly or semi-annual basis. This is generally done in a nonconfrontational manner that seeks only to improve the day-to-day running of your division. In the weeks leading up to your division's week in the spotlight, you, your chief, and your LPO should go over each of the areas that will be under review and make sure you are ready to go.

If your ship doesn't have a division in the spotlight program, you can still profit from the concept by conducting a self-run review of these aspects of your division's structure and process. Included in Appendix D is a sample division in the spotlight instruction that has been successfully used.

Naval Aviation Squadron Organization

An aviation squadron is organized much like a ship, but there are some minor differences. In most squadrons, the executive officer relieves the commanding officer midway in the latter's tour of command. This results in a smooth change of command, since the executive officer usually starts early in preparing the groundwork for his or her own tour in command.

About 70 percent of the rated enlisted personnel will be assigned to the Aircraft Maintenance Department of the squadron and so will most of the division officers. Above these division officers in the chain of command is the maintenance/material control officer, then the assistant aircraft maintenance officer, and finally the head of department, the aircraft maintenance officer. Some division officers may be tempted to avoid the chain of command in the heat of working on a critical project, but they should not do so. The maintenance/material control officer is the central figure in the department and must not be bypassed.

Since the highest standard of workmanship is of paramount importance, all work done on aircraft in a squadron is checked by quality assurance inspectors. These people are administered in a separate division and are a cross section of nearly all ratings in the squadron. An aviation division officer must accept having to assign one or more of his or her best petty officers to this control division. For more information, see the *Naval Aviation Guide*.

Chain of Command

Organization charts and functional guides are important, but they represent, for the most part, a theoretical ideal. A group such as a division rarely operates exactly along the lines of a chart drawn for it. One of your jobs is to see that your organizational directives are followed within reason, making necessary allowances for the characteristics and abilities of those involved.

In general, the chain of command must be followed. Seamen should have a special request for early liberty approved by their immediate superior, the petty officer for whom they work, and so on up the line. There are times, however, when this orderly procedure will not be followed. A person having serious marital troubles, for example, will usually go straight to the division officer.

Assignment of Personnel

The assignment of personnel to tasks within the ship is accomplished in three steps:

1. Assignment by name to departments and divisions as outlined in the ship's Personnel Assignment Bill.
2. Assignment to watches, stations, and duties within the department and division. These assignments are made by the division officer in accordance with the various ship's bills.
3. Dissemination of information on assignments of individuals. This is accomplished by posting the Watch, Quarter, and Station Bill.

Division officers have the major role in assigning personnel. They must make adjustments based on changes in manning level, on-board count, division assignments, and operating conditions. In making these adjustments, they must do the following:

1. Assign their people to sections, maintaining rates and numbers in each section as nearly equal as possible, in conformance with the Personnel Assignment Bill.
2. Arrange the rates in each section in order of seniority from top to bottom. Watches, duty stations (cleaning, maintenance, etc.), and liberty are assigned on the basis of sections.
3. Make a list of divisional responsibilities contained in each ship's organization bill, and indicate the number of people required for each station and duty.
4. Assign people from appropriate sections and of appropriate ratings or abilities to each station and duty listed in paragraph 3 above.
5. Fill out the Watch, Quarter, and Station Bill by following provisions of paragraphs 2 and 4. Post the completed bill and *ensure that all your sailors know* their assignments and duties. This is particularly important after considerable personnel changes have occurred. It is recommended that a methodical effort be made, after any long stay in port, to ensure that *all* new personnel have, in fact, been instructed in their assigned duties.

Watch, Quarter, and Station Bill

The Watch, Quarter, and Station Bill is the division officer's summary of assignments of personnel to duties and stations within each of the unit's bills. Its primary purpose is to inform division personnel of those assignments.—*Standard Organization and Regulations of the U.S. Navy.*

The *Standard Organization and Regulations Manual* has been described here in enough detail that by referring to a copy as you read this you should understand the major directives on which your own organization is based. As a division officer (or department head of a small ship), you now come to the heart of the matter—your Watch, Quarter, and Station (WQ&S) Bill, which is your summary of personnel assignments to duties and stations specified within the Battle Bill and each of the other ship's bills. Its primary purpose is to inform division personnel of those assignments.

The WQ&S Bill is standard for all ships of a type, and a supply

WATCH, QUARTER

COMPLEMENT				ALLOWANCE	ON BOARD				
BILLET NO.	RATE			NAME	CONDITION I	CONDITION II	CONDITION III	SEA WATCH DETAIL	SPECIAL SEA DETAIL
	COMP.	ALLOW.	ACTUAL						

Figure 3-2. Typical Watch, Quarter, and Station Bill. (Some details will vary in different types of ships.)

of blank forms is usually maintained on board each ship. The standard bill is bulletin-board sized—the bill for a cruiser, for example, includes 31 columns—and is too big to be reproduced here. A smaller mechanical form in common use is shown in figure 3-2. These forms are no longer necessary for units with the Shipboard Nontactical ADP Program (SNAP III) computer system on board. Authorized users need only request a printout of the most current WQ&S Bill for posting. Although a computer terminal replaces the pencil and eraser method of updating and/or creating a new WQ&S Bill, the procedures for such updates are basically identical to those listed below.

The bill allows one line for each person in the division, and shows his or her billet number, name, rate, compartment number, bunk and locker number, and cleaning and maintenance assignment. It lists duties for all condition watches applicable to the par-

& STATION BILL

PORT WATCH DETAIL	CLEANING STATION	FIRE		COLLISION- UNDERWATER DAMAGE	ABANDON SHIP		RESCUE & ASSISTANCE		LANDING FORCE	REMARKS
		STATION	PROVIDE		STATION	PROVIDE	PARTY	PROVIDE		

DIVISION   LAST CORRECTED

ticular ship. Next, it may list, as applicable, stations and duties for Special Sea Detail, Port Watch Detail, Rescue and Assistance, and so on.

The first step in making the bill for your division is to obtain from the ship's Personnel Assignment Bill the billet numbers for each section. Then, take from the Battle Bill the battle stations to be manned and fill in the other assignments in emergency and miscellaneous bills from the *Standard Organization and Regulations Manual.*

The next job is to assign someone to each billet number. Selection of personnel for the various billets is guided by the experience, training, and known capabilities of the individuals. This is your first major opportunity to exercise your judgment and to demonstrate that you know your subordinates. Of course, certain billets call for certain rates, but there are many ways in which you can organize. You should anticipate eventually losing your key people by transfer. For this reason, it is always wise to have your most promising younger petty officers in positions where they can learn more responsible jobs and gain the practical experience necessary to qualify for duties such as those of mount captains and section leaders.

There are, of course, other considerations that will influence your assignments. Often two or more sailors together make a strong team if they each have special qualifications. Let us assume, for example, that you have a mount captain who is a fine leader: aggressive, cool in emergencies, and full of competitive spirit during practice firings, but only fair on maintenance. You can then back him or her up with a junior petty officer who is a natural mechanic and keen on checks and upkeep. This, of course, is an extreme case, but there are opportunities in every unit to do something similar on a smaller scale.

The important point here is that, in assigning your crew, you must not look upon them as just bodies to fill billet numbers. Recognize and take the utmost advantage of their individual capabilities. If you have not served with your division long enough, or if you are not yet familiar with the new personnel in a large division, then ask your petty officers for advice and recommendations. It is often a good idea to do this anyway as a check against your own estimates. Never put your faith in snap judgments of people.

Battle Requirements Govern

There are several other aspects of the Watch, Quarter, and Station Bill that are worthy of note. As quoted from the *Standard Organization and Regulations of the U.S. Navy* at the head of this chapter, "The requirements for battle shall be the basis for organization of units." An obvious way to comply is to have Condition II and III stations. Cleaning stations should also, if practicable, be related to battle stations. This not only facilitates training, it also helps in reducing the time needed for your personnel to get to their General Quarters stations. It is particularly important to have all duties and assignments of the key people related to their battle stations in order to develop their battle efficiency. Those whose duties change, such as food servicemen and compartment cleaners, should be given relatively routine battle stations, such as handling ammunition.

Cleaning Bill

In assigning cleaning details on the Watch, Quarter, and Station Bill, the division officer has more leeway than in filling out the other bills. Only the spaces are assigned to each division: it is up to the division officer to see that they are kept clean.

It should be noted that there are certain accepted practices in sharing the work where the responsibilities of two divisions meet. Some of the more common practices are described below.

The insides of the hatch coamings are cleaned by those whose stations are in the compartment *into which* the hatch leads. The outside of the coaming and the knife-edges are cleaned by the top-side personnel. Doors are cleaned by those into whose compartments they open. Ladders are cleaned by those who keep up the space at the foot of the ladder.

In addition to listing each person's cleaning station opposite his or her name on the Watch, Quarter, and Station Bill, it is important for the division officer to make up a separate cleaning bill for the division, listing each compartment and space along with the names of those who work there and the name of the person in charge. The names of those detailed to clean a given compartment or area of deck space should also be posted on a card in that area. At first glance, this may seem to be just more paperwork, especially when these cards have to be kept up to date, but the results gained make it very worthwhile. It drives home to all your subordinates, without the possibility of a doubt, the exact nature and extent of their duties and responsibilities in regard to cleaning.

A final thought on organization may be helpful. There is no "one" organization in a command. A sailor may report to one senior for military matters and to another for cleaning and maintenance. At General Quarters and while on watch or standing a day's duty, there may be other seniors in charge. And with every activity of a ship, such as fueling and rearming, the sailor is required to adjust to a different chain of command.

4/Administration

Every officer must enhance the operational readiness of his unit within his area of responsibility. To be prepared to carry out this duty, he must have a clear understanding of the meaning of administration and the responsibilities involved.—Standard Organization and Regulations of the U.S. Navy.

Paperwork will ruin any military force.—*Lieutenant General Lewis "Chesty" Puller*

Administration is the act of managing, supervising, and controlling. It is a broad term, and applied to a division, it includes all the activities of the crew: their training, inspection, discipline, and welfare. Since these subjects are covered in detail in separate chapters, this chapter will focus on the methods of administration. Young officers need not know in detail the theories of administration; on the division level, they are really supervisors, concerned with the most efficient ways to get their division work done and their people trained for battle. A grasp of the essential principles of administration, however, should help a division officer in developing the art of efficient supervision.

Policy

Administration from a division officer's viewpoint is accomplished in three general ways: by *policy*, by *procedure*, and by *personal supervision*. Policy is a statement of intent, a statement of what action will be taken under certain circumstances. Most of the important policy in the Navy is established on a higher level. However, in many small ways, division officers can establish their own. A regular and well-understood system for granting leave is an example of policy. It may have been announced, for example, that two weeks' leave for half the division at a time will be approved for the Christmas holidays. Whenever practicable, policy should be in writing and should be made known to all hands, particularly to new personnel. Carefully written and well-understood policies, covering many of the day-to-day questions and problems of working and living, will go far toward a division officer's goal of having a happy and efficient unit. When policies are clearly stated, men and women will know where they stand and what the accepted rules of the game are. This tends to eliminate many minor misunderstandings and bickerings. When a petty officer can make a decision based on a well-known division policy, there will be no question of its ready acceptance. Policy must not be inflexible, however; circumstances often change, and individual questions often require special answers. Division officers must remember that they are dealing with human beings with human concerns. On the other hand, policy must not be so flexible as to render it useless.

Procedure

Procedure determines *how* the division is managed. How will a person or a group perform a particular task? What will their responsibilities be? In what order will they act? Established procedure, like policy, simplifies the daily problems of managing a group. Instead of problems to be solved each day, the matter becomes routine if established procedures are known. Junior enlisted personnel are inclined to feel secure; they are assured, in a sense, of fair and consistent action by their petty officers. This assumes, of course, that the division has first been properly organized. Procedure should be simple yet complete, and should be stated in writing. An example of division procedure would be a written statement of the steps necessary for someone to qualify for advancement. In contrast to policy, procedure should be rigid, and exceptions to established procedure should be rare. Since procedure establishes individual responsibility, failure to observe the procedure may deprive some individual of the opportunity to discharge his or her responsibility. If many exceptions to the routine become necessary, the procedure should be examined and revised.

Personal Supervision

The third way in which a unit is administered is through personal supervision. This is by far the most important method and is the one most often neglected by division officers who confuse paperwork with leadership. A division officer must, first of all, maintain contact with subordinates, know where they are and what they are doing. He or she must know their attitudes, hopes, desires, fears, and worries. He or she must know these things, not so much individually as collectively. People may behave quite differently as a group from the way they act individually under the same circumstances. These human factors are a division officer's primary administrative responsibility.

The demands of making reports, filling out forms, and answering correspondence often will appear so overwhelming that division officers are tempted to concentrate on their paperwork and neglect their people. Certainly, the complexities of the modern Navy result in a staggering burden of messages and directives, not only for division officers, but also for their superiors. In trying to meet this responsibility, the officer must not neglect his or her people. Divide the paperwork among your assistants and seek every legitimate shortcut. Concentrate on items of importance. At times you may have to do your paperwork after working hours—particularly on your duty day—if you cannot otherwise devote the proper time during the day to personal supervision. *The Armed Forces Officer,* a manual distributed by the Office of the Secretary of Defense, contains a very pertinent passage on this subject.

> They deceive only themselves who believe that there is a brand of military efficiency which consists in moving smartly, expediting papers, and achieving perfection in formation, while at the same time slighting or ignoring the human nature of those they command. The art of leadership, the art of command, whether the forces be large or small, is the art of dealing with humanity. Only the officer who dedicates his [or her] thought and energy to his [or her] men [and women] can convert into coherent military force their desire to be of service to the country.

In stressing the need for personal supervision, it cannot be emphasized too strongly that division officers must understand their sailors. The point has been made above that officers must be concerned about the feelings of their subordinates as a group, as well as their feelings as individuals. People in a group react to one another and develop group attitudes and sentiments in a way that is often quite difficult to understand. Not all these group feelings are logical or reasonable. Nevertheless, their existence must be acknowledged, since these feelings directly affect the efficiency and productivity of the group. As a division officer, you must keep group feelings in mind when making decisions. For example, one of your less efficient hands comes to you with a special-request chit for early liberty. The sailor's performance has been substandard and his personal appearance consistently needs improvement, about which he has been regularly counseled by his seniors. His chief and leading petty officer have quite properly disapproved the request. The sailor has business to do at the bank, and you may be tempted to be kindhearted and let him go ashore early before the bank closes. But, you must stop and consider the effect on his shipmates. They know his lazy habits only too well and may be very embittered to see him go ashore early when there is no known emergency, while they must stay aboard and do his work as well as their own. Also, consider the effect on the credibility of the divisional chain of command.

Group feelings are, of course, not all negative; it is just as easy to arouse strong, positive, cooperative sentiments—and here lies the real key to effective management. The major purpose of this book is to help you release in your subordinates this potential for cooperation and efficient work.

Control

Closely associated with personal supervision is the idea or philosophy of control. It is a most important concept and one that is vital to the success of any administrative effort. After a unit has been properly organized and its administration has been properly initiated by policy, procedure, and personal supervision, there becomes apparent a need for something else that is sort of an extension of supervision. This additional factor is *control*. By exercising control, a manager ensures that his or her policies and procedures are actually working. It is all very well to detail a group to clean and paint a compartment, but making sure that the job is done properly requires supervision (by a petty officer) and inspection by the division officer and the chief petty officer. In this example, control is exercised by inspection. Or perhaps your division provides a number of lookouts. You have organized this detail and directed a petty officer to assign the personnel and instruct them. Sometime later you should exercise control; check on these sailors on watch, see if they know their job by observing their watch-standing abilities and questioning them on their responsibilities. Also, provide positive reinforcement that their position as a lookout is extremely important and critical to the mission of the ship. If your engineering division provides someone for "after steering," drop back there every week to see if a qualified person is on watch and if he or she is alert. Failure to exercise control over division assignments and responsibilities means that sooner or later someone, being human, will let you down; and someone, perhaps the captain, will ask embarrassing questions.

Young officers too often accept at face value the reports made to them. Has the requisition for an important spare part actually left the ship? Is that critical equipment really beyond repair without assistance? Are your sentries, patrols, and lookouts really alert? Be skeptical and tough-minded; the best of people are only human and can, despite their good intentions, disappoint you. Make it clear that your skepticism and tough-mindedness are not an attack on their credibility in getting a job done, but a double check on the situation.

Delegating Authority

The preceding chapter on organization contained a few pointers on how to make use of junior division officers. As these officers learn the division and become acquainted with the personnel, give them increased responsibility and authority. Keep in mind that delegating authority to a subordinate does not relieve from responsibility the person who does the delegating. Seniors, in delegating, really create new responsibilities, which they place upon the shoulders of their subordinates. The senior's responsibilities to *his* or *her* seniors remain unchanged. This is a point worth stressing. Suppose that you, as a division officer, delegate to one of your petty officers the authority for maintaining a motor whaleboat. You cannot then assume that the motor whaleboat is no longer your responsibility; since it is assigned to your division, it will always be your concern to ensure that it is maintained properly. Say the executive officer notices that your boat needs repainting and calls it to your attention via your department head. You, in turn, will check on your petty officers. This point may seem obvious, but one of the greatest shortcomings of inexperienced division officers is delegating authority without continuing to supervise and control. On the other hand, do not go overboard and constantly hound your personnel about their assignments. Give them enough time to be creative and productive in their efforts to excel.

When things go amiss and you are reminded that a job has not been done or has been done improperly, do not make excuses that reflect on a subordinate. Division officers should never protest to their department heads, "Well, I told the chief to check those fittings before Friday." This will only irritate the department head, who has several divisions to worry about, who cannot become intimately involved in details of division administration, and who will not appreciate the division officer's efforts to avoid responsibility by passing the buck.

Good officers (those who can delegate authority effectively) absorb criticism from superiors without passing it down to their subordinates. They act as buffers and provide, if necessary, a less-troubled atmosphere in which their people can perform most effectively. They know their subordinates, particularly how far each can be trusted to act with initiative, and they are willing to let them make the kinds of mistakes by which people benefit.

The words of John Paul Jones are pertinent here, and just as applicable as they were two hundred years ago: "be quick and unfailing to distinguish error from malice, thoughtlessness from incompetency, and well-meant shortcomings from needless or stupid blunder." Meaningful delegation of authority implies that the division officer must be willing to accept some level of mistakes. This is not to excuse or justify error, simply to point out that error probably will occur, and to suggest that the division officer plan accordingly.

While you must retain your responsibility and thus must continue a certain amount of supervision, be free and comprehensive in your delegating; give your subordinates a big work load. People learn and develop by doing, and are happier and more efficient when given work that they feel is important and is theirs alone. As your assistants learn to handle their subordinates, give them more and more authority. Nothing is more shortsighted on the part of a superior than a reluctance to let go of some of the reins. It takes careful judgment to delegate efficiently and safely to the maximum extent, but mastering this technique will earn you much peace of mind and allow you the time for planning, which is most important.

This is a good opportunity to discuss a small, but often irritating, problem. What do you do when your department head, the executive officer, or some other senior officer bypasses you and goes directly to one of your subordinates with a complaint or order? The solution is not always simple, but in general you should direct your people to inform you of such incidents and to comply, of course, with any orders. If such incidents are rare, the best thing to do is overlook them; the officers concerned are busy and sometimes take direct action to save time both for themselves and for you. But if it seems to be a habit on the part of some officer to bypass you, then it is advisable to object to these actions, respectfully and good-humoredly. Be polite but firm, for repeated incidents of this nature tend to undermine your authority.

Another violation of the chain of command that sometimes plagues a division officer is the practice of sailors bypassing their immediate superiors and bringing a special request directly to you. Do not let them get away with this. Insist that the divisional chain of command, normally the chief and leading petty officer for whom they work, recommend approval or disapproval of any special requests. Unless your petty officers have real prestige and authority, they cannot be expected to assume full responsibility. This may seem to be a small matter, but it is vital that in your relations with your petty officers they feel secure in their authority. Petty officers of long service are understandably quite sensitive to any actions of a newly commissioned officer that could be interpreted as undermining their authority. Chief petty officers deserve special mention—they are a division officer's strong right arm. Give them as much responsibility as they can handle, and consult them frequently. Often they will be your only assistants and may act as junior division officers. Maintain a very good rapport with your chief petty officer, and benefit from his or her knowledge and experience to make your job less burdensome and a whole lot more enjoyable.

Planning Work and Drills

An important aid in administration is planning work and drills with care and foresight. Within the framework of the ship's organization, and limited by the Plan of the Day and Plan of the Week, a division officer always does the detailed planning to get the work done and the men trained for combat. There is no substitute for experience in developing the mature judgment needed to decide how much work to do and how long to train. There are certain general principles, however; understanding them will help you develop that judgment. These principles derive from years of study and experimentation in industry with groups of workers: measuring their output under different working conditions by changing such factors as hours of work, rest periods, lighting, and noise.

The first principle is that productivity—the relationship between the amount of work done and time spent on the job—depends largely on the attitudes of the workers, rather than on working conditions alone. In spite of high pay, short hours, and lots of rest periods, workers may produce less if they are distracted by some controversy or disgruntled with their leaders or foremen.

The reverse is also true; working conditions may be bad, but if the workers believe that their duties are important, and if they have been inspired to accept their hardships, their output will be high.

The application of this principle to division work is obvious. Within reasonable limits, men and women will do any amount of hard work under the worst conditions if they have the right kind of leadership. Workers will perform prodigiously for supervisors who plan the work intelligently, who go to bat for them when required, and who share their work by staying on the job. This statement is somewhat simplified, of course, as there are usually many other factors to consider. The major point here is that there is no easily determined limit to what people will do if they want to do it. A naval air station may suddenly be ordered to send all its planes to a hurricane refuge. Three-fourths of the sailors may have planned to go on liberty that evening, but all hands will turn to willingly and work all night if necessary to service the planes and secure the station.

This is an obvious example. More often you will have to use ingenuity and common sense to show your subordinates that a tough, unpleasant job needs to be done. It may be particularly difficult to keep them interested in doing the routine tasks of maintenance and cleaning aboard ship, and it is usually impossible to find any dramatic reason, like an approaching hurricane, for making a big effort. In such situations, careful planning and personal supervision are the only answers. Show all your crew that to you, at least, the work they are doing is important. You can usually find some small way to show your interest and enthusiasm. Frequent contact with the sailors is, of course, the best, and for this there is no substitute. Special marks of interest, such as getting permission for a certain hardworking detail to sleep in during the morning after working all night, or arranging for cold soft drinks on a hot day, are always worthwhile.

Long Hours

A second principle, particularly applicable to drills, is that when the crew's interest in a job is exhausted and cannot be revived, it will learn nothing further that day. In fact, its performance is likely to suffer if drilling is pushed beyond the interest point. Long hours are not a substitute for intelligently conducted drills. Again, it is a question of thorough planning and forceful, aggressive leadership. Sailors should never be permitted to doze during drills, which usually should be intense and relatively short.

Competition

A third principle in planning work and drills is that competition can significantly increase efficiency. This is true, however, only up to the point where the competition becomes an end in itself.

While competition is well regulated in our modern Navy, it is still possible to observe instances of the "tail wagging the dog." There is only one logical basis on which competition should be judged. Does it increase the fighting efficiency of the unit? Division officers and their crews are always engaged in some form of competition, because during peacetime, there must be some substitute for the rigors of fighting. In peace, you shoot for a score; in war, you shoot to destroy the enemy and to protect yourself. It is important for all officers to understand what competition strives to accomplish—to increase the fighting readiness and efficiency of the unit.

Cooperation among Divisions

A final general principle in planning the work and drills of a division is that cooperation with the other divisions is essential. No matter how well officers run their divisions, if they only give lip service to the coordinating efforts of the executive officer, they are not pulling their weight. This is not such an issue when a division is made up entirely of maintenance personnel or other specialists whose duties are clear-cut and confined to one space on the ship. But the healthy softball rivalry between two gunnery divisions or between a deck and an engineering division on a ship must not spill over into arguments over cleaning assignments or other administrative matters. Just as the Navy is much more important than a single ship of the fleet, so are the interests of a ship, squadron, or station more important than the interests of a single division.

The ship should be viewed as an entity, a combat system composed of interrelated and interdependent subsystems. Do not take someone from another division away from his or her assigned work at any time. If you have an important electrical problem in your spaces, do not grab, or have your people grab, the nearest electrician. Talk to your counterpart or have your chiefs work it out. It's the same for a ventilation problem. "A" Gang belongs to the auxiliary division officer. After all, you would not want someone using *your* men or women without your knowledge and approval. Each division provides a necessary service, and generally does so without much difficulty. It is at the interfaces among subsystems (divisions) that coordination problems may arise. The division officer must recognize that mutual support is not only reasonable but necessary. Occasionally, one division may have the technical expertise needed by another division to repair important shipboard equipment efficiently. For example, an electronics technician may be able to help the fire-control technician solve a particularly difficult problem, but only if the two division officers recognize the potential benefit. In other words, all of the ship's resources should be employed in a mutually supportive manner. This does not mean that one division should habitually do another division's maintenance, but rather that the division officer should recognize both the ship's needs and her assets. The best shortcut to harmony between divisions is a thorough understanding by the division officers of the work and responsibility assignments laid down in the ship's organization.

Directives

Efficient management of a division requires that the division officer be familiar with the current directives that apply to the duties of the division and to the division's personnel. No attempt will be made here to list all of the publications in which these directives are set forth, but the important ones will be mentioned. By far the most important, from your perspective as a division officer, is your own ship's *Standard Organization and Regulation Manual.* Read and be familiar with all sections pertaining to you and your division.

In addition, *U.S. Navy Regulations, 1973, Standard Organization and Regulations of the U.S. Navy,* the *Naval Military Personnel Command Manual* (the Coast Guard uses *Coast Guard Personnel Manual* COMDTINST 1000.6), and the *Uniform Code of Military Justice* are important.

The various systems technical manuals are also valuable, particularly the Naval Sea Systems Command (NAVSEA) technical manuals. If your duties involve a particular weapons system, then the NAVSEA technical manual relating to that system is an important aid to the division officer.

Most of the remaining directives are in the form of instructions and notices. The objectives of this Navy directive system are: to group together under a common subject number the directives from different commands concerning the same subject; to differentiate between directives of a continuing or permanent nature and those designed for brief use; and to improve general naval administration by using throughout the service a uniform format and numbering system. The system includes all directives, from those issued by the Chief of Naval Operations to those issued by a division officer on board ship. See chapter 10 of the *Standard Organization and Regulations of the U.S. Navy* for details on instructions and notices.

For special occasions, such as when someone inquires about a hardship discharge, a division officer should find the answer either in the *Naval Military Personnel Command Manual* or in an instruction or notice on file in the personnel office. A division officer must be informed on such matters as requirements for advancement in rate, shore duty eligibility, overseas shore duty, humanitarian shore duty, and transfers between ships.

Division officers who make the effort to obtain the answers, or who have their leading petty officers obtain them, not only will gain the respect and confidence of their people but probably also will receive much more cooperation from the personnel office, disbursing office, and other offices. Good officers who "run interference" will avoid sending their sailors to these offices for answers to questions such as "When will I be eligible for third class?" "Do I rate a good conduct medal?" and so on.

Division Personnel Records

The *Standard Organization and Regulations of the U.S. Navy* requires that a division officer "maintain a division notebook containing personnel data, training program data, a space and equipment responsibility log, the watch and battle stations required to be manned, and such other data as may be useful for the orientation of an officer relieving him and for ready reference."

Keeping the records of the personnel in a division is a standardized routine throughout the Navy, using the Division Officer's Personnel Record Form (figs. 4-1 and 4-2). These forms, filled out for each division member and assembled in a binder, constitute a division notebook, a most important tool for efficient personnel management. The personnel record form is valuable to help you know and record data about your subordinates. In the Coast Guard, these forms usually are kept in the ship's office. An advantage of small Coast Guard ships is that as a division officer you have ready access to the ship's office.

Note that many data are taken from the individual's official, permanent record, which is kept in the ship's office. These data are required, for example, when you assign duties and stations; when you consider leave, allotments, and special requests; and when you review job classifications. The form also provides space in which to record carefully the annual marks as a continuing record of performance without referring to the Enlisted Performance Record, filed in individual service jackets. The back side of the form provides blanks for logging training accomplishments.

There is a purpose for these spaces. The largest part of the responsibility for training rests upon division officers. They must keep adequate data on file to help discharge this responsibility. Some of the important items, such as the completion of a training course, are reported to the ship's office (sometimes via the training and/or administrative officer). There the information is entered in the individual's service record.

DIVISION OFFICER'S PERSONNEL RECORD FORM

PRIVACY ACT STATEMENT

Authority to request the information in this form is derived from 5 United States Code 301, Departmental Regulations. Purpose of this form is to provide the Division Officer with readily accessible data concerning personnel in his/her division. The information is used by the Division Officer to manage and administer his/her personnel; to determine training needed; to record training completed; to maintain readily accessible data concerning performance, work assignment, and other personnel data to enable the Division Officer to guide and counsel those assigned to him/her. Disclosure of the following items of information on this form is mandatory: name, rate, SSN, local address and phone number (if applicable), work center /berthing /bunk number (if applicable). Disclosure of the following items of information is voluntary; reenlistment intentions, rate desired, special qualifications, name of spouse, names and ages of children. Other items of information may be obtained from member's service record. Failure to provide those required items of information listed above may result in administrative action being taken; no action will be taken if the individual refuses to disclose those voluntary items of information.

NAME			RATE	USN USNR	SSN		NEC / PRI / SEC
DEPT / DIV		WORK CENTER	DUTY SECTION			BERTHING	BUNK / LOCKER #
DATE OF BIRTH		RELIGIOUS PREFERENCE				SECURITY CLEARANCE / ACCESS	
ADBD		DATE REPORTED	PRD	EAOS		U.S. CITIZEN	
GENERAL QUARTERS STATION		UNDERWAY WATCH STATION				PHYSICAL READINESS TEST	

SPECIAL QUALIFICATIONS OR INTERESTS

PERMANENT HOME ADDRESS AND PHONE NUMBER	LOCAL ADDRESS AND PHONE NUMBER

MARITAL STATUS	NO. OF DEPENDENTS	NAME OF SPOUSE / MILITARY ☐

NAMES AND AGES OF CHILDREN

NEXT OF KIN	RELATIONSHIP	ADDRESS AND PHONE NUMBER

PREVIOUS DUTY

DATE REPORTED	UNIT	DIVISION	DESCRIPTION OF DUTY

PERFORMANCE TRAITS

EVALUATION DATE	RATE KNOWLEDGE	RELIABILITY	MILITARY BEARING	PERSONAL BEHAVIOR	DIRECTING	OVERALL EVALUATION

NAVPERS 1070/6 (Rev 12-86)   S/N 0106-LF-010-7036

Fig. 4-1. Division Officer's Personnel Record Form (front)

AWARDS AND COMMENDATIONS

COMMENTS

FORMAL EDUCATION

HIGH SCHOOL		COLLEGE		MAJOR							
9 10 11 12		1 2 3 4									

HIGH SCHOOL GED		PART 1		PART II		PART III		PART IV		PART V	
COLLEGE CLEP											

ASVAB TEST SCORES

FORMS 5/6/7	GI	NO	AD	WK	AR	SP	MK	EI	MC	GS	SI	AI
FORMS 8/9/10	GS	AR	WK	PC	NO	CS	AS	MK	MC	EI	VE	

GENERAL PQS	DAMAGE CONTROL	DATE	3-M	DATE	FIRE FIGHTING	DATE	SHIP CLASS	REQUAL DC SHIP CLASS	REQUAL DC SHIP CLASS

NAVAL EDUCATION RECORD

ITEM	TITLE	DATE COMPLETED	MARK	TITLE	DATE COMPLETED	MARK
SERVICE SCHOOLS						
MILITARY CORRESPONDENCE COURSES						
OTHERS						

NAVY-WIDE EXAMINATION ELIGIBILITY SECTION

PARS		MILITARY LEADERSHIP		PROFESSIONAL COURSE		MILITARY COURSE		EXAMINATIONS		
RATE	DATE COMPLETED	RATE	DATE COMPLETED	RATE	DATE COMPLETED	RATE	DATE COMPLETED	RATE	DATE COMP	RESULTS

DATE PRESENT RATE		ELIGIBLE NEXT RATE		REC NEXT RATE	

NAVPERS 1070/6 (REV 12-86) (BACK)

*U.S. GPO: 1991-504-109/20718

Fig. 4-2. Division Officer's Personnel Record Form (back)

In addition to the division notebook, the division officer should maintain an informal division book in which Watch, Quarter, and Station Bill assignments are listed as well as muster lists for various drills and evolutions. The leading division petty officer should keep this book, ensuring all data are current and making recommendations for changes and updates to the chief petty officer and division officer as required. This book will serve as muster lists at Quarters and as checks for proper procedures at all drills. The books can be used not only to check assignments at drills but also to record minor deficiencies that might otherwise remain uncorrected.

To aid division officers and their assistants in keeping up with the ever-changing training required by or desired by their personnel, the *Standard Organization and Regulations of the U.S. Navy*, chapter 8, provides guidance and sample formats for scheduling and maintaining a divisional training schedule, a group record of training and skill qualifications, and a record of qualifications at battle stations. Chapter 8 also describes the use of the Personnel Qualification Standards. Several types of general record forms are illustrated, showing the flexible use of such forms to set down these vital training and qualification data. These forms, available in the supply system, are helpful in maintaining a comprehensive training and readiness status within the division.

By following a systematic procedure you will be able to plan more easily for training your crew on various stations and pieces of equipment. If you have determined and listed the schools and training courses available through the fleet training centers and other facilities, it will be easier for you to schedule your sailors for such training. If Personnel Advancement Requirement (PAR) forms are available to each person, together with lists of source materials for each rate, your sailors will be fully informed of the requirements for promotion. Last, through these efforts your people will realize that you are aware of their progress and, most important, that you are interested in their training.

All of the books and forms listed above are readily available to division officers assigned to units with the Shipboard Nontactical

ADP Program (SNAP III) computer system. The system maintains a database of division officer notebook information that can be easily accessed, reviewed, updated, and printed out.

Other Personnel Records

Service Record

The Enlisted Service Record reflects the career history of each enlisted person and is the property of the U.S. government, not the individual. These records are maintained in the ship's or activity's administrative office. They are always available for review by the individual and anyone with a need to review them. Entries can be made only by authorized personnel—usually the executive officer or administrative officer and his or her personnel.

Division officers should become intimately familiar with each of their sailors' service records and see that they are correct at all times. Any discrepancies should be reported immediately to the administrative officer.

The service record can be extremely useful to division officers both in taking care of their people and in learning about them. Each service record contains such information as time left in current enlistment, test scores, basic talents, educational level, record of schooling, record of transfers, summary of evaluations, and special remarks and qualifications.

The Enlisted Service Record consists of a flat-type folder with pages numbered 1 through 15, as necessary, on the right-hand side. Other official or unofficial papers (i.e., an up-to-date Service Group Life Insurance (SGLI) form, copies of orders, and previous evaluations) are filed in chronological order on the left-hand side of the folder.

Page 1: *Enlistment Contract.* Page 1 is the contract a person signs upon joining the Navy. Page lA records an agreement to extend enlistment. Page lB records an assignment to, and extension of, active duty.

Page 2: *Dependency Application/Record of Emergency Data.* Page 2 is one of the most important in a person's record, and it should always be kept up-to-date. This form provides the Navy with necessary information about next of kin, dependents, or other people who should be notified in case of death or other emergency.

Page 3: *Enlisted Classification Record.* Page 3 contains pertinent information about aptitude test scores, civilian education and training, personal interests, civilian experience, and such recommendations and remarks thereon that have military significance. This information is prepared from the data obtained by the naval training centers during the routine testing and interviewing of recruits.

Page 4: *Enlisted Qualification History.* Page 4 is a complete chronological record of the person's Navy enlisted classification (NEC) codes and designators, Navy schools attended, Navy training courses completed, educational experience level, Personal Advancement Requirements (PAR), performance tests, changes in rate or rating, education and vocational/technical off-duty training completed, decorations and other awards, other training courses/instructions completed, and Personal Qualification Standards (PQS) completed.

Page 5: *History of Assignments.* Page 5 provides a record of the ships and stations to which the sailor has been assigned, and of enlistments, extensions of enlistments, discharges, and amounts of reenlistment bonuses paid.

Page 6: *Record of Unauthorized Absence.* Page 6 is used to record periods of unauthorized absence in excess of 24 hours.

Page 7: *Court Memorandum.* Page 7 is used to report any court-martial action with a guilty finding, as well as any nonjudicial punishment that affects pay, including reduction in rate.

Page 9: *Enlisted Performance Record.* Page 9 is used to record chronologically the performance evaluations of enlisted members on active duty.

Page 13: *Administrative Remarks.* Page 13 (Coast Guard equivalent is page 7) serves as a chronological record of miscellaneous entries (i.e., specific indoctrination received or acknowledgment of an order or policy) not provided elsewhere or where more detailed information may be recorded in the clarification of entries on other pages of the service record. It includes entries on nonjudicial punishment not affecting pay, unauthorized absence less than 24 hours, and compliance with Article 137, UCMJ. These remarks sheets are not solely to record substandard performance, but are also used to document outstanding achievements. Such documentation is crucial to justify high marks, low marks, awards, punishment, discharge, or advancement. Such an entry can serve to document trends, build a case for recognition or provide future superiors with a lasting record of performance.

Page 15: *Certificate of Release or Discharge from Active Duty.* Page 15 provides documentary evidence of active naval service.

Enlisted Performance Evaluation

Evaluations mean a great deal to an enlisted person, just as a fitness report means a great deal to a division officer. One of the division officer's most important duties is the periodic evaluation of his or her people in such areas as professional factors, personal traits, self-expression, leadership, and management on a 4.0 scale. (The Coast Guard uses a scale of 1 to 7, with 7 being the highest mark.)

The Navy Enlisted Performance Evaluation Report is a periodic recording of an individual's qualifications, performance level in comparison to contemporaries, conduct, and prospects for increased responsibilities. It is the most significant personnel management tool in the enlisted record. Its primary use is by the Bureau of Naval Personnel in making advancement and assignment decisions. It is also used in determining eligibility for the Good Conduct Medal, reenlistment, and character of service at time of discharge. Various selection boards use performance evaluation reports to select members for advancement, continuation on active duty, retention, appointment to commissioned status, assignment to special duties, and enrollment in special educational programs.

The performance appraisal process cannot be overemphasized and demands command attention. Consequently, the division officer's evaluation must be neither casual nor routine. The evaluation should be made carefully, by following the descriptions in BUPERSINST 1616.9, and by comparing the individual with his or her peers, rate for rate and rating for rating. Be objective and discerning to ensure that only truly outstanding individuals receive outstanding reports. Provide adequate justification. Be sure to report shortcomings or deficiencies that signify unreliability. After the rough evaluation is completed, put it away for a day or so, then reread it. When you are satisfied with the evaluation, route it through the chain of command for review, smoothing, and the signature of the commanding officer. The whole procedure should be a leadership tool. The individual who is evaluated shall be given an opportunity to review, comment on, and sign the completed report. The division officer and chief or leading petty officer should be present while the individual evaluated reads through his or her evaluation. If the sailor doesn't agree with the report, he or she has the option of submitting, through the chain of command, a written statement concerning the disagreement.

Because of the importance of these evaluations and, perhaps, because of a feeling of inexperience, there is a tendency for new or careless officers to give all sailors who do their work satisfactorily a 4.0 across the board. This defeats the purpose of the evaluation, for it makes no distinction among average, good, and outstanding sailors. Extreme care should be taken so that marks are correct, strict, and fair estimates of ability, character, and worth. Only if this is done can the Navy select people efficiently for schooling, special programs, and promotions. The division officer, using the enlisted performance evaluation report-individual input form, and the specific aspects of performance checklist located in BUPERSINST 1616.9, coupled with a strong input from the chief or leading petty officer, can develop an accurate and fair evaluation of his or her personnel.

The Enlisted Performance Evaluation Report cannot be the sole method of advising service members of their performance. Throughout the evaluation period, the command must regularly counsel service members in regard to their professional growth and development. Positive feedback should be provided, specific weaknesses discussed, and suggestions for improvement delineated. Counseling is an integral part of the evaluation process and helps to give a performance appraisal the proper perspective and meaning. Commanding officers are urged to emphasize a constructive and continuing dialogue between reporting seniors and subordinates. To this end, division officers are most strongly encouraged to submit special performance evaluation reports on personnel in paygrades El through E3. Frequent submission of these reports will not only serve as an effective counseling aid, but will also provide a more meaningful summary on which commanding officers can base decisions regarding advancement recommendations, striker board selection, and reenlistment code assignment recommendations.

Enlisted personnel in paygrades El through E9 are normally evaluated annually, using the Enlisted Performance Evaluation Report from NAVPERS 1616/24. (The Coast Guard uses form CG 3788.) The evaluation section on the NAVPERS 1616/24 includes military knowledge/performance, rating knowledge/performance, initiative, reliability, military bearing, personal behavior, human relations including equal opportunity, speaking ability, writing ability, directing, counseling, management (E7/8/9 only), and overall evaluation. The following will be useful in making out the Enlisted Performance Evaluation Report:

• *Military knowledge/performance.* This measures the individual's knowledge of military customs, watch-standing duties, responsibilities within the chain of command, knowledge of and contribution to the command's mission, and his or her level of performance in these areas.

• *Rating knowledge/performance.* This measures the member's knowledge and level of performance of his or her job-related duties, application of technical and professional skills, problem-solving talent, and ability to accept instruction or direction. This block should be used to evaluate job performance whether or not the member is performing duties normally associated with his or her rating.

• *Initiative.* This evaluates the individual's ability to act appropriately, independently, and without specific direction, while exercising sound judgment. It also measures the member's ability to set goals and performance standards, both personally and for others. This block should also be used to evaluate the extent to which the member demonstrates resourcefulness and persistence in the face of obstacles.

• *Reliability.* This assesses the extent to which the individual can be depended upon to perform assigned tasks successfully, and the individual's ability to persevere to ensure timely completion of assigned tasks. This block is also used to evaluate the extent to which the member is at his or her assigned place of duty when needed, the degree of support for command and Navy policies and initiatives, and the individual's level of personal integrity.

• *Military Bearing.* This evaluates the member's personal appearance, including physical fitness, wearing of the uniform, and, when appropriate, neatness in civilian attire, knowledge and practice of military courtesies, and the way the individual presents himself or herself as a member of the Navy.

• *Personal Behavior.* This assesses the individual's personal behavior, conduct both on and off duty, and demeanor during the reporting period. In arriving at the final mark in this block, commanding officers should take into consideration any military or civilian offenses committed during the reporting period. This block should also be used to evaluate the extent to which the member presents a model of exemplary behavior, including the degree of self-control under stress.

• *Human Relations Including Equal Opportunity.* This measures the member's ability to work successfully with peers, subordinates, and superiors. It also measures the member's contributions to the morale of the command. Attention should also be focused on evaluation of the member's support of the Navy's Equal Opportunity programs and the command's Affirmative Action Plan.

• *Speaking Ability.* This evaluates the member's ability to use effectively the English language in expressing himself or herself orally. Correct usage of the language, clarity of speech, and organization and presentation of thoughts are also measured. Performance in formal presentations and/or informal discussions should be taken into account. For personnel in paygrades E1 through E3, a grade in this block is not required unless abilities are clearly demonstrated.

• *Writing Ability.* This evaluates the member's ability to make effective use of the English language in written communications. The quality of the written work, presentation of thoughts, and correct usage of English grammar are to be measured. For personnel in paygrades E1 through E3, a grade in this block is not required unless abilities are clearly demonstrated.

• *Directing.* This evaluates a member's skill at leading others to the successful achievement of a common goal. The ability to delegate, to gain commitment from others, to challenge and inspire subordinates while maintaining positive and realistic expectations should all be taken into account. Completion of this block is mandatory for personnel in paygrades E4 through E9. For personnel in paygrades E1 through E3, a grade in this block is not required unless abilities are clearly demonstrated.

• *Counseling.* This assesses the member's skill at counseling personnel. The ability to confront, where warranted, and praise, where justified, should be evaluated along with the individual's ability to assist subordinates in the resolution of professional and/or personal problems. The individual's support of the Navy retention programs should also be evaluated. Completion of this block is mandatory for personnel in paygrades E4 through E9. For personnel in paygrades E1 through E3, a grade in this block is not required unless abilities are clearly demonstrated.

• *Management.* This evaluates a chief petty officer's ability to successfully manage personnel, material, financial, and time resources under his or her control. It measures the member's ability to plan and organize, effectively use available resources, monitor results, create team spirit, and develop subordinates. Completion of this block is reserved exclusively for personnel in paygrades E7 through E9.

• *Overall Evaluation.* The overall evaluation mark entered in this block provides the reporting senior the opportunity to express an assessment of the member's overall value to the Navy. This mark should be consistent with the marks assigned in the above items; however, it need not be in direct agreement with the graded column that has received the majority of the marks assigned. The overall evaluation mark should not be determined through numerical averaging. The mark is a judgment by the reporting senior.

• *Not Observed.* The "not observed" box is used to indicate that the rater has been unable to observe the particular trait and cannot give a fair evaluation. This should be used sparingly.

• *Advancement Recommendation.* One of three choices—recommended, progressing toward, or not recommended—is required. This is an extremely important item to determine; therefore, a careful evaluation of the individual's capability to perform satisfactorily the duties and responsibilities of the next higher paygrade, regardless of the individual's qualification or eligibility for advancement, must be made by the division officer.

The evaluation report can be a powerful tool in persuading subordinates to mind their behavior. If you are troubled by shore-patrol reports concerning drunkenness and fighting, one of the most effective means you have of encouraging your men and women to tread the straight and narrow path is to let them know that their unsatisfactory behavior will be reflected in low periodic marks in military bearing and in personal behavior. This may not work for everyone, but it will be very effective for the majority of your minor offenders whose professional pride is reasonably well developed.

Marks reflecting conduct are assigned by the division officer and checked as the evaluation is being routed through the chain of command. Cases of nonjudicial punishment during a marking period normally require a mark of less than 3.0 to be assigned in personal behavior. The marks are reviewed by the department head and the executive officer. The completed evaluations will be signed by the commanding officer, who may authorize the executive officer or department head to sign, provided these individuals are of the grade of lieutenant commander or above.

Periodic marks and regular counseling periods are highly important in relation to performance and discipline, and they must never be considered just another item of administrative paperwork. Marks are one of the most effective means of rewarding good people, especially if they realize the importance of the marks. Poor marks, when deserved, effectively indicate your disapproval, and in some cases, they can spur the person on to improvement. Unless a decided difference is made in the marks given to poor, average, good, and outstanding personnel, there will be no way to ensure the promotion of efficient petty officers. The common complaint that "we have few good petty officers" is not a reflection on the American sailor or on the system of advancement, particularly in regard to training and somewhat in regard to periodic marks. If all officers were conscientious in training and marking their people, the Navy would, in time, have all the efficient petty officers it could use. There is no easy way to develop a large group of able petty officers; the only sure way is for every officer to develop all those under him or her to the full extent of their capabilities.

Evaluating Your Senior Petty Officers. In filling out the periodic evaluation forms for chief petty officers and first and second class petty officers, it is particularly important to be fair and just in following the standards laid down in the Milpersman and BUPERS 1616 series. There is a strong tendency for young officers to mark all their people too high. This misguided loyalty may backfire in later years, and you may find yourself saddled with an incompetent chief petty officer who has reached that position because of being given high marks by others every time for merely being pleasant and performing at a minimum level. A high rating should be based on good performance rather than just getting by.

The division officer should observe certain practices and writing techniques in order to be fair to the petty officers concerned and to make the job of the selection board more effective.

Tell exactly what primary and significant collateral duties the person had and how well they were performed. List special qualifications, service schools, and educational achievements. Do not describe how well the ship did on deployment, inspections, or competitions. Emphasize *ability, potential,* and *willingness* to accept positions of leadership. Indicate *why* someone should be advanced.

Keep all strong points and recommendations in the space provided. Continuation sheets are not acceptable. Remember that the first sentence sets the tone of the whole evaluation. Provide support for phrases such as "truly outstanding." Describe what he or she did, avoiding flowery adjectives by using clear, concise, specific statements in "bullet format." Use specific examples of the individual's work and its benefits to his or her ship. Underline significant phrases to emphasize important points.

If at all possible, compare "other" and "transfer" evaluations. State why an "other" report is being submitted.

Include *all* special goals, schools, duties, outside activities, community involvements, and awards. If you mark a person lower than his or her peers, tell why in the narrative. Do not recommend advancement just because the person has met the time in service/rate requirements. Comments on future duty assignments for which the member may be considered and general comments on the member's trend of performance and potential for advancement, retention, and reenlistment should be included in the evaluation comments. Finally, proofread your evaluation, and make certain you have marked all the blocks.

Enlisted Distribution and Verification Report

The Enlisted Distribution and Verification Report, EPMAC-EDVR-1080, serves as a rate or Navy Enlisted Classification (NEC) (see below) summary of the current and future manning status on board a ship, in an air squadron, or at a shore installation. This report is distributed monthly. EPMAC-EDVR-1080 gives division officers a summary of their allowance for personnel in numbers and by NEC, a view of their prospective gains and losses, and a common point of reference in any discussion of manning status. Division officers should review the report and ensure that it is correct for their personnel. Since this report is used in assigning personnel to the unit, errors in it may mean that needed personnel will not be assigned to the ship.

Navy Enlisted Classification (NEC) Coding

The purpose of the Navy Enlisted Classification system is to supplement the enlisted rating structure in identifying special skills and knowledge requirements. NEC codes express both the special requirements of ships and stations and the skills required by enlisted personnel. NEC coding has been integrated with the rating structure and enlisted distribution system in assigning personnel to ships and stations.

All organizations employing large numbers of people use some system for identifying and relating the skills of people with the skills required for all jobs. In military organizations, widely dispersed operations and constant training make it necessary to transfer large numbers of people periodically from job to job and from one type of command to another. The classification system, therefore, must serve more purposes than a similar one employed in a more static civilian organization.

The Army and Air Force use numerical systems to classify both personnel and jobs, but the Navy relies first on its traditional rating structure because each person must become as versatile and broadly qualified as possible. Only a given number of sailors can be berthed on a ship, yet all jobs must be accomplished—including the all-important one of manning battle stations.

The key word in the Navy system is *rate*. Navy rates are combinations of (1) ratings and paygrades (for example, FC2, fire controlman second class) or (2) apprenticeships and paygrades (for example, SA, seaman apprentice). There are six apprenticeships: seaman, fireman, constructionman, airman, hospitalman, and dentalman. Each has three pay grades (E1, E2, and E3), thereby comprising 18 rates. At paygrades above E3, there are approximately 80 general service ratings, which subdivide into rates at each paygrade.

Taken together, these rates provide a broad occupational classification system for identifying both job requirements and personnel. Since all personnel are advanced in pay grade under this system, the aims of versatility and broad qualification are basically attained.

On the other hand, many jobs are extremely specialized in nature. Some require long and expensive training; others are simply not numerous enough to warrant training everyone in a given rate. Classification of this type is attained by using NEC codes to identify both the job and the person able to do it. While NEC codes have nothing to do with your subordinates' advancement in pay grade, they often have a lot to do with their following duty assignments or their opportunities for advanced schooling. By referring to the EDVR, you can determine the rates, ratings, and NEC codes allowed your ship. You should verify that your allowance contains the necessary NEC codes. This will go a long way toward ensuring that the right numbers of people are trained in key specialties and that your ship receives a qualified replacement when your trained person is transferred.

It is easy to shrug off NEC coding as the responsibility of someone else—the personnel person, the department head, or even the type commander. However, this is not a matter to ignore. You have a major responsibility to your people, your command, and the Navy to see that your unit has the qualified people it needs to support mission accomplishment through a battle-ready team of capable, qualified, and trained personnel.

You must ensure that your people are identified correctly. The best times to do this are when you receive a new person, when you transfer someone, or when one of your subordinates completes a school for which an identifying NEC code should be assigned. Correct NEC code assignment requires service record review, personal interview, and observation of duties performed. Failure to ensure a correct NEC code assignment for each person may mean the loss of additional pay or incorrect additional pay to the service member. To be on the safe side, you must promptly review NEC codes of divisional personnel.

Watch, Quarter, and Station Bill

Another important administrative task for the division officer is keeping the Watch, Quarter, and Station (WQ&S) Bill up-to-date. In the preceding chapter on organization, the steps for making out the bill were described in detail. Keeping all hands informed of their assignments is equally important. One of the simplest ways to accomplish this is to have leading petty officers use copies of the bill when instructing their division. They might have each person initial the posted bill near his or her name. Whatever the method used, the goal is to make sure everyone understands the WQ&S Bill. Abbreviations used on the bill can be confusing and must be defined. The bill should be checked at frequent and regular intervals, particularly before getting under way, to ensure that all personnel have listings and that the transfer of personnel has been recognized and compensated for as well.

An important feature of a WQ&S Bill is permanence. Once you have considered all the factors and have written up your bill, do not change it. Nothing is more conducive to confusion than a WQ&S Bill that is always being revised. Training comes to a halt when different people are assigned different jobs each time the ship goes to sea. Changes should be made only for important reasons.

One of those reasons would be to aid training. Thus, you should rotate personnel at regular intervals if it would facilitate learning and if they are qualified for the new job. For example, all yeomen strikers might be rotated through enough battle stations and condition watch stations to prepare them for eventual duty as captain's sound-powered phone talker. Rotation for training is a necessity that should never be confused with the constant and aimless revision that is a symptom of poor administration.

All items on the WQ&S Bill (except the names and cleaning stations that are changed periodically) should be typed or printed in ink. Avoid ditto marks and fill in all items so that all people can see their assignments plainly.

Security

No chapter on administration in the Navy would be complete without a discussion of security. The division officer may have custody of classified messages, publications, charts, blueprints, microfiche, or pictures. She or he is also likely to be responsible for classified equipment, weapons, and ordnance. Thus, the division officer must be concerned with safeguarding classified materials. To do so he or she should be familiar with the following basic directives: *U.S. Navy Regulations, 1973*, the Department of the Navy Information Security Program Regulation, OPNAVINST 5510.1 series, and the Security Bill contained in the *Standard Organization and Regulations of the U.S. Navy*. Amplifying instructions may be issued by fleet, type, group, and squadron commanders. For division officers designated as custodians of classified material, which includes Communications Security Material System (CMS) material and Naval Warfare Publications (NWP), there are additional CNO instructions, notices, and guidance in the OPNAVINST 5510.1 series.

The second step in ensuring security in a division is to set up a systematic procedure for the stowage and use of classified publications. Classified material must be stowed as required by its degree of classification and as specified by regulations; when removed from stowage, classified material should be signed for on a card or in a book. This emphasis on security must not, of course, result in classified material being hidden from those who should use it either for their jobs or for their training. Good judgment and good practice must be applied here by the division officer.

In regard to classified equipment, weapons, or ordnance, such as radars, small arms, or powders and projectiles, the division officer should be vigilant at all times when visitors or guests are on board ship. He or she should ensure that critical spaces, such as the Combat Information Center (CIC), are locked or guarded, and that classified gear on deck is covered. Further guidance on general visiting and ship security in port is contained in OPNAVINST 5510.1 series and the *Standard Organization and Regulations of the U.S. Navy*, OPNAVINST 3120.32. Remember that classified publications can be used only within authorized or designated working spaces. Taking a classified publication home is specifically prohibited.

There are times when the ship must be secured against the wholesale disappearance of everything that is not welded down. One such occasion is when a ship enters a shipyard for overhaul. Before the ship enters the yard, a division officer should either stow all his tools and other portable equipment in a compartment where no work will be done, or pack the gear in boxes to be stowed ashore. Labeling tools and equipment with a division/ workcenter abbreviation is also a wise precaution to avoid loss. Among the hundreds of thoroughly honest workers there will always be a few who cannot resist taking a tool or a souvenir. Over a period of weeks or months such persons can effectively strip a ship. This condition becomes more acute, of course, in times of naval expansion, when many new workers are joining the shipyards.

Another occasion for special precautions is when the ship is open to large numbers of civilians, whether invited guests attending a ceremony or visitors during an Armed Forces Day open house. Under these circumstances, a division officer can keep some people on watch in all spaces, with instructions to discourage, courteously but firmly, the collection of souvenirs. At such a time your sailors also must be instructed to enforce no-smoking regulations, observe safety precautions, and keep visitors out of restricted or classified areas.

A reverse situation can occur too. It is the practice in many shipyards for the workers, while working on a ship, to leave their tools on board in locked tool boxes, usually stowed topside. Occasionally, sailors will break into these toolboxes. This infrequent, but embarrassing, occurrence can often be avoided by a forehanded division officer, who not only instructs his subordinates about leaving the workers' tools alone but also suggests that the toolboxes be locked and stowed in a secure area.

When in foreign ports, a ship's company must be particularly alert to prevent theft, not only by casual visitors, but also by ship's personnel. Where black market prices ashore are very high for medical supplies, electronic spare parts, and other desirable items, it is tempting for sailors to take material ashore. This problem can be greatly aggravated by the presence on board ship of civilians representing themselves as foreign merchants and traders, who may really be there for less-honest reasons.

Division officers should not overlook information security. They should caution their people to refrain from discussing anything of a classified nature either ashore or afloat—except, of course, in the pursuit of their duties, and only in an area where they cannot be overheard by others not involved. When in a liberty status ashore, officers and enlisted personnel must be particularly careful to avoid conversation about classified information, especially in crowded areas.

An increasingly important aspect of security on ships, squadrons, and submarines today involves automatic data processing (ADP). Much classified information is stored electronically on disks, both hard and floppy. There is potential, therefore, for individuals to take information by copying hard disks or carrying off floppies. All hands must be made aware of the danger of putting classified information on unmarked disks; and no disks should leave the command without being checked and cleared.

All of the above is only a bare outline and a suggestion of the many aspects of security that will affect a division officer. The main point is that everyone must be security conscious. They should be suspicious of everyone and trust no one, including themselves, when it comes to matters affecting the security of the United States. Sometimes, a conscientious observance of this principle becomes tedious and time-consuming. Any shortcuts, however, in matters of security are a poor reflection on an officer's sense of responsibility.

Administrative Details

Several other aspects of administration deserve discussion.

Special Requests

U.S. Navy Regulations, 1973, Article 0727, directs a commanding officer to afford an opportunity, with reasonable restrictions as to time and place, for the personnel under his or her command to make requests, reports, or statements to him or her, and also to ensure that they understand the procedures for making such requests, reports, or statements. Division officers carry out the last part of this directive by being sure that their subordinates understand the procedures, subject matter, and manner of making a request or statement. Even if the division officer believes that the request may waste the captain's time, it is important for the crew to feel free to exercise its rights as stated in *Navy Regulations.* The usual procedure is for people to write out their requests on a special request chit, available in the administrative office, and to submit it through their leading petty officer, chief petty officer, and division officer for routing up the chain of command.

Article 0727 also directs the commanding officer to ensure that noteworthy performance of duty of personnel under her or his command receives timely and appropriate recognition and that suitable notations are entered in the official records of the individuals. It is thus clear that division officers should bring such noteworthy performance of duty to the attention of their commanding officer for possible public recognition at an awards ceremony or Meritorious Mast, and that they should be meticulous in having such a commendation entered in the service record. The *Naval Military Personnel Command Manual* contains detailed instructions on this subject.

Chief Master-at-Arms

The chief master-at-arms, who is an important assistant to the executive officer, derives authority from Article 303.3 of the *Standard Organization and Regulations of the U.S. Navy.* It says that there will be assigned under the executive officer a chief master-at-arms [CMAA] and such other masters-at-arms [MAA] as may be required as his or her assistants, for the "maintenance of good order and discipline." Division officers are often called upon to furnish the assistants referred to above. All hands in a division should be informed about the authority of the masters-at-arms. There should be no basis, through ignorance, for your personnel to feel that masters-at-arms were invented to harass them. Everyone in the division should be familiar with the duties and responsibilities of these people. The duties of masters-at-arms are listed in the *Standard Organization and Regulations of the U.S. Navy.*

Liberty and Leave

It is important that leave and liberty policies be thoroughly understood. While these matters are primarily the responsibility of the executive officer, division officers often can do much within their units to stabilize these policies. If people are led to believe they will have a certain amount of leave at a certain time, nothing but a real emergency should deprive them of that leave. A firm and fair policy is often more important than any particular number of days allowed each person.

It is a great advantage for the division officer to have some discretion in granting liberty that has been authorized by the commanding officer. Many well-managed ships now have a policy of commencing liberty at a certain time *at the discretion of the division officer.* Liberty, then, is not an automatic right; it depends on the necessary work being finished. A division officer may then keep on board those who have not finished their work. A ship that follows this policy is usually able to grant almost continuous early liberty while in port and yet get the same amount of work done. The personnel have a goal; they know that if they turn to and get the work done, they can earn early liberty. By the same token, those who have not been pulling their weight in the ship can be kept aboard. In practice, division officers seldom have to deprive their sailors of liberty, but the very existence of this prerogative serves to remind the lazy and less-efficient hands that, if they do not produce, they are liable to be delayed in getting ashore.

Pay Problems

Problems involving pay records and Leave and Earnings Statements (LES) are common. Other pay problems involve housing allowances, sea pay, and recent advancement, for example. Your prompt assistance in these matters will be much appreciated by your people.

As a division officer, you must be aware of the Privacy Act of 1974, which affects everyone in government service who maintains records. The purpose of this law is to establish a property right for individuals in information about themselves. The law protects individuals against unauthorized uses or disclosures of information, assures them access to their records, and ensures that records will be accurate insofar as possible. A Privacy Act statement appears at the top of the Division Officer's Personnel Record Form (fig. 4-1, page 64).

Relieving or Being Relieved as Division Officer

Another administrative matter of some importance is that of relieving, or being relieved as, a division officer. When taking over a division for the first time, you have every right to expect that the sailors have a full sea bag, are up on their training, have their equipment and spaces in good shape, and that all division paperwork is in order. The sailors' progress in being prepared for advancement in rate should also be noted. The Administrative Inspection Check-off Lists, available in every ship, should be used as much as possible to cover administrative details. Of particular importance are: a close and thorough inspection of training records (PQS), equipment maintenance and history records (PMS and MDS), outstanding casualty reports (Casreps), individual inventory of controlled equipment, assigned personnel records, and spare parts records for assigned equipage. Only a few division officer billets such as Communications Officer, Damage Control Assistant, and Main Propulsion Assistant require a complete and accurate relieving letter. In any case, always be well informed and comfortable before you take over a division. Remember that once you have taken over, you will be held responsible for deficiencies that may be revealed to your superiors unless you have noted them in writing as part of the turnover procedure.

SNAP II

SNAP II (Shipboard Nontactical Automated Data Processing System, 2d Generation) is the system that is an integral part of today's surface fleet. This system was created to reduce the administrative workload of the officers and petty officers, and to create a database that can be shared by all users. The system's "user friendly" approach provides easy-to-follow instructions on the video screen to guide the user through each subsystem. The system handles unclassified information only, and information stored in the database is protected by the Privacy Act of 1974. The SNAP II database is divided into the following subsystems for access by its users: (1) administrative data management, (2) maintenance data management, and (3) supply and fiscal management.

The Ship System Coordinator is responsible for the overall management of the system. Duties of this position include (1) setting policy and priorities for system utilization, (2) maintenance of the system hardware and software, (3) monitoring security of the system, (4) training, and (5) determining who has access to the system and which subsystems will be available to the user. The ship system coordinator is usually dual-hatted as the ship's 3M coordinator.

Each subsystem of the SNAP II database has its own Functional Area Supervisor, who controls the database and access to particular usage areas within that portion of the database.

Administrative Data Management

The Administrative Data Management (ADM) subsystem Functional Area Supervisor will most likely be the administrative officer. Within this subsystem are the personnel and medical records of the entire crew. Once an individual checks aboard and the information from his or her records has been entered into the database, anyone with access to his or her divisional/work center files can review and possibly modify the information. The subprograms that make up this functional area include:

1. berthing records
2. career counselor records
3. department/division records
4. lifeboat assignments
5. medical records
6. personnel office records
7. watch bill information
8. security force management
9. training records (including PQS)

Each subprogram includes customized reports that can be generated by the Central Processing Unit for the user. Some of these reports include the social roster, recall bill, Watch, Quarter, and Station Bill, PQS reports, and the division officer's notebook. In addition to these subprograms, there is a separate subsystem to manage visitor access records and an area known as query, in which the user can construct a unique report for a particular need. The ADM Functional Area Supervisor will control the production of the printed reports through a line printer at his or her disposal.

Maintenance Data Management

The Maintenance Data System (MDS) subsystem Functional Area Supervisor will most likely be the 3M coordinator. The database for this area includes the ship's COSAL, configuration data, maintenance documents (2K, CK), and the ship's force maintenance files. The ship's configuration database, in the computer maintained at SPCC Mechanicsburg, Pennsylvania, is transferred to a SNAP II system during installation and becomes the Ship's Equipment File (SEF). This SEF contains data on every piece of equipment and equipage. Any maintenance document created will automatically be formulated with the SEF information within the database (i.e., noun name, APL/AEL, EIC, location, serial numbers). The four basic functional areas within the MDS subsystem include the production of:

1. Ship's Force Work List (SFWL) items documenting own ship's work
2. Deferred Maintenance/Material History Reporting (2K)
3. Trouble Log Reports to request assistance from other workcenters aboard the ship
4. Configuration Change Reports (CK) to document the addition/removal/change to equipment.

Within these areas, an individual user can produce requisition documents for parts/supplies, which will automatically be forwarded to the supply department for further processing. This system eliminates the need for a ship to use an outside data-processing facility, allows the ship to produce and update its own reports, and provides the capability to communicate with other computer systems on a tender or shore facility via magnetic tape. This subsystem can generate a number of management reports for use by both officer and enlisted supervisors.

Supply and Fiscal Management

The Supply and Fiscal Management (SFM) subsystem Functional Area Supervisor will most likely be the supply officer. The SFM area is used to process requisitions, produce departmental budget reports, and maintain supply stock inventory and storage records. For the most part, this area will be used by divisional personnel to check the status of parts and supplies that are on order.

SNAP III

The Navy is gradually shifting from SNAP II to SNAP III. The major differences between the two systems are as follows:

• SNAP III is run on a local area network (LAN) between Zenith 486 computers set up throughout the ship, instead of hard-mounted dedicated SNAP terminals. As a result, additional software can be loaded onto the computers, making them far more flexible and useful to the ship at large. The computers are connected either via hard-wire ("ported SNAP III") or fiber-optic cable.

• SNAP III is windows-driven, which means several applications can be viewed and used simultaneously, adding to the power of the system.

• SNAP III is far, far quicker—roughly 50 times faster than its predecessor, SNAP II. One of the major frustrations with SNAP II was the slow pace of the system, requiring users to wait—often for seemingly long periods—for data to process and products to be printed.

• Because it is on 486 computers, SNAP III provides a great deal of powerful computational space and permits the establishment of truly effective LAN message routing throughout the ship.

• Maintenance on SNAP III is greatly improved.

• Laserjet printers (versus line printers) greatly speed up printing tasks.

Otherwise, SNAP III functions in a similar manner to SNAP II, with the same basic functions and uses.

5/Training

> Your people have to be extremely well trained. They can't
> do any better in battle than they can do in peacetime. You
> can't expect performances in battles that are superior to
> that in an exercise—*Admiral Arleigh Burke*

In peace and war, training is a primary naval objective, one sur-
passed in wartime only by that of victory, for which training is the
essential preparation. A ship's state of training is a major factor in
her ability to carry out assigned operations. Her personnel must
be able to operate and maintain all of the installed equipment and
systems. They must also be able to function continuously as a combat team, as a cohesive group. As ships, aircraft, and weapons become increasingly sophisticated, training becomes more crucial
and more difficult. But computers and space-age weapons are useless without skilled hands and well-trained minds to operate them.
It is clear, then, why division officers must train their subordinates.

Shipboard training can be viewed as a composite of several
kinds of training. First, there is individual in-rate maintenance
training, conducted at recruit and apprenticeship training facilities ashore before assigning a sailor to a fleet unit. Individual in-
rate operator training, also traditionally conducted ashore in the
service-school setting, prepares sailors to operate the equipment
they will be called upon to work with aboard ship. Once sailors
reach their ship, they will participate in watch-station training designed to teach them to function as part of a watch team. Finally,
systems training (such as ASW and AAW team training) for both
individuals and watch teams is conducted both ashore and on
board ship. Normally, the basic training is done ashore, and advanced training to maintain proficiency is performed on the ship.
However, a great deal of advanced training, especially in combat
systems, can be accomplished at fleet schools. The importance of

advanced training ashore must be kept in mind when at-sea time is limited.

As far as the division officer is concerned, the various types of training—whether for advancement in rate or shipboard training in general—are practically the same. That is, they have the same objective, to get the crew members to operate better in the billet to which they are assigned or to which they may be assigned. The fact that the BUPERS has set forth in a manual the requirements for advancement in rating does not make such training different. The division officer's problem is to conduct training so that the division operates at maximum efficiency.

The real value to the Navy of everyone preparing for promotion is that it improves combat readiness. Thus, division officers are not just "looking after their people" when they closely supervise and encourage the sailors' preparation for promotion; they are at the same time improving the efficiency, performance, and readiness of their ship or crew.

Training Definitions

Naval standards are the general qualifications, both knowledge and practical factors, for Navy men and women concerning discipline, ceremonies, uniforms, first aid, and responsibilities under the *Uniform Code of Military Justice.*

Occupational standards are the skills and knowledge expected of sailors in their specialty, their rate and rating: for example, typing for yeomen, signaling for signalmen. Both military and occupational standards will be found in the *Navy Enlisted Manpower and Personnel Classifications and Occupational Standards Manual,* Section I (NAVPERS 180680).

Rate training is designed to teach professional qualification for a specific rate.

Individual training is any training (including all rate training) that improves a person's usefulness to his or her unit.

Functional training relates to a specialized task or function, such as teaching sailors to operate a specific weapon or machine.

Team training involves teaching groups of enlisted personnel and officers to work together in CIC, ASW, and others.

Enlisted technical schools provide individual technical training. They have the following designations and functions:

1. *Class R-recruit training* is the basic training that each new enlistee undergoes to accomplish the transfer from civilian life to the Navy.
2. *Class A* provides basic apprentice and job-entry-level training to prepare personnel for the lower petty officer rates (paygrades). An NEC code may be awarded.
3. *Class C* trains personnel in a particular skill or technique not necessarily peculiar to any one rating.

Group or team training is provided by the following types of schools or programs:

Functional schools provide training, often to a group or team that includes both officers and enlisted personnel, in specialized tasks or functions that are not normal to the rating training of enlisted personnel nor to the professional training of officers. They also provide training on weapons of new or advanced design that have not reached fleet usage.

Fleet schools ashore are shore-based fleet training activities, assigned to fleet commanders, that provide refresher and team training to fleet personnel who normally are members of ships' companies.

Training cycles are the sequences of events and exercises through which a ship passes continuously between forward deployments. The cycle includes a *basic phase,* an *intermediate phase,* and an *advanced phase.*

In the *basic phase,* the ship conducts a *CART*—Command Assessment of Readiness and Training—which determines what exercises and events it must undergo before moving through the training cycle. The basic phase also includes four phases of TSTA, which is Tailored Ship's Training Availabilities. TSTA I, II, III, and IV are the ship's opportunities to prepare for the "final exam," the *Final Evaluation Period.* What used to be called REFTRA, or refresher training, is now a part of the basic phase of cycle training.

Assistance is provided to the ship by a large organization on each coast called the *Afloat Training Group,* which provides trainers in every aspect of shipboard operations.

The ship will then move into the *intermediate phase,* which is conducted on a battle group level in a large exercise called a COMPTUEX. Finally, the ship will complete a *final phase,* which is conducted through the FLEETEX. The ship then deploys with the battle group/joint task group.

Additional terms the division officer should be familiar with include the *operational sequencing systems,* which include primarily those for engineering (EOSS) and combat systems (CSOSS). Various *casualty training teams* on the ship include those for engineering (ECCTT), combat systems (CSTT), seamanship and navigation (NDSTT), and damage control (DCTT). Division officers in engineering and combat systems may be on the various teams, and will certainly be in contact with the sequencing systems.

Off-duty training assists individuals in enrolling in Navy correspondence courses or foreign language study, or prepares them for eventual enrollment in the Naval Academy or NROTC programs.

Training services are organizations in the fleet set up to provide training to fleet units, such as tractor aircraft (for AA gunnery), drone control (for missile exercises), fleet tugs and towed targets (for surface conventional gunnery), towed submarine targets, and shore fire-control parties (for naval gunfire-support training).

The Training Program

The ship's training officer is responsible for organizing and executing a vigorous training program. In doing so, she or he is working for the executive officer, and with the department heads, first lieutenant, damage control assistant, personnel officer, and educational services officer, as members of the Planning Board for Training.

When developing the training program, the training officer's first step is to establish long-range goals that cover the ship's competitive training cycle, with a series of intermediate short-range goals that recognize the ship's operational commitments. These goals must then be meshed with personnel resource requirements, that is, the required personnel and NEC codes, shore-based training, watch stations, and systems qualifications. Finally, he or she must establish a schedule for ship training that meets the goals and allows specific, measurable accomplishments. The ship's long-range training program, which normally covers the period between deployments, encompasses an integrated set of standardized exercises for that period. These exercises are normally major evolutions, involving the entire battle organization of the ship, or at least a major portion of that organization. Thus, the long-range training program is the framework around which the departments, and subsequently the divisions, construct their individual training programs.

The long-range training program is not made up in a vacuum; the training officer will meet with the executive officer and the other department heads on the Planning Board for Training. This committee coordinates all training. The required exercises are well defined, but do not cover all the training that must be accomplished over the projected year. The advancement-in-rate program, team training, fleet schools, the operational schedule and maintenance workload, and overseas deployment plans will be considered, and each department will have training requirements that are unique to its role in the overall combat system. As a result, the training officer will prepare a Long-range Training Plan, which consists of a detailed list of training events, exercises, drills, General Military Training (GMT), lectures, seminars, inspections, and assist visits. The Planning Board for Training may sit down with this document at the beginning of the month and prepare a Short-range training schedule (fig. 5-1) showing all unit training, evolutions, and operations scheduled in the Long-range Training Plan. From this plan the division officer will build his or her own training plan.

With the Short-range Training Schedule, you have a leg up on your own divisional plan. You may need to add some material to

Engineering Department	1993						
Month of OCT / **Month of NOV**	03 10	17 24	31 07	14 21			
	03	10	17	24	31	07	14	21
Employment	Sea Trials		ISE		Plane Guard			
Major Inspections/ Evolutions		Zone Insp	Heavy ECC					
	Prac Facs							
Casualty of the Week (self study)	Loss Feed	Loss SSTG	Loss of L/O	High Salin				
System of the Week (self study)	Elec Distr	Lube Oil						
B Div	Feed/ Cond							
M Div	Feed/ Cond	Lube Oil						
E Div	MMR/FR Lgting	Loss SSTG	Salin					
A Div	Loss of pwr	AC&R						
R Div	Loss of pwr	Firemn						
Repair Locker 2	Inves- tigatn	A fire wkthru	Exer- cise					
Repair Locker 3	Inves- tigatn	A fire wkthru	on fan -tail					
Repair Locker 5	Inves- tigatn	A fire wkthru	with hoses					
Department wide	Class A/B	Elec distr						
	fires							

Fig. 5-1. Short-Range Training Schedule

the plan; specifically, you must determine what training is required for your watch standers, what instruction is needed for equipment maintenance, and what professional and military training will be necessary. For example, if you are the OI division officer, you will probably decide that your operations specialists need instruction in surface and air plotting, radio-telephone procedures, security of classified publications, radar operation and preventive maintenance, the *Uniform Code of Military Justice,* and so on. You will have determined this by considering the jobs your people need to do, the equipment they will use, and the military knowledge they need to have. Sources of information include the *Manual for Qualifications for Advancement,* the division's responsibilities under the Battle Bill, the ship's operating schedule, and the list of general military training (GMT) topics contained within OP-NAVINST 1500.22 series. (GMT will be discussed in greater detail later in the chapter.)

Within the framework discussed above, your training responsibilities as a division officer are basically concerned with *organizing your division's time* in order to get all the required training done. Two rules should apply: (1) you need to make each person proficient first at a particular job and then as a member of a combat team; (2) "doing" is the most effective method of training. Both of these imply a certain progression.

Your training program will begin with individualized instruction under the supervision of petty officers. Each person will be assigned a particular billet and station on the Watch, Quarter, and Station Bill of the entire division. If an operations specialist is assigned to operate an air-search radar console, training must show him or her everything needed to operate the console. To accomplish this, the petty officer in charge will use his or her own knowledge, the Navy training course for operations specialist, console operating instructions, and the CIC doctrine book. Shipboard training probably will be supplemented by a week at a fleet school in one of the specialized courses.

You, as division officer, will see to it that the person gets the required console time and is assigned the right petty officer as an instructor. You will have to coordinate this with watch and cleaning duties, and general evolutions such as working parties, all of which complicate your training program. Your senior petty officers might tell you that it takes three weeks of daily instruction for an average operations specialist to become proficient at this particular job; you must see to it that this time is available in spite of interruptions, and that this is made a matter of record.

When proficient, the sailor is ready to advance to team training and becomes proficient at coordinated operations of the CIC team. This type of training will require that your entire division train at the same time. This would be difficult for you to schedule, but this is the point where your training plan comes into play. The plan provides for scheduled team training, by division, during the quarter. You simply take advantage of this scheduling, and work up your CIC team-training sessions accordingly. Remember, your responsibility as a division officer is to get *all* the training done, and the quarterly plan should give you an opportunity to do just that if you are prepared to participate.

In addition to training related to your own departmental combat systems, training such as a first-aid lecture or military indoctrination will be scheduled in the ship's quarterly training program. Since your planning was based on the ship's quarterly plan, time already will have been allotted for this kind of training. Your responsibility is to see to it that your subordinates attend these sessions. Keep in mind that practical factors and military standards for advancement-in-rate include many aspects of training that your specialized divisional program may not cover, but that the ship's programs *do* cover. This gives your people a visible incentive to make effective use of both kinds of training opportunities.

One rule that holds true all the time on board ship is that things are always changing, so the best-laid plans may have to be altered. To keep the training program for the ship current, the training officer, in cooperation with the executive officer and other department heads, will publish a Plan of the Week, which is usually attached to Monday's Plan of the Day. It should list "all-hands" evolutions planned for that week and significant changes to the ship's schedule or training plans. The weekly plan allows you to update your own training plans at the beginning of the week, so that your training sessions are not disrupted by an evolution you could not or did not anticipate.

The most difficult aspect of training is measuring your program's effectiveness while it is in progress. You will have to employ a variety of resources to get a feel for how the training is going. Your chief or first-class petty officer will be able to give you a very good idea of the program's strengths and weaknesses; these people have been in the training business for a long time. The attitude of the sailors is another measure. If they find the training program challenging, they will apply themselves with interest and seriousness. The smoothness of team training is yet another measure: an efficient combat team will perform its jobs quickly, quietly, and correctly the first time around. When you think the division is up to speed, ask your department head to sit in and observe; if you are having problems, ask for help.

Training Records

The record-keeping requirements for a successful training program are not elaborate. Recent initiatives have greatly reduced the redundancy of many previously required records. It is more important that your records be functional than impressive.

You can use a simple method of record keeping for participation at lectures and training evolutions. This is best done on a computer, using a simple word-processing or database management program. Most ships have a standard program they use to record training—check with your ship's training officer. If your ship has SNAP III, the local area network (LAN) will have a database management program that will work well.

Another important aspect of your training program is evaluation of training quality. This can be monitored by any officer or chief for any given lecture or training evolution. A simple form should be used and routed up to the executive officer (see fig. 5-2).

The record of Available Off-Ship Training is used to assemble, for easy reference, information on all Navy schools of interest to the division. Information on available schools is published in the *Catalog of Navy Training Courses* (CANTRAC). This information is also maintained in the computer database of the Shipboard Nontactical ADP Program (SNAP II/III). Most ships assign a collateral duty petty officer or CPO as schools officer to assist the training officer in maintaining this list of schools and coordinating off-ship training. The Ship Manning Document and NMPC 1080-14 list the NEC codes that you should have within the division, and the type commander may specify additional formal school requirements. It is up to you, the division officer, to take advantage of these schools. You should determine what your requirements are and request school quotas from the training officer or schools officer. This may be done in writing or, for those ships with SNAP II/III, it may be done by selecting a school from the computer's database and assigning that school to a member of your division, by name. The schools officer will arrange for quotas, transportation, berthing, and orders.

The Division Officer's Personnel Record is kept in BUPERS (Bureau of Naval Personnel) 1070/6, and records a number of items of interest. Space is provided for administrative information, such as date reported, expected loss date, personal data, previous duty stations, performance marks, awards, educational achievement, advancement, and general remarks.

A divisional Personnel Qualification Standards (PQS) progress chart is a record of individual PQS training. It reflects, for all divisional personnel, the progress at each watch station, including theory and systems progress. More detailed guidance for filling out the chart can be found in the *PQS Manager's Guide* (NAVEDTRA 43100-lC). Generally speaking, PQS progress is maintained on a computer (e.g., SNAP III) instead of a paper chart.

Officers assigned to aircraft squadrons will find in OPNAVINST 4790.2 series, Naval Aviation Maintenance Program, detailed information about training for aviation ratings, including specific instructions for keeping training records.

```
From:    _____
                  (Monitor)
To:      Executive Officer
Via:     _____
              (Head of Department)
         _____
                (Instructor)

Subj:  CRITIQUE OF INSTRUCTION

1.  I monitored _____ on _____
                                                      (Date)
I evaluate the _____
               (Lecture, seminar, OJT title)
training as effective/not effective.
```

	U	N/I	S	G	E
Classroom environment readiness					
Readiness of material and presentation					
Voice projection					
Poise (professional, but relaxed)					
Clear statement of lesson objectives					
Ability to hold group attention/interest					
Engaged student interest through skillful questioning					
Distracting mannerisms (speech or gestures)					
Ability to clarify material when questioned					
Provided useful training aids					
Objectives met					

```
Remarks:  (Comments on "Unsat", "Needs Improvement", or
   "Excellent" areas are highly  desired.)
                              _____
                              (Monitor Signature)
U - Unsatisfactory, N/I - Needs Improvement, S - Satisfactory,
G - Good, E - Excellent
```

Fig. 5-2. Critique of Instruction

Personnel Qualification Standards (PQS)

The Navy has developed an excellent tool for shipboard training, the Personnel Qualification Standards. These standards describe the skills and knowledge a sailor needs to do a particular job. They are somewhat similar to programmed texts in that they provide a detailed, step-by-step breakdown of the learning process; however, the PQS contain no answers. They are something like an exam; the standards tell what must be known, studied, and done.

These standards were developed as the need to provide detailed training guidance became apparent. In the past, such guidance had been provided by officers and petty officers. But as the Navy's ships and aircraft became more sophisticated while the operating schedules remained rigorous, it became increasingly difficult for the officers and petty officers to provide detailed direction. To assist in this task, PQS was developed.

The Coast Guard also uses the PQS system for watch-station training, although the administrative requirements are different. In many cases, the same PQS used by the Navy is used by the Coast Guard. Due to differences in equipment and procedures, not all PQS can be used by both services nor has PQS been developed to meet all of the Coast Guard's requirements. To fill the gap, Coast Guard units develop particular Job Qualification Requirements (JQR) using the PQS format.

The PQS program is designed as one element of the ship's training program. It will not supersede the division training normally conducted, but it will act as a guide for much of the maintenance and watch-station training. The division officer still must schedule and conduct a divisional training program, but the PQS will be a part of it. The standards are broken down into several sections: Introduction, Glossary of Qualification Standard Terms, Table of Contents, 100 Series—Fundamentals, 200 Series—Systems, 300 Series—Watch Stations/Final Qualification, Bibliography, and Feedback Forms.

The format and organization of the PQS are explained in the

Introduction. Throughout the PQS system, the terminology has been standardized, and the key terms and phrases are defined in the Glossary. The Fundamentals section specifies information with which personnel should become familiar before proceeding. For example, the division officer PQS Planned Maintenance System Fundamentals section asks the division officer to explain the following terms and how the contents of each are used:

1. MRC (Maintenance Requirement Card)
2. EGL (Equipment Guide List)
3. . . .

The 200 Series—Systems then breaks the material down into sections that can be studied and tested separately. Continuing with the previous example of the division officer PQS, the division officer is asked to "explain the purpose and objectives of the PMS (Planned Maintenance System) as stated in the 3-M Manual (OP-NAVINST 4790.4, volume I)."

The Watch Stations section asks the sailor to work with the system, to operate or maintain it. For the division officer 3-M requirements, he or she is asked to fill out the weekly schedule, record a completed maintenance requirement on the weekly schedule, and so on.

PQS Record Keeping

Under the PQS system, the qualification entry in the individual's service record and the Qualification Progress Record Chart form the necessary records. Many units are now maintaining PQS records (other than the service-record entries) in the SNAP II/III system. Some are using personal computers. Both methods work well. As each person completes the entire qualification package and is certified by the commanding officer, a page 4 service-record entry is made (see fig. 5-3).

To avoid duplication in record keeping, the completion of training that is covered by PQS need not be recorded elsewhere. For the areas where PQS is implemented, the following records may be eliminated: Division Drill Schedule, Group Record of Prac-

NAVY OCCUPATION/TRAINING AND AWARDS HISTORY
NAVPERS 1070/604 (REV. 11-81)   S/N 0106-LF-010-6948

14. PERSONNEL QUALIFICATION STANDARDS COMPLETED

DATE COMPLETED TITLE	PQS/WATCHSTATION NO.	PQS TITLE/WATCH STATION OFFICER'S INITIALS	
	BASIC DAMAGE CONTROL COMMS	43119-2F 301	
	BASIC DAMAGE CONTROL	" 302	
	BASIC FIREFIGHTING	" 303	
	FIRE WATCH	" 304	
	BASIC CBR-D	" 305	
	DIVISION DCPO	43119-5A 301	
	3-M MAINTENANCE PERSON	43241-F 301	
	3-M REPAIR PARTS/SUPPLY PETTY OFFICER	" 302	
	3-M WORK CENTER/GROUP SUPERVISOR	" 303	
	3-M DIVISION OFFICER	" 304	
	SHIP CONTROL AND NAVIGATION	43492-2B	
	SOUND POWERED TELEPHONE TALKER	" 2301	
	LOOKOUT	" 2302	
	BEARING TAKER	" 2303	
	BEARING RECORDER/RADAR NAV RECORDER	" 2304	
	LOG KEEPER	" 2305	
	LEE HELM	" 2307	
	HELM	" 2308	
	AFT STEERING HELMSMAN	" 2309	
	MASTER HELMSMAN	" 2310	
	QMOW/NAVIGATION SUPERVISOR	" 2312	
	NAVIGATION DETAIL PLOTTER	" 2313	
	ASSISTANT NAVIGATOR	" 2314	
	ENLISTED SURFACE WARFARE SPECIALIST	43390-B 301	
	DECK WATCHES INPORT	43397-A	
	MESSENGER	" 303	

NAME (Last,First,Middle)	SOCIAL SECURITY NO.	BRANCH AND CLASS
DOOR, WALTER TITUS	123-45-6789	USN

Fig. 5-3. Workcenter Tailored PQS, Page 4

tical Factors, Supplementary Record of Equipment Qualification, and Individual Drill Record.

This means that the division officer will maintain two sets of records: one for the PQS-covered areas (the Qualification Progress Record Chart); the other, standard records, for any additional shipboard training.

The Shipboard Nontactical ADP Program (SNAP II/III) enables the division officer to make PQS assignments and to review and update them quickly and easily. All applicable PQS standards are maintained within the computer's database and may be located quickly to make PQS assignments to members of your division. Once this information has been entered, the status of all assignments may be reviewed for satisfactory progress and updated to show the current status. Then a Qualification Progress Report may be printed out for posting.

Training Principles

The division officer must determine when, where, how, and by whom his training plan will be carried out. Several general principles should be observed here. First, instruction should be "on the job" as much as possible. During General Quarters, condition watches, and routine underway and in-port watches, at cleaning and maintenance stations, and at drills, there is time to conduct most of the required individual and team training. Petty officers must be taught how to take advantage of every opportunity for training their subordinates. This point cannot be stressed too heavily; it is the key to efficient and relatively painless training. Many inexperienced young officers look upon training as something separate from day-to-day duties and then complain because they have no "time" for training. In fact, training is an integral part of all activities.

While cleaning, repairing, and maintaining spaces and equipment, your personnel, if properly supervised, should learn as they work. The frequent, inevitable standby periods are excellent opportunities for important training. There are dozens of topics that can be profitably discussed at an impromptu session of this sort, from the authority of shore patrol to next quarter's employment schedule. Damage control, NBC defense, federal housing loans for those on active duty, and the benefits and advantages of a naval career are just a few of the topics on which your people either should be informed or would like to be informed. Much of the knowledge gained this way will pay off directly—for instance, in a future battle problem when all your sailors will be expected to know the rudiments of nuclear defense. If your subordinates are standing by under less-formal circumstances, such as a deck division during replenishment while the ship's approach is made, you can conduct first-aid and resuscitation demonstrations and have each person checked out in certain minimum requirements. It is not hard to get your men and women interested in this sort of training by appealing to their self-interest, and it is far better to have them learning something useful than lounging around being bored. It will not be an annoyance if you arouse their interest and respect their leisure time after normal working hours.

Petty officers must be responsible for training their sailors during watches, on battle stations, and in all other situations where they exercise command. It should be made clear to the petty officers that training is one of their most important duties, and that their performance in this activity will be reflected in the marks they receive for proficiency in rate and leadership.

A second principle is that training must be planned, organized, and controlled. Instruction must be orderly and complete. To accomplish this, the division officer must first devote time to a plan of instruction and to the proper training of the petty officer instructors.

A third principle of training is that it must not be rammed down the throats of the sailors; it must be presented logically, reasonably, and with a certain amount of salesmanship. The position of division officers is sometimes a difficult one, since they are usually on the receiving end of a long and elaborate series of directives. Allowing oneself to become stampeded by this pressure is self-defeating. People can comprehend and retain just so much, and the amount depends to a large extent on attitudes. If the reasons for the instruction are not obvious, explain them. It is not difficult to relate all training to some need in battle, to necessary economies in material or labor, or to such matters of self-interest as survival. It is understandable that in the fast pace of day-to-day operations this need to keep personnel informed is sometimes overlooked.

A fourth principle of division training is that the plan should be realistic and not too ambitious. It must be coordinated with the employment of the unit. Inexperienced officers sometimes try to do too much in order to have a comprehensive plan on paper to impress their superiors. Such self-deception is rarely effective, even for a short time, and in the long run, it is far less worthwhile than a modest plan that is well executed.

Effective Training

Successful division training programs depend on division officers who know what they are trying to achieve and are enthusiastic about training their personnel. Enthusiasm is always infectious; if you are really interested in molding a group of people into an effective fighting unit, they will respond. You can display your interest best by being present at as many training sessions or lectures as possible. You will have many duties on board ship, but you have the advantage of being able to arrange your daily schedule to a great extent. Foresighted planning should help you avoid being called away from a training session.

One problem you will face in initiating a training program is that you may not know as much on a particular subject as some of the people being trained under your direction. This is not as significant a problem as it might first appear. Your senior petty officers represent a reservoir of technical knowledge. Your job is to tap that reservoir and to apply their experience and know-how to the education of the less-experienced sailors.

When you are assigned as a division officer, examine the existing training program. Satisfy yourself that it is effective and that your people are getting better at their jobs as a result of the training. If your predecessor had a vigorous and successful program going, don't discard it just to change things. Sit down with the chief or leading petty officer and examine the whole program. See if it is complete, that is, if it covers the requirements of the ship's training program. Does it complement the division's advancement-in-rate program? Is it going at the right pace, or should it be slowed, accelerated, or discarded altogether? Ask yourself: are the sailors really interested or has their training become monotonous and mechanical? Size up your petty officers: do they really know more than their subordinates or are they out of their depth? Is the program attempting to cover something that might be taught more effectively at a specific formal school? Search the catalog of Navy training courses for those that fit your area of training and compare what the schools offer with what you can accomplish on board.

These measures will get you involved, and the existing program will slowly become your program. Discuss training with your department head, who has been there before you and who can evaluate your proposals. In one sense, you are competing for school time; if you have an integrated and well-balanced training program, your chances are much better for convincing your department head that your men and women should get the school quotas.

Effective Speaking

Speaking to your sailors is something you cannot escape. There will be a number of occasions during the division training program on which you will personally deliver a lecture or briefing. This can be satisfying or embarrassing, depending on your personality and experience. Speaking comes harder to some officers than to others, but all can teach themselves to do a reasonably good job. The important point is to be relaxed, friendly, and natural. Look upon your speech as a sort of conversation, and talk in an easy manner directly to your subordinates. At first, talk to and look at one person, forgetting the others. Then learn to address individuals in turn, shifting from one to another. Do not bother with introductory remarks or closing salutations. Do not tell jokes unless you are very sure of yourself, but do bring in all the humor and light touches that you appropriately can. Humor relaxes your audience, and their relaxation will relax you. Say what you have to say simply and sincerely, and you will get across. Avoid the pitfalls of profanity; most people may laugh at it, but they do not respect officers who can express themselves only by swearing. Above everything, avoid being trite and long-winded.

Speaking, like writing, is a basic way to communicate with people and is important to success in any profession. The surest way to learn to speak easily and effectively is to take every opportunity to do so. There are many occasions to practice speaking in training situations. Lectures must be introduced and drills must be explained. The success of a drill may depend, in large part, on your ability to motivate your subordinates. Your real opportunity to speak comes during the critique of an operation or event, when you can summarize the lessons learned in such a way that the time spent will not have been wasted.

For all but the shortest and most informal talks, make an outline indicating the key points to be covered. Rehearse the talk, but do not attempt to memorize it; refer freely to your notes. Rehearse it by writing it over two or three times. Try out your talk on a tape recorder if you have the time.

Training Instructors

The selection, training, and supervision of instructors is most important. The best designed training will be a resounding failure if you choose poor instructors. Choose petty officers who are able to communicate. If they have not been to instructor training school, check them out yourself using the *Manual for Navy Instructors* as a text. Remember that your sailors must be persuaded to learn; it sometimes takes a great deal of skill on the part of instructors to hold the group's interest and teach it anything.

Find out if your chief or senior petty officers are Navy master training specialists. This means they are graduates of instructor training school and have proven themselves. Use them not only to lecture and train, but to train the trainers!

Imagination in Training

One important part of a division officer's training duties is divisional and departmental drills. Here your sailors must work as a team whether they are involved in weapons, engineering, or tracking drills. The team organization allows you to use your imagination to enhance the degree of realism in drills.

The division officer's enthusiasm and imagination can affect everyone. An otherwise dull drill can come to life when every last bluejacket can imagine the situation vividly. As an inspired director commands the best performances from his or her actors, so the officer who leads with energy, enthusiasm, and a vivid imagination brings to drills a reality that, though temporary, can double their effectiveness.

Weapons Exercises

Weapons exercises are probably the most important general drills conducted aboard a warship. They are held both in port and at sea, usually in a progression from walk-through rehearsals in port to live firings at sea. The ship's long-range training program includes a schedule of the exercises to be conducted; your job as division officer is to see that your people are prepared individually and as members of their combat team to handle the drill and the eventual live firing. In addition, periodic small-arms qualifications are required for security forces, weapon guards, and, in the Coast Guard, boarding personnel.

The conduct of proper drills is dependent on the enthusiasm and effort of division officers. They know best the state of training and readiness of their people and thus are in the best position to organize weapons drills. In most ships, the distinction between weapons and operations departments has blurred significantly. The operations department handles target detection, tracking, identification, and designation to a particular weapons system for engagement. The weapons team then acquires, tracks, solves the fire-control problem, and launches weapons against the target. The management of this whole progression is in CIC; thus, weapons exercises and the drills for them are usually run in combination with operations drills, even when they are extremely rudimentary.

A good drill takes careful preparation. The division officer needs to know what is to be accomplished, that is, the training objectives for each person participating and for the team as a whole. Many complex machines are involved in weapons exercises, but sailors still run the machines and make the important decisions; they must know your training objectives and the purpose of the drill. You must explain what will take place and describe the exercise. If it is being graded or evaluated, you must describe the evaluation points to your team. Above all, you should know the exercise thoroughly.

Training aids that may be useful in increasing the realism of drills include audio tapes for sonarmen, video tapes for search and fire-control radars, and complete battle problem scenarios for many different combat situations. Your department head makes a good adversary when you feel that your team is ready to handle unrestricted drills by imposing equipment and personnel casualties as your sailors run through the drill. An exercise they know fairly well becomes quite realistic and challenging.

The basic rule of training still applies in actual drills—each person must know his or her own job before the team can work together.

Emergency Drills

While emergency drills are scheduled by the ship or unit, the division officer has important responsibilities for the performance of subordinates at these drills. As with almost every other activity in the Navy, successful drills are a product of intelligent and careful planning. If each division officer assigns sailors accurately, and follows up to see if they know their assignments, then even the first emergency drills held should be moderately successful. From here on, the division officers continue to instruct their people at their stations, and, most important, keep the assignments up-to-date. As individuals are detached and new sailors report, a check must be made at regular intervals (and always before getting under way) to see that the Watch, Quarter, and Station Bill is correct.

One factor of paramount importance in emergency drills is the manner in which they are conducted. Division officers must show why the drills are important. Aggressive and enthusiastic leadership is required to avoid the pitfalls of boring, lackadaisical, and nonproductive drilling. Ideal drills are short, well planned, and full of purposeful activity.

Safety Instructions

> The Commanding Officer shall require that persons concerned are instructed and drilled in all applicable safety precautions and procedures, that these are complied with, and that applicable safety precautions, or extracts therefrom, are posted in appropriate places. In any instance where safety precautions have not been issued or are incomplete, he shall issue or augment such safety precautions as he deems necessary, notifying, when appropriate, higher authorities concerned.—*U.S. Navy Regulations, 1973.*

Safety demands a special kind of training. The daily routines of handling ships, operating aircraft, and dealing with machinery and power tools all involve a certain amount of hazard. Division officers must be responsible for safeguarding their personnel against accidental death and injury. It is not enough to know all the safety regulations and have them posted, or even to obey solely the letter of these rules. Safety must be taught so that the division becomes safety conscious.

For example, it is not enough to see that sailors working over the side wear life jackets. Each one should wear a kapok life jacket, and the ties holding the collar up must be secured to support the head above the water. People have fallen into the water and been knocked unconscious. A kapok or fiberglass-filled jacket with the collar tied will keep a person from drowning even when uncon-scious.

Ammunition, jet aircraft engines, aircraft propellers, fuel, and chemical and atomic fission products all require special precautions that are listed in official publications.

Personnel must be kept alert at all times to the risks that surround them and their jobs. It is tough enough to lose your people in battle; it is worse to lose them in peacetime. The best way to avoid this is to keep pushing your safety training. The *Standard Organization and Regulations of the U.S. Navy*, Article 361, states, "A division officer will . . . instruct subordinates in applicable safety precautions, and require strict observance." For full details on shipboard safety see OPNAVINST 5100.19, *Navy Safety Precautions Manual for Forces Afloat.*

Electric Shock

The use of privately owned electrical equipment on board naval ships creates a fire hazard as well as personal safety hazard. In addition, radios, phonographs, and other electronic equipment emit signals that may compromise the ship's radio security. Therefore, no privately owned electrical equipment may be used on board naval ships except when specifically authorized by the ship's executive officer, and then only after it has been inspected and approved by the engineer officer or a designated representative. The electronic material officer will make a similar inspection of all electronic equipment.

A steel ship is quite different from a house in its ability to conduct electricity. Most of us learn to handle electrical appliances at home, and may learn habits that can be fatal aboard ship. Standing on a dry wooden floor at home is quite different from standing on a steel deck; the latter is usually an excellent conductor. The careless handling of ungrounded tools has led to considerable loss of life in the Navy. Even though grounded outlets and plugs are now supposed to be standard, one may have been missed in your spaces. Or one of your people may bring on board a small iron or hair dryer and be electrocuted before it has been inspected and fitted with a grounded plug. Look up your ship's directive on this subject and impress on your sailors how much more dangerous an electrical accident can be aboard ship than ashore.

Safety Training

Because of the importance of shipboard safety and safety training, the ship's commanding officer will have set up a safety program, under a safety officer, to implement Navy safety policies and procedures. The safety program will provide for dissemination of general shipboard safety precautions, instruction of all personnel subject to special hazards, and supervision of personnel in matters of safety. It is your responsibility to implement this program within your division. Among other things, this requires that you appoint a senior petty officer, E6 or above if available, to act as division safety petty officer, and that you ensure that your people receive accident prevention training. See chapter 7 of the *Standard Organization and Regulations of the U.S. Navy* for a specific listing of your safety duties.

Your division training program must include accident prevention, and should make use of such assistance as Navy training films, safety notes, and publications issued by the Navy Safety Center. Your instruction should be tailored to the ship's schedule and cover items of interest at appropriate times. For example, a shipyard overhaul, getting under way after a long in-port period, and seasonal or unusual weather changes should each prompt a training session. As a minimum, your training program must include the following subjects, from chapter 7 of the *Standard Organization and Regulations of the U.S. Navy:*

Electrical safety
Damage control/fire fighting
Industrial/job-related safety
Protective devices/equipment
Explosive ordnance safety/ammunition handling
Hazardous materials
Fuels

Boat handling/deck seamanship/cargo handling
Small arms training
Personal hygiene/first aid
Food service
Toxic gas/oxygen deficiency
Motor vehicle safety
Recreational safety
Aviation safety

Naval Aviation Safety

This section is applicable in general terms to all division officers afloat and ashore. As a naval aviator, you will be extremely safety conscious and will receive highly specialized training in all aspects of casualty and accident prevention. It is your job as a division officer to learn about safety as quickly as possible and then to ensure that those for whom you are responsible learn and observe the rules, policies, and procedures so vital to save lives. There is a Safety and NATOPS (Naval Air Training and Operating Standardization) Department in all squadrons, which is concerned with highly specialized procedures and training. This is fully described in the *Naval Aviation Guide* (Naval Institute Press).

New Personnel

Enlisted Sponsor Program

When someone is ordered from one duty station to another, a sponsor program form will indicate whether or not a sponsor is necessary. If so, the new station will usually designate someone of equal rank, who becomes the point of contact at the new station. A sailor may hesitate to write to the executive officer, but will feel quite at ease with someone he or she will work with at the new ship or station. The sponsor writes to the new sailor, usually at a leave address, and sends a welcome aboard packet of information concerning the ship or station, housing, quarters, schedule, and so on. This packet is provided by the personnel office. The division officer is notified when a sponsor is being arranged, and should help the sponsor; it is not difficult, and it makes a very good impression on a newly reporting sailor when the command takes the initiative in helping out. The assigned sponsor also meets the new sailor on arrival, ensuring that berthing is arranged, initial interviews with key members of the command are made, and a brief tour of the new duty station is conducted. The sponsor is charged with making the new sailor's first impressions of the ship, cutter, or squadron enthusiastic and positive. In some commands, the division officer also writes to the new arrival.

Orientation Training

The indoctrination of newly reported personnel is an important and necessary task of the division officer. Frequently new people on a large ship are assigned to I Division as soon as they report to the ship. I Division functions administratively under the executive officer. Its purpose is to instruct new people in their individual responsibilities, duties, and opportunities, and to acquaint them with departmental and special office facilities and functions. The I Division officer coordinates training for the new sailors on such matters as the ship's mission, organization, regulations, schedule, and advancement and educational opportunities. Since the number of new personnel fluctuates, I Division may be discontinued from time to time. On smaller ships, I Division is a one- to two-week all-day course of instruction that acquaints the new arrival with the ship's routine. In any event, the continued indoctrination of new personnel is a responsibility of the division officer.

Once sailors have completed indoctrination with I Division, they still must be oriented in the division to which they are assigned. It is important to take your new sailors in hand as soon as they report. This is especially true of recruits, who are more easily squared away if some of the polish of the recruit training center is still upon them. One way of introducing a new person is to assign a "buddy" to show him or her the ropes. Clearly, the "old hand" selected should be one whose appearance, conduct, performance, and attitude are worthy of imitation.

The new sailor should be shown around the ship, squadron,

or station, and should be fitted out with a bunk, locker, and a place on the Watch, Quarter, and Station Bill as soon as practicable. Positive means, such as a checklist, should be used to ensure that the new crew member has passed over all administrative hurdles, from having his or her identification card checked to getting up-to-date inoculations.

The last and most important step in the orientation program is a personal interview with the division officer. This interview may be postponed for a good reason, but should never be omitted. In a very large unit, personal interviewing could be shared with a responsible assistant such as a junior division officer. Review each person's record before the interview.

The interview has three major objectives: to establish your position of leadership and responsibility in the new sailor's mind, to discover special characteristics or aptitudes that may not be included in the record, and to show that you have a personal interest in the new arrival. The interview should be friendly, not too formal, but thorough. Take notes that can be used in assigning duties.

Starting someone off with the right attitude is a tremendous advantage for you, not only insofar as training is concerned but in terms of discipline as well. New sailors, fresh from recruit training, are bound to fall in with some of the less-talented types in your unit. They may be tempted to believe that the smart way to get along is to avoid work and look for a soft job. This is why it is particularly important to get new hands squared away on the proper track. By showing that you are interested in them yet making it plain what you expect from them, you make it much more difficult for them to accept poor advice from some of their new shipmates.

Basic Skills

Most newly enlisted sailors reporting on board ship are designated strikers. They have gone straight from recruit training to a Class A school and possess the basic skills of this rate. (This is true for practically all technical ratings such as operations specialist, radioman, fire-control man, electrician, and gunner's mate.) This preparation greatly simplifies training, since these new sailors already know something about the equipment aboard your ship. What they need more than anything else is on-the-job experience, training in military duties and watch standing within their rate, and shipboard indoctrination. They will stand quarterdeck watches and have fire-party assignments, replenishment and sea detail stations, and many other duties not covered in school. This kind of training is also your responsibility, whether or not you personally supervise it. You control their time and their working day, and thus you will have to work with other division officers (such as the damage-control assistant in the case of fire-party training) to round out their training as seagoing sailors.

General Military Training

General military training is another responsibility of the division officer. It is by nature nontechnical and applicable to all ratings. If properly conducted, this training can improve the sailor's appreciation of his or her role in the Navy, both as a member of a combat unit and as an individual citizen. OPNAVINST 1500.22 series lays down these objectives of general military training:

1. An appreciation of the unique role of the U.S. Navy in American history, including its contributions to peacekeeping
2. An awareness of the benefits, rewards, and responsibilities of a professional career in the Navy
3. An appreciation of the fundamental principles of American government and the forces that threaten its security
4. An appreciation of the rights and obligations of citizenship—at home and overseas
5. An awareness of Navy policy, personal responsibility, and assistance available in the conduct of personal affairs
6. An understanding of the principles, practices, and techniques of naval leadership
7. An awareness of the medical, legal, and social aspects of drug, nicotine, and alcohol abuse, and physical inactivity

As division officer you can contribute to this program by offering your personal interest and guidance. You should act as moderator or lecturer during these military training sessions. OP-NAVINST 1500.22 lists and outlines discussion topics and indicates available reference materials. Of all training conducted on board ship, general military training can prove the most interesting, informative, and challenging. The challenge is to the division officer, since the material at first glance appears so fundamental that everyone should already be familiar with it. A second, closer inspection will indicate how little we really do know about the origins of our government, the reasons for certain policies, and many other things that we take for granted. You, as division officer, will find at first a challenge and then satisfaction in being able to lead your personnel in down-to-earth discussions of what the Navy is all about. All of them will gain, as they participate, a deeper understanding of why their jobs matter, what their ship is doing, and how the success of the whole depends upon the smooth functioning of each part.

The last subject—drug and alcohol abuse—merits some additional emphasis here. Drug and alcohol misuse is increasingly prevalent in our society, and consequently finds its way into the Navy as well. Division officers can play an effective role in educating their personnel about the hazards involved, both to the person and to the ship. It is hoped that increased awareness of these problems, and of the Navy's programs for dealing with them, will help reduce and eventually eliminate drug and alcohol abuse within the Navy.

Advancement in Rating

A major part of a division officer's training activities is concerned with the sailors' advancement in ratings. Almost without exception, advancements are made on the job, that is, as a result of in-service education and training. This is one of the factors that makes division officers so important in the Navy. They are the key people in the whole system of skill development and education so vital to the efficiency of the fleet.

First of all, officers and petty officers must encourage subordinates to prepare for advancement. At times, sailors, particularly young ones, are reluctant to work for promotion. They may feel that the increased pay is not enough incentive, and that the increased responsibilities and complications of a higher rate are not worthwhile. One obvious cure for this lack of motivation is to increase the position and prestige of petty officers. Treat your petty officers as junior assistants; allow them to pass the word to their own personnel and give them all practicable privilege in decisions about leave and liberty, bunk and locker space, and so forth. Ask for their recommendations when it comes to promoting the sailors under them. Convince them that only those who have earned promotion should be recommended. The hands should be fully aware that their leading petty officers make these recommendations on the basis of merit and that the standards for recommendations are high.

A generally reliable method of motivating others to work for advancement is to explain the long-term benefits of doing so. Remind them that a superior education usually speeds advancement in all walks of life, and make sure that you provide exact information on all requirements for advancement. Every ship, squadron, and station ashore has copies of the NMPC publications and effective directives, which give this information in detail. This material must be given to the sailors; they should not have to ask for it.

The division officer follows definite procedures for advancement. A brief outline of eligibility requirements for advancement in rating is furnished below for guidance.

Service requirements relate to required time in rate and rating before a person is eligible for advancement. Current service requirements are as follows:

Pay Grade	Time in Grade
E1 to E2	9 months
E2 to E3	9 months
E3 to E4	6 months
E4 to E5	1 year
E5 to E6	3 years
E6 to E7	3 years
E7 to E8	3 years
E8 to E9	3 years

PAYGRADE	E-1 TO E-2	E-2 TO E-3	E-3 TO E-4	E-4 TO E-5	E-5 TO E-6	E-6 TO E-7	E-7 TO E-8	E-8 TO E-9
TIME IN RATE (TIR)	9 MOS. AS E-1	9 MOS. AS E-2	6 MOS. AS E-3	12 MOS. AS E-4	36 MOS. AS E-5	36 MOS. AS E-6	36 MOS. AS E-7	36 MOS. AS E-8
PARs			MANDATORY FOR E-4 THROUGH E-7					
NAVY LEADERSHIP COURSES						LPO COURSE	CPO COURSE	
PERFORMANCE MARK CRITERIA			3.0 MINIMUM PERFORMANCE MARK AVERAGE (PMA)					
PERFORMANCE TEST			NAVPERS 18068-F LISTS THE RATINGS THAT MUST COMPLETE PERFORMANCE TESTS BEFORE TAKING NAVYWIDE ADVANCEMENT EXAMINATIONS					
EXAMS		APPRENTICESHIP EXAMS	PASS MILITARY/LEADERSHIP EXAM (E-4/5/6/7)					
			PASS NAVYWIDE ADVANCEMENT EXAM (E-4/5/6/7)					
INDOCTRINATION COURSES			COMPLETE POIC			COMPLETE CPOIC		

Table 5-1. Eligibility Information by Paygrade

Additional requirements are listed in table 5-1.

The Personnel Advancement Requirement (PAR) form is a checklist of the minimum qualifications for advancement in rate (fig. 5-4).

Completion of Navy training courses prepares enlisted personnel for advancement. These courses cover most of the ratings and military requirements. They are primarily designed to satisfy the knowledge-factor qualifications and are an invaluable aid in preparing for advancement. Completion of certain Navy training courses is mandatory except when specific schooling has been completed satisfactorily. Division officers should consult *Training Publications for Advancement,* NAVPERS 10052, to determine which courses are mandatory if their men and women are to be eligible for advancement. This publication also lists study materials and courses recommended for each rating. This information should be available to your people.

Required service schools apply to certain ratings: hospital corpsmen, dental technicians, musicians, and legalmen.

Recommendation of the commanding officer is the most important requirement for advancement in rating. If the sailor has completed all other requirements, he or she must still be recommended for advancement by the commanding officer before be-

```
NOTE: SEE YOUR ESO ABOUT OTHER MANDATORY ADVANCEMENT REQUIREMENTS:
      *  PROFESSIONAL TRAMANs/NRTCs  *  MILITARY/LEADERSHIP EXAMS
      *  MILITARY TRAMANs/NRTCs      *  PERFORMANCE TESTS
```

PERSONNEL ADVANCEMENT REQUIREMENTS

FIRE CONTROLMAN THIRD CLASS (FC3)

INITIAL DATE

A. WEAPONS HANDLING
A4.001 PREPARE FOR WEAPONS HANDLING
     REF # 5, 16, 26, 32

B. FIRE CONTROL SYSTEM TESTING/ALIGNMENT
B4.001 ASSIST WITH OVERALL COMBAT SYSTEMS OPERABILITY TEST (OCSOT)
     REF # 1

C. FIRE CONTROL SYSTEM MAINTENANCE
C4.001 PERFORM MAINTENANCE AND TESTS ON GUN/MISSILE FIRE CONTROL (G/MFC)
     SYSTEMS
     REF # 1, 12, 13, 14, 24
C4.002 ISOLATE FAULTS IN G/MFC SYSTEMS
     REF # 1, 20, 24
C4.003 OPERATE GUN FIRE CONTROL SYSTEM DURING SURFACE/AIR ENGAGEMENT
     AND NAVAL GUN FIRE SUPPORT (NGFS) OPERATIONS
     REF # 1, 19
C4.004 OPERATE MISSILE FIRE CONTROL SYSTEM DURING SURFACE/AIR ENGAGEMENT
     REF # 1, 19

D. TARGET DESIGNATION/WEAPON DIRECTION SYSTEM
D4.001 CONDUCT TESTS, PERFORM MAINTENANCE ON AND ISOLATE FAULTS IN
     TARGET DESIGNATION (TD) EQUIPMENT
     REF # 1, 12, 14, 20
D4.002 PERFORM TESTS ON FIRE CONTROL SYSTEMS DATA INDICATING/TRANSMISSION
     DEVICES
     REF # 1, 14, 20
D4.003 PERFORM STATIC/DYNAMIC ACCURACY TESTS ON TD WEAPONS CONTROL
     EQUIPMENT
     REF # 1, 14, 20
D4.004 ADJUST AND ALIGN CIRCUITS IN TD EQUIPMENT
     REF # 1, 10, 12, 14, 20
D4.005 PERFORM MAINTENANCE AND CONDUCT TESTS ON WEAPONS DIRECTION (WD)
     EQUIPMENT
     REF # 1, 14, 20
D4.006 ISOLATE FAULTS IN WD EQUIPMENT
     REF # 1, 14, 20
D4.007 TEST/ALIGN/REPLACE FCS DATA INDICATING DEVICES DURING WD
     MAINTENANCE/OPERATION
     REF # 1, 14, 20
D4.008 TEST/ALIGN FCS DATA TRANSMISSION DEVICES DURING WD
     MAINTENANCE/OPERATION
     REF # 1, 14, 20
D4.009 TEST WD WEAPONS ORDER EQUIPMENT
     REF # 1, 14, 20
D4.010 ANALYZE WAVEFORMS IN WD EQUIPMENT
     REF # 1, 13, 14, 20
D4.011 ADJUST/ALIGN ELECTRONIC CIRCUITS IN WD EQUIPMENT DURING
     MAINTENANCE
     REF # 1, 13, 14, 20

Fig. 5-4. Personnel Advancement Requirement (PAR) Form

ing eligible to compete in the servicewide advancement examinations. The senior petty officers must consider the sailor capable of performing the duties of the higher rate, and his or her overall performance mark must be no lower than 3.0. The division officer must act as primary adviser to assist the commanding officer in making this decision. The division officer, in turn, should solicit the opinions of responsible petty officers to ensure that each person gets fair consideration. Examinations are no longer required for advancement to senior (E8) and master (E9) chief petty officer. These top petty officers are now appointed by selection boards.

Career Counseling

The career counseling program provides a single source of information on the wide variety of career opportunities. On each ship, an assigned career counselor supervises and coordinates the program under the direction of the executive officer. Working for the career counselor in collateral duty billets are departmental and divisional career counselors, who become contacts for the various divisions. The career counselor has all the information on programs such as SCORE (Selective Conversion and Retention), GUARD (Guaranteed Assignment Retention Detailing), and nuclear-power training. The career counselor will interview your personnel periodically to determine career intentions, inform them of Navy programs, and so on.

When sailors have less than six months of obligated service remaining, the career counselor will automatically interview them. The idea here is to have division officers identify the best prospects for retention in the Navy; such people are then given a comprehensive look at what the Navy has to offer them. The career counselor in a sense works for division officers in that he or she is familiar with all the programs, while the division officers know which of their subordinates are best fitted for retention. Obviously, only the best are wanted in career programs.

Training for Officer Status

Leading petty officers should be given some training that not only will assist them in improving their present performance, but also will fit them for duties of greater importance—perhaps promotion to warrant or commissioned status. The division officer shares the responsibility for bringing these programs to the attention of eligible sailors and assisting them as necessary in submitting applications and meeting requirements.

A course in the duties of the division officer, using this guide as a text, might be appropriate. Emphasis should be placed on teaching petty officers how to train their personnel. Talks on leadership problems and topics of current interest are also recommended. As in all training, it is important to assess the students' existing knowledge of the material so that teaching time is used effectively. Presentation should be lively and compelling.

Educational Services Program

The educational services program is set up on a ship or station basis, but can succeed only if it is actively supported and encouraged by the division officer. The purpose of the educational services program is to raise the educational level of all active-duty Navy personnel. This in turn will increase their value both to the Navy and to the country. To this end, the educational services officer (ESO) assists personnel in obtaining high school, college, business, and military education credits. The ESO conducts high school equivalency tests, sponsored by the Defense Activities Nontraditional Educational Support Office and may organize off-duty classes in English, mathematics, and foreign languages as the sailors' interests dictate. The ESO works with the division officer in executing the program and in conducting the necessary counseling and interviews.

Educational benefits available through the Veterans Administration are now extended to active-duty personnel and may be used for undergraduate or graduate courses at most colleges. Such benefits can be a great retention factor, as a sailor can earn a college degree while on active duty rather than waiting until discharge. Consult the educational services officer in all matters relating to formal education for your personnel.

Training Directives

Training directives originate with the Chief of Naval Operations, under whose direction training policies are made and responsibilities fixed for both shore and shipboard training. All training activities, with the exception of medical training, have been combined under the command of the chief of Naval Education and Training (NAVEDTRA). Fleet commanders, through their training commanders and type commanders, are responsible for the conduct of shipboard operational training and team training ashore.

Coast Guard Training

Training for the Coast Guard can be complicated. The turnover of enlisted personnel is greater than in the Navy, and schedules are less regular. Required courses for each class of cutter are listed in Commandant Instruction M 1500.10, *Coast Guard Training and Educational Manual.* As the division officer, it is your job to send your subordinates to the right school at the right time. Consult the *Coast Guard Training and Education Manual* and your ship's ESO, but check school dates yourself for recent changes.

Training References

A list of training references is found in Appendix C.

6/Discipline

A Division Officer will . . . be responsible, under the head of his department, for the proper performance of the duties assigned to his division and for the conduct of his subordinates, in accordance with regulations and the orders of the commanding officer and other superiors.— Standard Organization and Regulations of the U.S. Navy (OPNAVINST 3120.32)

Military justice is to justice what military music is to music. —*Georges Clemenceau*

Discipline has many definitions, one of which is punishment, but the most important meaning is expressed by the term *attitude.* Good conduct, high morale, smart appearance, and, above all, combat readiness are the results of good discipline, and a high state of discipline is the direct result of the right kind of attitude on the part of the division. As a division officer, you are responsible for the conduct and appearance of your subordinates. When they shoot a high score during weapons practice or present a perfect appearance at captain's inspection, you take the credit, and quite rightly so. Similarly, when they fail to look their best or when some of them get into trouble with the masters-at-arms or with the civil authorities ashore, you must accept the implication that you have not done your job properly. Either you have not informed or indoctrinated your personnel thoroughly or you have not succeeded in persuading them that it pays to look good and behave properly.

Good Discipline Depends on the Right Attitude

The right attitude makes crew members willing, eager, and determined to follow orders, to fight courageously, to behave in a military manner, and to take pride in their Navy, in their ship, and especially in their division. It is a fair assumption that most Navy personnel have the right attitude. The fighting reputation of the Navy is proof of this spirit. The small percentage who get out of step causes the trouble. *Standard Organization and Regulations of the U.S. Navy* and the *Uniform Code of Military Justice* are written not only for this small group but for all Navy personnel. Remember the primary reason for having a Navy is also the reason for maintaining a well-disciplined ship: combat readiness.

Responsible Supervision by Petty Officers

For the relatively few who never seem to get the word, who leave their gear adrift, who tend to go UA, who can be counted on to appear at mast, there is only one answer: responsible supervision. If these few problem sailors are not concentrated, but are scattered throughout the division, petty officers who are on the job can usually straighten them out. It often takes hard work and ingenuity on the part of the petty officers, but someone who deserves the rate of petty officer must be able to direct productive work and maintain order and discipline. This does not mean, of course, that the petty officer should mistreat personnel, or assign punishments such as extra duty. But by example, reason, persuasion, influence in recommending promotions, and power in assigning duties and work details, the petty officer has ample means to demonstrate that being a contributing member of the team is the best way to enhance one's own position and privileges.

Petty officers must be convinced that they are personally and directly *responsible* for the conduct and appearance of their sailors. Those who do not accept this should be removed from positions of responsibility and reevaluated in terms of their ability to perform the duties of petty officer. The first step in developing a highly disciplined unit is to train the petty officers to accept their responsibilities.

One of these responsibilities in connection with discipline is keeping the hands informed. They must be kept abreast of ship's orders and of all directives that might affect their conduct. For example, if the time of expiration of liberty is changed at the last minute because the ship is getting under way sooner than expected, everyone going ashore must know about the change and the reasons for it.

The second step is to increase the prestige and authority of the petty officers. One way to do this is to tell your petty officers first about changes in the employment schedule, any special tasks, entertainment, or events. Let them pass the word down the line.

Let the petty officers know that they have a share and a voice in the management of the division. This can be done in many small ways without interfering with your own military authority as a division officer. For example, your division may be allotted 15 tickets to an entertainment ashore. Divide the tickets among your petty officers for distribution. They will be gratified by your confidence in them, and the sailors will note that rewards, as well as work details, flow from petty officers. Another way to increase the prestige and authority of your petty officers is to grant them special consideration in locker and bunk space, leave and liberty, and such. Sometimes these matters are beyond the division officer's control, but there will be other ways for an alert division officer to show confidence and trust in petty officers. Above all, back your petty officers in all matters. If you do not completely approve of the way something was handled, there will be time later to tell the responsible petty officer privately how the matter could have been handled better.

Punishment Is Not Discipline

Punishment, the second term associated with discipline, often is used incorrectly as a synonym. The two words should not be confused. Punishment follows a *failure of discipline.* A perfectly disciplined military unit would have no trials by court-martial, no captain's mast; in short, it would have no punishment. Fear of punishment is often an important factor in the conduct, appearance, and performance of any military unit.

People can be careless and irresponsible. Such offenses as gross disrespect for authority, willful disobedience, and sleeping on watch must be punished swiftly, impartially, and sternly. These offenses require the attention of the commanding officer. In case of such offenses, prompt action is particularly important for its effect on others. As a division officer, you must thoroughly investigate the circumstances and should be prepared at captain's mast to shed all possible light on the offense. You may be asked for an estimate of the person's reputation or for a recommendation regarding punishment. In recommending or awarding punishment, the objective always should be improved performance. Avenging a wrong will never right it and will almost always work against your interests.

Investigation of Offenses

In any case of wrongdoing or negligence, your investigation should be as thorough and painstaking as possible. Except for very serious offenses, which must be investigated by the Naval Criminal Investigative Service (NCIS) (see SECNAV directives), the division officer is obliged to investigate all the details and background relating to an offense committed by one of his or her sailors. No one so quickly wins scorn and loses trust and respect as an officer who accepts all reports at face value and just passes them along to the commanding officer. Even when your people are completely and obviously in the wrong, you must learn all the facts of the case. Someone reported for fighting after being slurred or insulted is not in the same class as someone who is written up for beating up a shipmate while in a drunken rage. Some of your sailors may have grown up in a part of society in which fighting is the way to resolve differences of opinion. Others may have learned to tell the truth only when it is to their benefit and expect the same of others. You should encourage these persons to demand more of themselves and point out that the Navy will demand more if they intend to advance. While you cannot condone their conduct, you can often help them get squared away in Navy life. This means that you must learn to manage your sailors efficiently, with an understanding of their human strengths, weaknesses, and cultural differences.

Your sailors are a reflection of the society from which they come. The young people now entering the armed forces face demands for performance and personal qualities that are very different from those of civilian society. Their reaction to the personal sacrifices the military life requires must be viewed with consideration of their backgrounds. The nature of a fighting force does not allow us the same privileges as our civilian counterparts.

Division officers have a special relationship with their sailors and know them better and should understand them better than anyone else. When they get into trouble, every possible effort should be made to see that they get a fair deal. This means more than a plea to the captain or executive officer for leniency; it means getting *all* the facts together and being prepared to make a specific recommendation about punishment.

Unofficial Punishment

Punishment in the armed services is a responsibility and duty of the commanding officer alone. It is not proper, nor is it legal, for the division officer to punish subordinates. An officer tempted to violate the spirit of this rule should remember that sailors are usually well aware of the regulations. Any punishment that is not legal or justified will be quickly resented, and the damage to the morale of the division will far outweigh the good effect that the punishment might have on a few individuals. There is never any justification for unofficial punishment.

The reason why punishment is awarded only by the commanding officer or by courts-martial is to maintain a consistent standard of fairness. Imagine the confusion among the crew if every officer and petty officer could hand out extra duty or curtail liberty according to his or her own standards. The division officer has ample means, in the form of administrative sanctions, to control all but the most hardened cases of bad conduct. Delaying opportunities for advancement, assigning unpleasant work, and denying special requests—such as those for early liberty, exchange of duty, or special pay—are some of these means.

Extramilitary instruction (EMI) after working hours is perfectly legitimate if the strict rules for its use, found in type command instructions, are followed. Generally, up to two hours of EMI per day may be awarded by officers and senior petty officers for a total number of days allowed by command regulations. To be legal, EMI must serve a useful training purpose and be directly related to the deficiency of the individual. It may not be used as a cloak for unofficial punishment. An example of proper EMI would be assignment of several hours of extra painting for a person who did a sloppy job at the assigned painting task. An improper EMI order would be the assignment of several hours of bilge cleaning to the person who painted improperly. The major point here is that division officers must recognize their own means of maintaining discipline, and must use these means instead of bringing all their problems to mast. An officer who does resort unnecessarily to mast is quickly recognized as weak and lazy. EMI should be supervised and scheduled outside normal working hours after normal liberty starts. It should not be done on Sundays, holidays, or on the sailor's own Sabbath. Most ships require that the executive officer be informed of EMI.

Another administrative sanction, although one that is rarely exercised, is the loss of one or more of the following privileges for a specified period: commuted rations, single basic allowance for quarters (BAQ) and variable housing allowance (VHA), wearing civilian clothes, driving and parking privileges, special liberty, duty standbys, exchanges of duty, club privileges, access to movies, exchange and commissary use, and hobby shop access. Final authority to withhold privileges rests with the commanding officer.

Division officers in aircraft squadrons embarked on a carrier have a special problem in that the carrier commanding officer may, if he chooses, personally hold all the mast cases, although he usually shares this task with squadron commanding officers. However, this arrangement does not affect the principles discussed above.

New Personnel with Poor Records

There are several other aspects of discipline that should be considered. One of them is the problem of new personnel who have poor conduct records. In looking over the records of new hands, you may discover a history of offenses or a marked change in performance at some point. A proper course of action is to call them in and tell them frankly that you have seen their record, but that their past will in no way influence their future in the division. Make it plain that you expect nothing but the best from them and that they will start off with clean slates. This reassurance will be important to help them make a new start. All of us know sailors who have "fouled up" at one time or another, but who have done very well since. It is sometimes difficult for people to stay out of trouble if they feel that they have two strikes from the start. It is important to understand that people with poor records will usually want to talk about it and tell you their side of the story. Listen with sympathy; let them get it off their chests even though you may not believe it all. Above all, really listen, don't just go through the motions. Make a firm effort to see life for a few minutes through their eyes—see how their problems look to them, not just the way they seem to you. The rewards you will have for tuning in on their frequencies for a short while may be astonishing.

Interviewing Disciplinary Cases

An important aspect of discipline is the private interview or talk with a sailor who is in trouble. Obviously, the sooner you can spot people who are not well adjusted, and find out what makes them tick, the better are your chances of straightening them out. Sailors who are still in their teens, as well as those who are new to military life, often get off on the wrong foot. Their minor difficulties may be brought to your attention by the petty officers. Sailors with good records of performance and conduct may also fall out of step with the division and become disciplinary problems. There is a reason for their unsatisfactory behavior, and most of the time you can do something about it. The important thing is to find out where their troubles lie.

A private, informal talk is a good way of doing this. There should be no suggestion of a lecture or a "chewing out," although at another time such a procedure might be useful. Try to make them feel comfortable; they may have trouble relating their problems if they feel threatened by the interview or feel their actions and attitudes are being judged as foolish or inappropriate. Remember that something they consider important will have an important effect on their actions. Many seemingly insignificant problems can become important to another person. If you treat that matter with the importance the individuals have placed in it, they will know that you respect them and are interested in their well-being. During the interview, if they wander from subject to subject let them ramble; sometimes people will only hint indirectly at the real problem. Sometimes the very subject avoided, the things not said, may be significant. An offhand remark as they leave may present a clue. Remember that you are trying to find out what they *feel;* do not be too concerned with the accuracy of the statements. Above all be relaxed, sympathetic, and a good listener. You can do all these things without being overly familiar. Just be natural, sincere, and always honest.

Personal Relations with Your Subordinates

The question of whether or not the sailors may themselves become too familiar and informal often concerns young officers. There may, of course, be an occasional character who will presume upon your interest and be disrespectful. A firm yet calm reminder of military manners will usually square him or her away. But this will be extremely unusual. Almost invariably an officer who is dignified and sensible in manner and speech will have nothing to fear on this score. Most sailors shy away from disrespect or bad manners.

Relations with sailors ashore sometimes pose problems for junior officers. In general, it is best to avoid social activities with enlisted personnel. It is very hard for a young officer to maintain status as the leader of a group if he or she becomes too intimate with subordinates ashore. Of course, this does not preclude participating in athletics, or enjoying a few beers after a softball game. Nor does it mean that people who are related by blood or marriage, or who were good friends before entering the Navy, must avoid each other because one is an officer and the other an enlisted person. But it does mean that officers should habitually pursue their social life ashore apart from their sailors.

You may occasionally be invited to a divisional party at the house of one of your sailors. You should certainly stop by early, have a beer or two, and then politely depart. Show you are interested and then move on.

Self-Discipline

> The commanding officer and his subordinates shall exercise leadership through personal example, moral responsibility, and judicious attention to the welfare of persons under their control or supervision. Such leadership shall be exercised in order to achieve a positive, dominant influence on the performance of persons in the Department of the Navy.—*Navy Regulations, 1973.*

Division officers cannot favorably influence their people's attitudes on behavior and conduct unless they set a good example themselves. They must look the part of professional officers and must act in a reasonably military manner. Sloppy and nonregulation junior officers often gain the affection of their sailors, but they cannot gain the confidence and respect so necessary for real efficiency and discipline. When sworn in, each officer assumes an obligation to wear a uniform correctly, with dignity and decorum, and to behave as sailors expect an officer to behave.

The principle of setting a good example goes to the very heart of effective leadership. Officers who behave badly in foreign countries or who come on board drunk are hardly in a position to encourage their sailors to good conduct. Officers who behave immorally not only are failing to lead effectively but are in direct violation of Navy regulations.

Self-discipline includes the moral courage to correct your subordinates. No one likes to be unpopular, but it is often necessary to point out to your subordinates their shortcomings. This is sometimes difficult when the subordinate is a close associate and even a companion, as in the case of a junior officer. But that is part of your job, and is a duty that requires self-discipline.

Another example of self-discipline involves the division officer who simply passes along an unpopular order, taking the easy way out by blaming it on the higher levels in the chain of command.

There should never be a suggestion that "the captain says" or "the exec wants." The order must be passed along and backed up with more than lip service.

The test of self-discipline comes in times of unusual stress. A leader who demonstrates this quality under pressure will gain the confidence of the sailors he or she commands, and will show them the value of discipline. A prime example of the value of this quality is seen in the experiences of people who have been prisoners of war. The records and statements of repatriates from POW camps clearly show that those who appreciated the value of self-discipline proved able to resist and were far more apt to survive the ordeal.

The development of self-discipline is, after all, the ultimate objective of all externally applied discipline. The totally dependable person who fulfills responsibilities under any and all circumstances without direct and immediate supervision is the one who is able to discipline herself or himself. It is such people who carry on the battle when their leaders and shipmates have fallen.

A Division Officer Must Be Accessible

As a division officer you must instill in your subordinates the feeling that if anything is troubling them they can speak to you in private and off the record. This does not mean that you should bypass your petty officers and encourage the sailors to come to you for every minor gripe or grievance. It does mean that the sailors should feel that if they have a real personal problem, they can tell it to their division officer. Some division officers pass the word around through the petty officers that they are available upon request for a talk. Others set aside time on certain days when anyone is welcome to come and talk things over. Avoid, if you can, having your sailors come into wardroom country. Details will vary with individuals and circumstances, but the principle of a division officer being accessible should always be observed.

In a command survey, it was found that approximately 80 percent of the sailors who had been sent to mast for relatively serious offenses had started these offenses in a comparatively nonserious manner. When asked why they had not gone to their division offi-

cer for help, most stated they had no idea that their division officer would be willing to help them. If you do not know the answers
to all the questions or problems brought up, find the answers.
Avoid any suggestion of brushing off your subordinates.

Try to be aware of the troubles that sailors endure even when
they have not revealed these troubles directly. This awareness is a
sort of preventive medicine, and is characteristic of really capable
leaders who know their subordinates well enough and know human nature well enough to be able to detect and help those who
are in trouble before a crisis occurs.

For example, you may observe or hear that one of your quiet,
studious men is becoming careless about his work and is also hit-
ting the bottle pretty hard on liberty. This does not seem at all in
keeping with his past habits of sobriety. You understood that he
was saving money to marry his girl back home. A few questions
may reveal that he has recently received a "Dear John" letter from
his girl and this has hit him quite hard. You can ignore the matter
(and sometimes this may actually be the best course) or you can
try to help him through the situation; a friendly talk, a week's
leave, or a new and more interesting job assignment may do the
trick. This positive action on your part might forestall an addiction
to alcohol or drugs and the inevitable incident involving the police or shore patrol.

The point is that young people often need help in hurdling
life's obstacles. It is more than humanitarian to help them, it is efficient management that pays off in more productivity, better behavior, and greater satisfaction from your job than you can imagine.

Importance of Group Feeling

In the first part of this chapter, discipline was defined as a certain
kind of attitude. An officer who has built up such an attitude and
has gained the trust and support of his or her sailors will find in
the force of group opinion the power that runs the outfit. The
sailors will not want to go against the feelings of their shipmates,
and the fear of punishment may not be needed. This is the true
kind of discipline that pays off, and the only kind suited to the

sailors. Encouraging and building this group feeling are important duties of division officers.

Athletic and social events enjoyed by the division together are real aids in this direction, as is competition in training and inspections. Your divisional PQS progress chart is an excellent tool for training competition since the responsibility for completion rests with the individual. When the progress chart is conspicuously posted and you and your petty officers make it clear that you are interested in each person's progress, the entire division will respond and profit from the training and attention.

Most important of all is your attitude as division officer and that of your assistants. In many small ways, you and your petty officers can show your enthusiasm for and pride in the division and your strong sense of identification with it. The importance of setting an example cannot be overemphasized. It is not only the key to proper discipline in peacetime, but is the most vital factor in leading people in battle. If the officers complain of hardship or seem to lack vigor and aggressive spirit, then their crew members will quickly exaggerate these weaknesses and lose their effectiveness. Inexperienced young officers often relieve their feelings by complaining and griping in the presence of their sailors. You will be hard-pressed to find loyalty, obedience, and trust for authority if you do not present a good example in your own behavior. If you complain about the directives of your superiors or about the demanding schedule, your men and women will assume the same privilege. Nothing could be worse for discipline.

Remember that people cannot be assessed and treated as individuals alone. They must be treated as members of a group, for it is a group of sailors, a division, that you are managing, as well as a collection of individuals. A sailor can be taken out of a group, but the influence of the group cannot be removed from the sailor. In talking to a person, remember that he or she is hearing you against the background of the voices of the group. The sailor's attitude toward what you are saying is determined, to a large extent, by the goals and attitudes of the division. This is why decisions about individuals must be made with consideration of how these decisions will affect the group.

A valuable aid in assessing group feeling is the responsible petty officer who will represent the true feelings of the sailors to the division officer. This is not, of course, the vindictive type, the one trying to curry favor by carrying tales, or constantly complaining about the others. It is the sincere and concerned subordinate who will discuss such matters objectively and frankly with the division officer. The division officer must make certain that such a petty officer feels free to speak frankly.

Informal Groups

Every military unit or command, and a ship in particular, has a complicated social structure. It is made up of interacting groups that have their own leaders and that respond to many stimuli within the framework of the formal, visible organization. These informal groups can have a profound effect upon discipline as well as efficiency. Their existence should be recognized and their behavior studied by all division officers. Informal groups cut across the visible lines of authority and responsibility. Often they center about a coffee pot in a workshop or compartment, or on the bridge. They may result from friendships on liberty or between families, or because of common hobbies or technical skills. Whether they are a force for good or for bad discipline depends on many factors; usually they are beneficial in that they increase their members' feelings of belonging. By observing those groups, an officer can sometimes spot individuals who are potential leaders. If an occasional malcontent or loudmouth begins to dominate such an informal group, the sailor should be given special attention and perhaps transferred to another area. The important point is that division officers must be aware of informal, undefined groups, and be as quick to take advantage of their good features as to take action when they become troublesome.

Regulations

Another point should be covered in any discussion of discipline. Some young officers are prone to set up their own standards of conduct as being superior to those required by appropriate authorities. Nothing can lead more readily to poor discipline. Regulations were written by capable and experienced officers based on the accumulated wisdom of generations of good leaders, and they have the status of law as it pertains to the naval service.

There is only one way to run a division, and that is in a regulation manner. It may not seem irregular to wink at gambling, for example, as a harmless diversion, but a frequent sequel to gambling is theft. Aside from the moral and legal issues involved, gambling is against regulations. Running a division in a regulation manner is a most important requirement for good discipline. This must apply to officers, of course, as well as enlisted personnel. The old saying that a taut ship is a happy ship is still true. On a taut ship, the sailors and officers know where they stand and what is expected of them. Work, hardship, and recreation all are shared. Sailors can depend on their shipmates, because slackness is not accepted. Officers and petty officers are on the job and require their subordinates to be on the job as well.

Among the most important results of administering a military unit in a regulation manner are pride and job satisfaction. People have a profound sense of professional pride and integrity; they take pleasure in belonging to a unit that is run well and by the book. They know that they are good at what they are doing when the rules do not have to be stretched for them to measure up. A division officer must, of course, be familiar with all applicable regulations.

Appearance and Deportment

While it is impossible in a short guide like this to cover every disciplinary problem facing division officers, it is worthwhile to discuss some of the more common ones. The first of these, appearance and deportment, includes cleanliness and dress, as well as general behavior taboos, such as leaning on the lifelines, throwing trash and cigarette butts on deck, and so on.

These matters often harass a division officer unnecessarily, with the result that he or she sometimes harangues the division ineffectually at Quarters, often admonishing them in vague terms. The correct action is simple and effective: use your chain of command. Get your section leaders together and tell them exactly what you expect in the way of everyday appearance and conduct. Direct the section leaders to use their subordinate petty officers, down to the last petty officer, to enforce these standards. Make it clear that if someone steps out of line, you will hold the immediate petty officer and all petty officers up the line responsible. This will keep all your petty officers reasonably alert to the appearance and conduct of their sailors; and if the division is properly organized, it will attain your high standards.

When you have to reprove someone for not doing his or her job to your satisfaction, be careful not to arouse resentment unless the case is a flagrant one and you decide that frank or even caustic remarks are needed. The latter should be needed very rarely. For example, suppose you have the first division on a guided-missile cruiser and the quarterdeck for which you are responsible could stand a little improvement. Your Boatswain's Mate 2C Harris is in charge of the quarterdeck. A good approach to Harris (assuming he is a competent petty officer) would be: "Boats, the Quarterdeck needs some work. Have someone shine up the brass on the picture board and scrub the mats, please." Harris should be chagrined enough at your specific suggestions, which impugn his judgment or alertness, to take adequate action. Or you could say: "Harris, the quarterdeck has improved in appearance, but let's push along further. Here are a few ideas. . . ." If you wish to make it a bit stronger, you can say: "Harris, the quarterdeck is not up to standards of appearance for this ship. If you cannot keep it up properly with the men you have, let me know and we'll look into a shift of work details here." If this does not get results, you should consider either replacing Harris or assigning more people. Note in the above examples that no personal attack is made on Harris; he is in no danger of losing his self-respect. This may seem an obvious point, but it is most important. It is almost fatal to put a subordinate in a position where she or he loses her or his self-respect. If you do so, your future relations with him will probably be marked by resentment and only minimum cooperation.

In learning to exercise authority, a division officer should not cling to outmoded behaviors that he or she may erroneously believe to be standard or proper usage. Poor personnel management often results from a mistaken idea of how leaders should behave. Bad manners, arrogant and sarcastic language, or a tough, heedless, peremptory approach are *not* the normal tools of a boss or leader. The democratic, productive division officer exercises authority and power with dignity and moderation, with consideration for the welfare and personal integrity of subordinates, and in an atmosphere of optimism and approval.

Unauthorized Absence (UA)

The most common disciplinary problem is that of unauthorized absence. A properly organized and administered unit should not have unauthorized absences except under the most unusual circumstances. Sailors sometimes respond to a personal emergency with an unreasoning urge to go home. Unless they understand that requests for emergency leave will always be considered sympathetically and granted if at all possible, they will often yield to their first impulse and depart. If, however, they know that their division officer will do everything possible to help them—including helping with financial and travel arrangements, if required—they will be inclined to request emergency leave.

Other people "go over the hill" because they feel a grievance against the leave policy or the employment schedule. Often efforts by division officers to establish a sound leave policy and to inform their sailors of the reasons for the inconvenient deployment of their ship or squadron can reduce the cases of UA. Of course, there will always be stubborn individuals who prefer to have their own way, no matter what action their officers take. These people can be dealt with only by their commanding officer at mast.

Examine all cases of unauthorized absence critically to detect any evidence of misunderstanding or misinformation. Be sure your personnel know what will happen if they are unauthorized absentees. Their pay (including all allotments) will be stopped immediately; the time they are UA will be "bad time," which will extend their enlistment day for day; they will be punished upon return with the possible loss of liberty, pay, and rate; and they will face the anger of their fellow workers who had to take on the extra burdens of work.

An excellent tool for the division officer in cutting the UA problem is to place a phone call to the service member's family as soon as the absence is discovered. Often the parents have been told that he or she is home on leave or liberty. When they find out the absence is unauthorized, they will see to it that he or she returns on board promptly. Merely knowing that a division officer will call the next of kin will stop many a service member from going UA.

UA generally happens in three ways: (1) failure to go to place of duty; (2) departing from place of duty; or (3) absence from unit, organization, or place of duty. UA requires no specific intent to be absent, while the offense of desertion requires proof of specific intent to remain away permanently.

Theft

Another common disciplinary problem is theft. Its relation to gambling has been mentioned. A division officer can reduce theft by making it as difficult and risky as possible. Crew members should be required to keep their lockers locked, and should not be permitted to stow clothes and other gear in their bedding. Peacoat lockers and bag stowage should be left open only when necessary —and then under supervision. Compartments where thefts have occurred should be patrolled and well illuminated, even at night. When personnel draw large sums of money on payday, such as upon the return from a long cruise, special steps should be taken to prevent stealing. One of these steps is to discourage the sailors from carrying large sums of money on their persons. This is easier to do if arrangements are made for stowing money safely until it is needed, encouraging bank accounts, and promoting direct-deposit programs. The installation of automated teller machines (ATMs) on most ships has reduced theft. Encourage your people to deposit their money via the ATM and withdraw it only as it is needed.

If a theft is reported and you suspect that the stolen property is in the locker of one of your sailors, you should immediately report the facts to the commanding officer, or to the officer delegated to order searches, in order to obtain specific permission for a locker search. In most cases, searches must be personally authorized by the commanding officer of the unit. Unless the search is properly authorized, the evidence will probably not be admissible at court-martial, and you might be held personally responsible for violating command search regulations. Always try to consult your unit legal officer before performing a search or questioning a suspect to ensure that you are following the latest rules regarding search and seizure and ensuring no violation of constitutional rights.

A thief can have a devastating impact on crew morale. A thief on the loose generates worry, suspicion, and distrust throughout a ship or barracks.

Homosexuality

On 22 December 1993, the secretary of defense released new Department of Defense (DOD) regulations on homosexual conduct in the armed forces. Reflecting a law enacted by the passage and signing of the FY-94 DOD authorization bill, the new regulations emphasize that DOD judges the suitability of persons to serve in the armed forces "on the basis of conduct and their ability to meet required standards of duty, performance, and discipline."

This is a very complicated area of policy, and should be approached very carefully. This section will merely provide an overview. If you are dealing with a possible homosexual conduct case, discuss it with the chain of command before taking any definitive action. Your executive officer will probably want to discuss it with a Navy lawyer from the local Navy Legal Service Center (NLSO) before proceeding.

In addition, bear in mind this is an area that has seen a great deal of policy change and controversy since 1991, and more change may be ahead. Your ship's office or local NLSO can ensure you have all the current references and regulations.

Several definitions are germane, all quoted here from NAVADMIN 010300Z MAR 94, published by the Chief of Naval Operations:

Homosexual: A person, regardless of sex, who engages in, attempts to engage in, has a propensity to engage in, or intends to engage in homosexual acts.

Homosexual conduct: (1) Any bodily contact, actively undertaken or passively permitted, between members of the same sex for the purpose of satisfying sexual desires; and (2) any bodily contact that a reasonable person would understand to demonstrate a propensity or intent to engage in such an act as described above.

Sexual Orientation: An abstract sexual preference for persons of a particular sex, as distinct from a propensity or intent to engage in sexual acts.

Propensity: Propensity to engage in homosexual acts means more than an abstract preference or desire to engage in homosexual acts; it indicates a likelihood that a person engages in or will engage in homosexual acts.

The basis for separation will be homosexual conduct. Homosexual conduct includes homosexual acts, a statement by a member that demonstrates a propensity or intent to engage in homosexual acts, or a homosexual marriage or attempted marriage. A member's sexual orientation, on the other hand, is considered a personal and private matter, and is not a bar to continued service unless manifested by homosexual conduct.

There are many complicated nuances to this policy area, particularly when the possibility of discharge is involved, but the simplest broad construct is as follows:

Homosexual conduct is grounds for discharge; sexual orientation is a personal and private matter and is not grounds for discharge.

If an individual is discharged for homosexual conduct, the discharge will be the type warranted by service record unless the homosexual act occurred under the following circumstances: (1) under force, coercion, or intimidation; (2) with a person under 16 years of age; (3) with a subordinate in circumstances that violate customary naval superior-subordinate relationships; (4) openly in public view; (5) for compensation; (6) aboard a naval vessel or aircraft; or (7) in another location subject to naval control (e.g., a naval base) under aggravating circumstances that have an adverse impact on discipline, good order, or morale compared to the impact created by such activity aboard a vessel or aircraft.

Only the member's command is authorized to initiate fact-finding inquiries involving homosexual conduct, not, for example, the Naval Criminal Investigative Service (NCIS). A commander may initiate a fact-finding inquiry only when he or she has received credible information that there is basis for discharge. Commanders are responsible for ensuring that inquiries are conducted properly and that no abuse of authority occurs.

It is worth noting that credible information leading to an inquiry does *not* exist when the only information consists of the opinions of others that a member is homosexual; or rumor, suspicion, or capricious claims against a person; or associational activity such as going to a gay bar, possessing or reading homosexual publications, associating with known homosexuals, or marching in a gay rights rally in civilian clothes. The latter activity, in and of itself, does not provide evidence of homosexual conduct.

On the other hand, credible information *does* exist, for example, if a reliable person states that he or she observed or heard a service member engaging in homosexual acts, or saying that he or she is a homosexual or bisexual or is married to a member of the same sex; or when a reliable person states that he or she heard, observed, or discovered a member make a spoken or written statement that a reasonable person would believe was intended to convey the fact that he or she engages in, attempts to engage in, or has a propensity or intent to engage in homosexual acts; or a reliable person states that he or she observed behavior that amounts to a nonverbal statement by a member that he or she is a homosexual or bisexual.

Revisions to the MILPERSMAN, which explain all of this in detail, are in place and should be reviewed with all other applicable references. All hands should, at least, be generally familiar with Navy policy in this area.

Drugs

It is the policy of the Navy to prevent and eliminate the use of marijuana, narcotics, and other controlled substances by preventing their sale; by publicity, counseling, and instruction relating to drug abuse, including information concerning possible administrative separation or criminal liability; and by stressing the responsibility of commanders for initiating disciplinary or administrative proceedings in drug-abuse cases. The division officer has a vital role to play in enforcing this policy, especially in counseling. To do this, he or she must be well informed on the subject. Here are a few key facts:

1. Federal law includes in the term *controlled substances* all narcotic and nonnarcotic products that the attorney general finds have a potential for abuse.
2. *The Uniform Code of Military Justice* (UCMJ) prohibits the unauthorized manufacture, possession, sale, transfer, or use of any controlled substance. The latter means amphetamine, cocaine, heroine, lysergic acid diethylamide (LSD), marijuana, methamphetamine, opium, phencyclidine, and barbituric acid, including phenobarbital and secobarbital. It also includes other substances listed in the Controlled Substances Act of 1970.
3. Under the UCMJ, the use or possession of more than 30 grams of marijuana or narcotics is a felony, punishable by dishonorable discharge, confinement at hard labor for five years, forfeiture of all pay and allowances, and reduction to the lowest paygrade. It is the duty of the division officer to instruct subordinates regu-

larly on the dangers involved in drug abuse and the administrative action or criminal liability that can result.

The Chief of Naval Operations has emphasized that there will be no use (zero tolerance) of marijuana or other drugs in the Navy. New and positive means of detection, including urinalysis, are being used, and first offenders will be separated from the Navy at once. Regardless of what happens among civilians, the Navy cannot meet its responsibilities for combat readiness with personnel who use drugs. The sooner your people know that you are very tough and determined about this, the sooner they will get the word. It is not wise to debate with them the pros and cons of drugs and alcohol. They must accept the total prohibition of drug use that the Navy imposes.

Alcohol

Although the use of alcohol is not illegal by those of age (except, in general, on board ship) in the Navy, its abuse presents serious problems to the individuals involved and to those responsible for supervising their work. Your men and women are separated from home and their normal system of psychological supports much of the time. For some, this may be their first experience on their own. This and other factors (notably peer pressure) may lead to alcohol abuse. Dependence upon or compulsive abuse of alcohol is considered alcoholism. This can lead to great suffering for the abuser and is always detrimental to good discipline.

Someone who is an excellent sailor aboard ship, but cannot handle liquor ashore, needs and deserves your help. People who perform poorly as a result of alcohol abuse can become valuable members of your organization if you help them with their problem. Alcoholism is a complex condition that can sometimes be conquered, but it is not easy, either for the victim or for those who want to help.

Alcoholics may not be able to live up to the responsibilities of their jobs. Others, therefore, may have to do their work. This inevitably leads to hard feelings, and if allowed to continue will ruin discipline in your division.

As the division officer, you should take action as soon as you suspect that alcohol abuse may be becoming a problem for any of your sailors. As noted in chapter 2, in counseling you should approach the matter from the standpoint of performance of duty. Let your people know that you will not tolerate poor performance as a result of alcohol abuse. This should not be presented as a condemnation of all drinking but as an instruction in the hazards of alcohol abuse. Its effects on both the individual and the group are your concern as division officer.

OPNAVINST 5350.4B series sets forth Department of the Navy policies on alcoholism and alcohol and drug abuse among Navy personnel, and establishes responsibility for implementing those policies. Subordinate echelons of command have issued specific guidelines for administering local programs for alcohol abusers.

It is the responsibility of all Navy personnel to avoid alcohol dependence and to seek assistance for alcoholism. The Navy, however, attempts to identify and treat alcoholics whether they seek treatment or not. Alcoholism itself is not reason for discharge on the ground of unsuitability, since it can be controlled. If an individual does not cooperate with rehabilitation efforts, he or she may be administratively separated. Remember that drunk and disorderly behavior, drunk driving, and drunk on duty are all violations of the UCMJ and will result in serious punishment.

Uniform Code of Military Justice (UCMJ)

This is not the place for a full exposition of the UCMJ. A division officer uses the code every day when handling sailors, and must understand it in relation to disciplinary problems. Some aspects of the code, however, may not be covered in a course on military law.

Bringing someone to mast (making out a misconduct report) should be the last resort, used only when all other administrative and disciplinary means have failed. At times, however, the gravity or frequency of an offense leaves you no choice.

It is sound practice to have officers and petty officers under you obtain your concurrence before placing one of their people on report, and to settle your problems within the division if at all possible. If the case involves someone from another division, consult that division officer before you place the person on report for a serious offense; you may not be aware of some aspects of the incident. Consulting your fellow division officers before taking action is a mark of courtesy.

In order to become familiar with the UCMJ, Coast Guard division officers should consult the Coast Guard supplement to the *Manual for Courts-Martial*, U.S. Coast Guard regulations (CG 300), and all relevant unit instructions and standing orders. Naval personnel should consult the *Manual for Courts-Martial*, 1984 (MCM).

Apprehension and Restraint

An officer must know the difference between *apprehension* and the three degrees of *restraint*.

The officer of the deck will take custody of personnel charged with misconduct. They may be delivered by the shore patrol or by an officer or petty officer on board ship. They may even deliver themselves for minor offenses, such as being out of uniform. The officer of the deck must know the legal meanings of the terms involved, and what action to take.

All officers, petty officers, and noncommissioned officers of any service have authority to apprehend offenders, subject to the UCMJ. Other enlisted personnel may do so when assigned to shore patrol, military police, and similar duties. *Apprehension* means clearly informing the person that he or she is being taken into custody and at the same time of what he or she is accused. It should be noted here that apprehension, in the armed services, has the same meaning as *arrest* in civilian life. Just as a police officer informs a citizen that he or she is under arrest, a naval officer tells a sailor that he or she is being apprehended or taken into custody. *Custody* is temporary control over the person apprehended until delivery to the proper authority (on board ship: the officer of the deck). In general, persons who have authority to apprehend may exercise only such force as is actually necessary. Petty officers should apprehend officers only under very unusual circumstances, such as to avoid disgrace to the service, to prevent the escape of a criminal, or when another officer directs them to do so.

Restraint involves limiting the free movement of an individual. There are three degrees of restraint: *confinement, arrest,* and *restriction in lieu of arrest.* The degree of restraint used should be no more severe than that necessary to ensure the offender's presence at further proceedings. Thus, even though someone has committed an offense or is suspected of such, he or she need not be restrained to any degree if his or her presence is assured at future proceedings.

Persons apprehended on board ship are delivered to the custody of the officer of the deck, together with a misconduct report. The officer of the deck informs the executive officer (or command duty officer) and receives instructions as to the nature of restraint, if any, to be imposed. This, of course, normally depends on the gravity of the offense. Assuming that formal restraint, such as arrest, is ordered, the officer of the deck makes sure that the offender understands the nature of the restraint and the penalties for violation of restraint. The officer of the deck secures the offender's written acknowledgment of the notification by his or her signature on the misconduct report slip, and then turns the offender over to the master-at-arms. The matter is logged, of course, with full details.

Only the commanding officer may impose restraint on a commissioned officer or a warrant officer. If an officer must be restrained, the commanding officer must be notified.

Only officers may ordinarily impose restraint on an enlisted person. However, the commanding officer may delegate this authority to warrant officers and enlisted personnel.

Confinement is actual physical restraint imposed in serious offenses to ensure the presence of the person. *Pretrial confinement* involves placing the accused behind bars in a brig and should be employed only when necessary to ensure the presence of the accused at a special or general court-martial. It may not be used awaiting a mast or summary court. The requirements for legally confining an accused before trial are found in the *Naval Corrections Manual, The Manual for Courts-Martial 1984,* and in local type command instructions. They include a mandatory determination by the accused's commanding officer not later than 72 hours after the confinement was ordered as to whether the confinement should continue. A review of the adequacy of the probable cause to believe the prisoner has committed an offense and of the necessity for pretrial confinement shall be made by a neutral magistrate within seven days of the imposition of the confinement. Failure to follow the requirements to the letter can result in the confinement being declared illegal and can jeopardize the proper punishment of the accused.

Arrest is the moral restraint of a person, by an order, oral or written, to certain specified limits pending disposition of charges against him or her. It is not imposed as punishment. It is imposed only for probable cause, based on known or reported facts concerning an alleged offense. Arrest relieves a person of all military duties other than normal cleaning and policing. Arrest is imposed by telling a sailor (or officer) of the limits of the arrest, orally or in writing.

One of the disadvantages of placing accused persons in arrest is that they may no longer be required to perform their military duties. If the authority ordering this type of restraint requires the accused to perform military duties, the arrest is automatically terminated. Consequently, a lesser form of restraint is allowed. This is called restriction in lieu of arrest.

Restriction in lieu of arrest, often called pretrial or premast restriction, is restraint of the same nature as arrest, imposed under similar circumstances, but it does not involve suspension of military duties. Although the *Manual for Courts-Martial* (MCM) gives authority to any officer to restrict enlisted personnel, most command instructions require that restriction orders be approved personally by the commanding officer or executive officer. A restricted person performs full military duties.

The MCM states that an accused person may be required to remain within a specified area at specified times either because his

or her continued presence pending investigation may be necessary or because it may be considered a wise precaution to restrict
him or her to such an area in order that he or she may not again
be exposed to the temptation of misconduct similar to that for
which he or she is already under charges. Thus, if the offense is
relatively minor, and the accused has shown no tendency to attempt to leave the area to avoid trial, no restraint is necessary.

Once imposed, restraint may not be lifted except in the following circumstances. Arrest and restriction in lieu of arrest may
be lifted by the authority ordering the restraint, or by a superior in
the chain of command. Any commanding officer of a prisoner, a
military magistrate, or a military judge detailed to hear the accused's court-martial may release the accused from pretrial confinement. On board ship, the authority generally ordering the
confinement is the commanding officer.

When discussing an offense, or a suspected offense, with a
sailor, be meticulous in informing him or her of rights under the
UCMJ. The suspected offender should be warned that he or she
need not testify or say anything at all, and that whatever he or she
does say may be used. He or she should further be told that he or
she has the right to have an attorney present during the interroga-
tion and that, if desired, an attorney will be appointed by the Navy
at no cost. He or she should also be told that, if he or she consents
to questioning without the presence of counsel, he or she may ter-
minate the questioning at any time. Failure to observe this requirement may result in the acquittal of someone charged with a
serious offense, even though the evidence indicates that he or she
is guilty.

Article 137 of the UCMJ requires that each commanding officer explain certain parts of the code to every enlisted person beginning active duty, after six months of active duty, and upon reenlistment. A copy of the code should be posted on the ship.

All your sailors should understand the gravity of offenses involving unauthorized absence and missing ship. The extent and
limitations of nonjudicial punishment should also be understood.
The standard manual for the three services is the *Manual for*

Courts-Martial, United States, 1984. There is also a *Manual of the Judge Advocate General,* issued by the secretary of the Navy, chapter 1 of which implements in the naval service various sections of the UCMJ and the MCM. Especially useful for officers with limited legal experience is *Military Law,* published by the U.S. Naval Institute, which offers a concise, thorough review of the MCM.

Your major disciplinary problem will probably be the few immature young persons who are characterized as malcontents. This small percentage is evident in almost every command and is a seemingly constant source of unrest. These sailors can often be reformed and persuaded to become useful, but there may be a few who will never become useful members of the naval service. These hopeless cases are eventually separated from the service, either by court-martial or administratively. In either case, the division officer must decide about these people and, if they are beyond redemption, recommend their separation to the commanding officer. There is nothing to be gained by avoiding the issue; if no useful work can be obtained from a sailor, the sooner he or she leaves the Navy, the sooner a more useful person can be trained.

Remember that, although nonjudicial punishment is not legally considered a criminal conviction, it can be introduced at a court-martial for later offenses to show the accused person's character of service and may justify the awarding of a much harsher punishment than would have been awarded to a person with a clean record. Nonjudicial punishment also is used when evaluating the need for the adverse administrative discharges specified in the NMPC Manual.

In handling the few incorrigibles who cannot stay out of serious trouble, you may run into a few who appear to welcome a bad-conduct discharge. It often sobers these sailors to learn how serious a bad-conduct discharge really is. The impact a bad-conduct discharge carries into civilian life—upon veterans' rights and privileges, upon getting a job, upon parents and friends at home, and even upon one's children—is worth mentioning to sailors who claim that they don't care how they get out of the Navy.

The Effects of a Punitive Discharge

Punitive discharges are those awarded by special and general courts-martial. A special court-martial may award a bad-conduct discharge (BCD). A dishonorable discharge (DD) may only be awarded by a general court-martial. The real meaning of a bad-conduct discharge and its consequences are often not clearly understood by enlisted personnel.

This is probably because of the distinction between a bad-conduct discharge awarded by a general court-martial and one awarded by a special court-martial with respect to entitlement to federal benefits. A bad-conduct discharge awarded by a general court-martial always results in loss of benefits under federal laws.

A bad-conduct discharge awarded by a special court-martial may be termed a discharge "under dishonorable conditions" by the Veterans Administration, and this may also result in loss of most benefits under federal laws.

The following benefits are always denied to members of the naval service who are separated with a bad-conduct discharge awarded by a special court-martial:

Travel allowance
Right to retain and wear uniform
Honorable service lapel button or pin
Honorable discharge button
Certificate of satisfactory service
Shipment of household goods or trailer
Reemployment rights
Civil service preference
Burial in a national cemetery

The following benefits may also be denied in a case of a bad-conduct discharge awarded by a special court-martial upon determination by the Veterans Administration that the discharge was under dishonorable conditions:

Federal vocational rehabilitation
Educational rights (such as assistance in going to school, GI bill)
Loan guarantee (which includes GI loans for home or business)
Employment assistance (aid in getting federal or private
    employment)
Service-connected disability compensation
Pension for disability not service connected
Hospital care in Veterans Administration facility
Medical care and prosthetic appliances (such as false teeth, limbs)
Compensation for death due to naval service
Pension for death not due to naval service
Burial allowance
Burial flags
Right to join veterans organizations requiring
    honorable discharge

There are other serious consequences that stem from a bad-conduct discharge in addition to the loss of benefits under federal or state laws. Many employers, particularly large corporations, base the hiring of former members of the naval service in part upon the type of discharge. Thus, a bad-conduct discharge can affect the individual's whole future.

The consequences of a dishonorable discharge are as serious as a BCD and can be worse. It is a discharge reserved for those separated under conditions of dishonor after having been convicted of felony offenses or offenses of a military nature requiring severe punishment.

A division officer should be generally familiar with the administrative procedure for separating sailors from the Navy. Those whose conduct has been poor and whose performance of duty and value to the Navy are limited can be discharged under honorable conditions by the NMPC. Division officers should nominate for administrative discharge those whose contributions are negative and whose reform and improvement seem unlikely.

Nonjudicial Punishment

The terms *nonjudicial punishment, captain's mast,* and *NJP* are used interchangeably in the fleet. All refer to certain limited punishments that can be awarded for minor disciplinary offenses by a commanding officer or officer-in-charge to members of the command. NJP is both administrative and nonadversarial in nature—it is not a trial—and when punishment is imposed, it is not considered a conviction. Sailors assigned to shore duty can refuse NJP and take a courts-martial instead; if assigned to a ship, they must take NJP.

Captain's mast is run differently on various ships, but in general, it is held in a limited space (classroom, training room, bridge in port) with a podium at the head of the room. The commanding officer stands behind the podium and the sailor is marched into the room, stops and salutes the CO, and is read his or her rights. The CO will ask questions of witnesses, ask the chain of command about the sailor's performance, consider the case, and award punishment.

At this point, the division officer has the chance to make a statement about the offense, the performance of the sailor, and a recommendation. The CO will generally weigh very heavily the words of the division officer, and you should consider them very carefully.

Liberty Risk Program

Another important aspect of maintaining good order and discipline within your command is the liberty risk program. It is used only while forward deployed, and provides a means for the command to ensure that sailors who have exhibited problems in behavior are not permitted to go ashore in foreign countries.

Due to the extremely sensitive nature of foreign liberty visits, a commanding officer can—as a proactive measure—limit a crew member's liberty to minimize the potential for any liberty incident. The basis for this determination may be formed by the crew member's previous conduct either ashore or afloat, current medical evaluation, or any other reason deemed appropriate by the commanding officer.

There are generally several categories of liberty risk as follows:

Class A: No alcohol may be consumed during liberty and the individual must report to the officer of the deck before departing and upon return from liberty.

Class B: No alcohol may be consumed during liberty, the individual must report to the officer of the deck before departing and upon return from liberty, a petty officer escort of equal or higher paygrade is required and liberty expires on board at 2400.

Class C: The same as Class B, except liberty expires on board at 1800 and is limited to certain areas ashore.

Class D: No liberty is granted.

Being placed in a liberty risk status is an administrative rather than a disciplinary proceeding, therefore no hearing, presentation of evidence, or other process is required. Generally, a sailor can review the action via the request mast process.

Hazing

Navy and Coast Guard policy strictly prohibits unauthorized hazing due to the potential for death or injury to personnel. Hazing is not tolerated in any form, and is defined as any action that subjects a shipmate to any act of physical or verbal abuse. The issue of whether the service member is consenting or volunteering is irrelevant if the action has not received approval from the chain of command.

Past examples of hazing have included actions such as wrestling shipmates to the ground to give them "red bellies," so-called blanket parties, taping or tying a member's arms or legs; handcuffing members to fixed objects; placing or pouring foreign substances or liquids on personnel; "tacking on crows," forcing members to strip or consume substances; or forcing the consumption of alcohol. Unfortunately, this is not even close to an all-inclusive list—but it at least provides examples of inappropriate behavior.

Make it clear from the start to your division that you will not permit any form of hazing!

Conclusion

In the end, the best means of providing good order and discipline to your division is by taking care of your people. Listen to them, sort out their problems before they develop into crises, remain a steadfast example to them, be steady and firm in the application of discipline, and keep the chain of command informed as you work to keep your division running smoothly.

7/Assessments and Inspections

The division officer shall by personnel supervision and
frequent inspections insure that the spaces, equipment,
and supplies assigned to his division are maintained in a
satisfactory state of cleanliness and preservation.
—Standard Organization and Regulations of the U.S. Navy
(OPNAVINST 3120.32).

You get what you *inspect,* not what you *expect!*—*Naval saying*

General

Over the past years, the idea of "inspections" has shifted somewhat
in the fleet more toward "assessments and inspections." This is
meant to imply a "kinder, gentler" approach from off-ship inspection teams coming aboard—more teaching, preparation, positive
interaction, and explanation as part of the process. To a degree,
this is a result of total quality leadership (TQL), and to a degree it
is simply part of the gradual shift in organizational approach felt
throughout industry, business, and society at large.

It doesn't in any way obviate the old saying, "you get what you
inspect, not what you expect." This is particularly true at the deck
plate level where the division officer works. Navy regulations and
the *Standard Organization and Regulations of the U.S. Navy* (SORM)
still strongly emphasize the requirement for division officers to get
out into their spaces, inspect their personnel, and generally evaluate and assess the running of their divisions on a constant basis.

Division officers should take literally the directive to make
"frequent inspections." There is no substitute for periodic visits to
all the spaces for which you are responsible. These visits not only
ensure that work and training are progressing satisfactorily, they
also indicate your interest in your subordinates and give them a

chance to see you and talk to you. *Frequent inspections do not imply frequent criticism or carping.* Be friendly and praise work well done unless you note deficiencies. Remember that an atmosphere of approval results in maximum cooperation.

Anyone can go through the motions of inspecting without really seeing anything. Such inspections serve no purpose and waste everyone's time. *Inspection* means careful and critical examination. To examine carefully and critically requires considerable knowledge, hard work, and judgment. You may have to develop your knowledge as you go along in a new job, so do not hesitate to ask questions. Your people will appreciate your interest and honesty. As you learn all about your machinery and ordnance, compartments and spaces, or the personnel for whom you are responsible, your knowledge will help you develop judgment. "Do my sailors look as smart as they should? Is my gear as well maintained as that in the other ships in the squadron? Are my compartments cleaned satisfactorily? Should I paint the living compartment or touch it up again?" There are no simple answers to these questions. Many factors have to be considered, especially the policies of your superior officers. Find out what they want and then give it to them.

Other considerations may influence your judgment—funds available for paint, the past and future employment of the unit, and the demands of drills, leave periods, and similar interruptions to your maintenance schedule. Following the policies of your superiors should not, of course, stifle your own initiative.

Internal and External Inspections

As a general premise, there are two types of inspections a division officer needs to understand. One is the *internal inspection* conducted within the lifelines of the ship by a member of the ship's company, with the highest report provided to the commanding officer. Examples include the executive officer's daily messing and berthing inspection, zone and material inspections, division-in-the-spotlight inspections, formal and informal personnel inspections, seabag inspections, and health/comfort or locker inspections. These generally do not require the generation of a plan of action and milestones (POA&M) or the involvement of the entire ship at one time. They are a direct responsibility of the division officer.

The second broad category of inspection is the *external inspection* conducted by an organization from outside the lifelines of the ship. The final report, in this case, is forwarded to the squadron or air wing commander, the type commander, or the fleet commander. Examples include InSurv (inspection by the Board of Inspection and Survey), command inspection, propulsion examining board inspections, logistics management assessment, aviation readiness evaluation, or combat systems assessment. These are generally shipwide evolutions requiring the construction and execution of a detailed plan of action and milestones. As a division officer, you may be tasked with some segment of the POA&M, or occasionally, in the case of a smaller inspection like the Aviation Readiness Evaluation, be in charge of the entire evolution.

Internal Inspections

Many types of inspections will involve you in one way or another. You will conduct some inspections yourself; the petty officers in your division will hold others. Some inspections will be formal and extensive; others will be informal and rather cursory.

Division officers commonly hold personnel inspection, daily material inspection, and locker and seabag inspection in their divisions, and they sample rations in the general mess. There are no special procedures for holding such inspections, but this should not lessen their importance. In addition, your division will have to prepare for several graded, formal inspections by senior officers.

Executive Officer's Messing and Berthing Inspection—The executive officer will inspect all messing areas, galleys, and berthing compartments daily—usually at about 1000, after the food servicemen and compartment cleaners have them in order—and will be accompanied by the chief master-at-arms, possibly the corpsman, and occasionally the command master chief or the chief of the boat. The exec's main concern is to discover major hazards to health and safety in the messing and berthing spaces, but the appearance and condition of stowage and preservation in such spaces are also inspected.

When the executive officer inspects a berthing compartment, the regular compartment cleaner should be standing by to present the compartment and accompany the exec through it. Your presence may not be required during such inspections, but it is a good idea to show up for some of them so you can get an idea of what the executive officer's standards are, and see how your spaces compare. You should also check the compartment before the inspection, and take care of any last-minute items.

In the Coast Guard, the tendency toward berthing the leading petty officers together can result in a leadership vacuum in the berthing spaces. As a Coast Guard division officer, you and your petty officers must maintain a presence in the berthing compartments to ensure good order and cleanliness.

On larger ships, in addition to the executive officer's messing and berthing inspection, an assigned medical officer will routinely inspect the unit's messing, food service, living, berthing, and working spaces to monitor sanitary conditions. The medical officer is required to submit to the commanding officer a weekly written report on discrepancies noted during the inspection. On smaller ships, the corpsman will inspect and fill out the weekly written report.

Zone Inspections—Frequent zone inspections are necessary to ensure proper maintenance of machinery, spaces, and equipment. The commanding officer will hold periodic zone inspections. These inspections may be formal, with your people presenting the spaces, or informal, with your sailors working in the spaces. Regardless of the type chosen, the importance of this inspection remains unchanged.

Since most ships are too large for one officer to inspect completely in a short period, the ship is divided into zones, and the captain assigns other officers to inspect the zones he or she cannot cover. The captain will aim for a general impression of the ship, but may check for specific items that are potential problems.

As division officer, you will either stand by your spaces or accompany the inspecting officer through them. You must also ensure that all lockers, stowage cabinets, drawers, and so forth are unlocked and open for inspection. Remember that a zone inspection is not the time to be looking for the keys to unlock something the inspecting officer wishes to see.

Before reporting to your department head that all assigned spaces are ready for inspection, you must assign personnel to stand by. In preparing for a zone inspection, follow the procedures set forth for the executive officer's messing and berthing inspection and the material inspection. The zone inspection will closely resemble the significant parts of each.

After the zone inspection, a discrepancy list will be distributed for your corrective action. You will be required to prepare and submit to your department head a report on the status of all discrepancies.

Material Inspections

Preparing for an inspection of the machinery or spaces for which you are responsible involves the same principles of meticulous supervision described above in preparing for personnel inspection. The first step in preparing for a material inspection is to obtain copies of the checklists to be used by the inspecting party. There is nothing secret about these lists, which should be consulted daily for guidance in ensuring material readiness. The second most important aspect of preparing for material inspection is to learn how to inspect. This will help you define the correct standards for your division.

Material inspections can be divided into two major parts: (1) inspection of decks, compartments, and voids or spaces; and (2) inspection of machinery, ordnance equipment, electronic gear, and so on. A typical compartment on board ship will be discussed first. Unless you, the division officer, make a more thorough inspection of your spaces than any of your seniors will make, you cannot expect to be successful. The first thing to look at in entering the compartment is its overall appearance. Then go over all details, methodically and carefully. Look into, under, over, and behind everything. It is in the corners, over and under lockers, and behind pipes and fittings that you are likely to find dirt. You can be sure that if you do not find it, someone senior to you will. Have all lockers, drawers, and switch and control boxes opened up. Take nothing for granted; wear a working uniform and get down on your knees if you have to.

Nothing is so likely to infuriate senior inspecting officers as finding dirt, cigarette butts, and other trash under a locker or other piece of furniture. Their immediate and logical reaction is that the young officer responsible for the cleanliness of this space either is too lazy to bend over or is ineffectual.

In addition, the neatness and condition of the paint must be noted, as well as the absence of paint from gaskets, brightwork, pipe threads, nameplates, electric leads, knife edges, and other areas. Check all movable fittings such as fans, ventilation gear, valves, fire-fighting equipment, for freedom of operation. Inspect electrical wiring for frayed insulation. Test all standing and emergency lights and lanterns. Check electric plugs and receptacles for proper grounding connections. Inspect all damage-control fittings such as gaskets and dogs; these not only must be clean and free of corrosion, but, most important of all, must be in condition to function properly in damage control.

This is only a very brief mention of a few of the important points in checking a compartment. Living compartments, as well as other division spaces, should be inspected daily. There is no shortcut to making a good inspection. It takes knowledge, hard work, and judgment. When you are new on board, go out with your department head and see how he or she does a compartment inspection.

Another major kind of inspection concerns machinery, ordnance equipment, and electronic gear. Again, the key to success is personal attention to detail. The emphasis must be on the material condition of the machinery, as well as on the overall appearance of the compartment or battery. If the ship's employment has kept your gear operating, with little time to scrub and polish, appearance obviously suffers. But nothing should interfere with upkeep and maintenance that is within the capacity of the ship's force. All current directives about alterations, repairs, maintenance, safety precautions, and operating instructions should be followed meticulously. Allowances can sometimes be made for cracked paint or dull brightwork, but it is inexcusable for an inspecting party to find evidence of faulty lubrication or the omission of required maintenance checks.

In preparing for a material inspection, do not forget to check that calibration data are on gauges, test equipment, and thermometers. Such equipment must, of course, be in good operating condition. Labeling must be correct and complete, and include flow-direction markers, remote-controlled equipment, and all handwheels.

A list of all out-of-commission equipment must be available with all pertinent information such as the casualty report, if applicable, and the proposed plan to correct the deficiency. All Planned Maintenance System records must be available so that machinery clearances and such can be verified.

Before formal material inspections, make a detailed last-minute check that all lockers, files, drawers, etc., are open. The difference between a mark of "good" and a mark of "excellent" often depends on the last-minute efforts of those who are standing by, waiting for the inspecting officers.

Formal Personnel Inspection—The commanding officer or another senior officer makes formal personnel inspections. Unless otherwise specified, sailors should wear their best uniforms and shoes. You will be required to muster them in military formation and formally present them to the inspecting officer. See the end of this chapter for the proper procedures. As in other formal inspections, a discrepancy list will be published after the inspection for your action.

To ensure a high standard of appearance at formal inspections, the division officer should inspect regularly and frequently. Insist that your sailors maintain a reasonably neat and regulation appearance. The sooner this habit is instilled, the better. Take a few minutes in the morning to check for haircuts, cleanliness, frayed and soiled clothing, and dilapidated and nonregulation shoes.

In working to improve the appearance of your sailors, you should first deal with them through their petty officers. If these petty officers are made to feel responsible, they will take appropriate action. Step in only if a petty officer reveals an inability to straighten out one of your sailors.

Personnel inspections are sometimes a problem for division officers. Sailors often work long hours and then, with very little time to prepare, are expected to fall in and look smart, clean, and regulation. An inexperienced officer might be inclined to sympathize in this case and feel that it is unfair to expect the sailors always to look their best. This attitude is never justified. If the personnel are properly organized they should be able to present a regulation appearance with short notice.

The secret is to ensure that every person not only maintain a regulation seabag, but have at all times a complete inspection outfit. This means fairly new, clean, pressed suits of blues, whites, and dungarees; a good pair of shoes capable of taking a high gloss; and a new hat or cap, white shirt, and tie. All items must, without exception, be regulation issue and marked in accordance with *Uniform Regulations.* The suit of blues or whites must, of course, be complete with rating badges, hash marks, ribbons, etc. Once sailors get in the habit of keeping one good complete outfit of each uniform on hand, they never have to scramble before an inspection, and their division officer's problems are greatly simplified. Also, the requests to be excused from Quarters will decline sharply. Sailors may need to be reminded to get haircuts for a special occasion, but if they acquire the habit of having their hair cut regularly, the division will never look shabby for a surprise inspection.

Of course, officers and petty officers should present an immaculate appearance at all inspections. This is a military and moral obligation that not all young officers and petty officers may fully appreciate. Young sailors are very impressionable and tend to imitate in dress, action, and speech the leaders whom they respect.

Make an inspection with a positive, confident attitude, rather than a negative, complaining one. Commend those who look particularly smart. Teach your subordinates to take a positive attitude as well. For example, if a petty officer notices a pair of shabby shoes flanked by two pairs of well-polished ones, he or she could sharply reprimand the owner of the shabby shoes and might get results. A more certain and dignified way to handle this is to tell the offender that he or she is known to be as capable of shining shoes as any of the crew, and will be expected to do so in the future. Appealing to a person's pride is usually more effective than criticism. Of course, there will be times when sterner methods are required. The point is to try the positive approach first.

How to Present Your Division

There is much that a division officer can do to make personnel inspection a success. You may not realize it, but you are the first person to be inspected as you salute the inspecting officer and present the division. First impressions are always important. You should have a good uniform with bright gold for special occasions such as formal inspections. In addition to looking very smart, you should present yourself and your division in a snappy, alert, and military manner. The exact method of presentation varies a little throughout the Navy. The presentation should be uniform for each division in a ship. An accepted shipboard procedure is as follows:

When Officer's Call is sounded, all hands not on watch or specifically excused will fall in at their division quarters location. On completion of the muster, division officers will prepare their divisions for inspection. Sailors will be formed in either two or four ranks, according to height, with the tallest in each rank at the end of the division the inspecting party will approach first. Junior division officers and chief petty officers will form a rank or file in the rear of the division, with the junior division officer at the same end of the division as the tallest person.

The division should be given the command to open ranks, deck space permitting. The sailors can then stand at parade rest while waiting for the inspecting party to arrive.

The division officer will fall in so that the inspecting officer will approach from the right. When the inspecting party approaches, the division will be called to attention. When the inspecting officer is within six paces, the division officer will salute on behalf of the division, and then greet the inspecting officer with, "Good morning, captain (commodore, admiral)."

The division officer then will address the inspecting officer as follows: "____ division, ready for your inspection, sir/ma'am. ____ men, no unauthorized absentees (or the number of absentees)." The division officer must be prepared to provide the inspecting officer with an exact breakdown of his or her personnel, stating the number and their disposition, if requested.

As the inspecting officer and party inspect, the division officer will precede the inspecting officer through the ranks.

At the request of the inspecting officer, the division officer will give the command "uncover," permitting the inspecting officer to check haircuts.

Upon completion of the inspection, he or she will command the division to "cover."

The division will stand at parade rest until the inspecting party is clear of the next division being inspected, then the division may be allowed to stand at ease.

Divisions will remain at "division quarters" until the entire personnel inspection has been completed, unless otherwise directed by the executive officer.

Here are a few points that experienced officers note when inspecting personnel:

White hat, with unrolled brim, square on the head
Hair cut in accordance with current policy
Matching trousers and blouses, blues and whites
Shoes shined along soles, heels
Good posture, no exaggerated brace
Ribbons in proper order
No cigarettes, comb, etc., showing in pockets
Sailors should look straight ahead during inspection.

Locker and Seabag Inspections

> Commanding officers shall require the clothing of all nonrated personnel to be inspected by division officers at regular intervals to ensure that each person possesses his prescribed outfit. Clothing of petty officers may be inspected on an individual basis if appropriate.—*U.S. Navy Uniform Regulations*

Two other inspections deserve brief mention: locker and seabag inspections. No special methods are recommended; the important point is that these inspections must be scheduled regularly. People must learn to stow their lockers neatly and keep them that way. Only by learning to keep in their possession a minimum amount of gear, neatly stowed, can sailors adapt comfortably to the crowded living conditions aboard ship or in barracks. Many of the younger people have never learned to keep their personal effects in order either at home or in school. If they are permitted to live aboard ship in the same confused manner, they will always have gear adrift, will look sloppy at inspection, and will be disorganized in general.

The importance of requiring sailors to maintain a regulation full seabag cannot be stressed too heavily. Inexperienced young officers are inclined to be indulgent and to overlook some deficiencies. This indulgence is not justified; sailors get a clothing allowance and must be required to maintain a full seabag. Ships can and do receive sudden orders that may involve radical changes in climate. See *U.S. Navy Uniform Regulations* for a list of items in a full seabag.

All clothing that is part of a uniform must be regulation. Officers are sometimes tempted to overlook an occasional suit of "tailor-mades" or a pair of nonregulation shoes. For the sailor's own interest, nonregulation items should not be permitted. Regulation issue clothing is far better in quality and usually less expensive than articles purchased ashore. Personnel should be thoroughly informed on this score and should also be given frequent and regular opportunities to buy small stores. To ensure full seabags, small stores should be drawn shortly after payday, while the sailors still have funds. Those on watch and stragglers should be checked as soon as possible after the division seabag inspection.

An important point is to ensure that all clothing is clearly and properly marked. Marking instructions from *U.S. Navy Uniform Regulations* should be given to each person, and this standard marking should be insisted upon. This uniformity will add greatly to the appearance of your division at inspection. The practice of marking dungarees with mottos, slogans, nicknames, names of hometowns, etc., is not permitted. Unless dungarees are marked in a regulation manner, your division will present a very poor appearance at an inspection in which dungarees are specified as the uniform.

External Inspections

InSurv Inspection—The Board of Inspection and Survey is the closest thing to a group of professional inspectors that you will see in the Navy. The board's members, appointed by the inspector general of the Navy, are senior officers and petty officers experienced in their respective fields. Collectively they conduct comprehensive inspections on every item of the ship's equipment and material. These inspections normally are held shortly before a ship is scheduled for shipyard overhaul or at least once every three years. The findings of the board are used to determine overhaul requirements and to gain an overall idea of the condition and capabilities of a ship.

You want your spaces and equipment to make a favorable impression during an InSurv inspection, but don't try to cover up problems. They will probably be discovered anyway, but problems that are missed will not be dealt with at the shipyard and will continue to be problems.

Preparation for an InSurv is the name of the game. The degree of effort expended in preparation is directly proportional to the ease with which the inspection goes. A well-organized plan with milestone dates and the use of a checklist are considered normal procedures for an InSurv inspection. In preparing for an InSurv, use the guidelines issued by the InSurv Board, your fleet commander, the Navy Safety Center, and previous InSurv inspection reports from your ship. If there are discrepancies that cannot be corrected prior to the inspection, they must be documented in accordance with the Maintenance Data System (MDS), using the 4790/2K form. Preparation for an InSurv inspection or the lack of it is addressed in the report the InSurv Board makes. Cleanliness will also be addressed. Even if your ship is old, she can be clean!

Command Inspection Program—The objective of the Command Inspection Program is to ensure the readiness, effectiveness, and efficiency of commands. It will also assess the quantity, quality, and management of resources provided to the command for performing its assigned missions. The command inspection includes the following segments:

1. General—This segment evaluates the command's mission, functions, tasks, resource adequacy, and various management areas such as personnel, equipment, supply, training, and funding.
2. Maintenance/Material—This segment evaluates the condition and adequacy of machinery, equipment, and support facilities. Possible recommendations include repairs, alterations, and changes or developments that will ensure satisfactory readiness of the command. The results of recent InSurv inspections conducted by the Board of Inspection and Survey of Ships may be used to serve as the maintenance/material portion of command inspections.
3. Administrative—This segment evaluates the command's administrative methods and procedures to determine the degree of compliance with directives of higher authority and how well the command utilizes its resources. Many other inspection requirements are integrated into this segment such as medical, dental, communications security material system, communications, crypto, and security.
4. Items of Special Interest—This segment evaluates general or technical areas of particular interest to the immediate superior in command or as directed by higher authority.

Propulsion Examining Board (PEB) Inspections—These inspections are administered to engineering departments on steam-, gas-turbine-, and diesel-powered ships. Their emphasis is on determining the safety of the propulsion plant and the training state of the engineering watch standers. There are two types of inspections given by the PEB:

1. Light Off Examination (LOE)—An LOE is administered whenever a ship has been in an availability of four months or greater duration prior to lighting fires in any boiler or activating any gas-turbine or propulsion diesel engine. The PEB members will evaluate the physical condition of all main propulsion and auxiliary machinery. This includes an overall evaluation of the cleanliness and preservation of the spaces as well.

Ships must be prepared to conduct applicable material checks using PMS, EOP (Engineering Operating Procedures), technical manuals, or locally prepared procedures to demonstrate cold plant checks of equipment and systems.

In addition, all supervisory personnel and the Engineering Casualty Control Training Team (ECCTT) members will receive oral examinations. All watch standers will be administered a written examination covering the areas of general damage control and engineering topics. The PEB will determine the effectiveness of the ship's watch qualification program. Other areas of interest to the PEB are electrical safety, tagout, heat stress, hearing conservation, training, boilerwater/feedwater chemistry, lube oil and fuel oil management, and fire-fighting ability in the main spaces.

2. Operational Propulsion Plant Examination (OPPE)—OPPEs are conducted within 6 months of completion of an evolution that qualifies a ship for an LOE and then once every 12 to 18 months until the ship reenters any 4-month or greater availability that qualifies her again for a Light Off Examination (LOE).

During an OPPE, the PEB will observe normal watch-standing procedures and request that certain major and minor casualty drills be conducted upon each steaming watch section by the ship's ECCTT.

The engineering plant will be operated in accordance with

ship's directives, Engineering Operating Procedures (EOP), Engineering Operational Casualty Control (EOCC), and technical manuals. Responsibility for the safety of personnel, material, and propulsion-plant operations will at all times rest with the command officer.

Other areas evaluated during an OPPE include the evaluation of watch-section and repair-party ability to combat a fire in a main propulsion space, various engineering department administrative programs, level of knowledge (oral and written examinations to watch standers), material readiness of equipment, PMS maintenance checks, and boiler flexibility tests for steam-propelled ships.

Refresher Training (REFTRA)—REFTRA is a training evolution that is conducted by the Fleet Training Group to determine a crew's ability to fight the ship. This includes various drills such as general quarters, damage control, man overboard, and abandon ship. All readiness areas are evaluated during this training evolution/inspection that will normally last for several weeks. For more information, see the chapter on training.

Combat Systems Assessment—The CSA is a demanding assessment of the entire ship's ability to successfully conduct combat. It looks at every aspect of training, material readiness, administration, and capability related to the combat system. Both the submarine and aviation communities have roughly equivalent inspection/assessments, as does the Coast Guard.

The assessment team's size will vary depending on the size of the ship, but will be around 15 for a destroyer/frigate ship. They will ride the ship underway for two or three days and evaluate every aspect of the combat system, including observing live ordnance firing, multiple warfighting training scenarios in CIC, and thorough inspections of the entire combat/operations material suite. Results are reported via the squadron to the type commander and fleet commander.

While the focus of the assessment is on the combat systems or weapons department, the operations department is almost equally involved. The engineering, supply, and navigation/administration departments likewise have key roles to play in supporting this evolution.

Like the OPPE or InSurv, this is a command-level assessment that requires the generation of a complete, thorough, and detailed POA&M. Most ships will conduct monthly—and, as the assessment approaches—weekly or daily round-table reviews of progress, generally chaired by the executive officer or even the commanding officer.

The division officer's role can be a very large one if he or she is a member of the combat systems or operations department. In addition to ensuring the material and training readiness of the division, the officer will probably have a watch station to stand in the combat organization—so quite a bit of self-study and training is required as well.

The CSA—like the OPPE and InSurv—requires looking out ahead at least six months to adequately begin preparations for and achieve a successful conclusion.

Aviation Readiness Evaluation—This is a somewhat specialized, one-day evaluation of a ship's ability to conduct flight operations. It is conducted by the surface type commander, although the primary inspectors will be naval aviators assigned to the type commander staff.

It requires the production of a detailed POA&M, and the best approach is to use the associated checklists that the inspectors bring aboard as the basis for the POA&M. The checklists are readily available from the type commander instructions on aviation in surface ships.

Generally, the ship's aviation coordinator (a collateral duty of the operations officer or first lieutenant) will be in charge, but engineering, combat systems, operations, supply, and administration will all have a role to play.

The inspectors—about five for a destroyer-sized ship—will spend a day on board examining all aspects of aviation safety and readiness. Their results are reported via the squadron to the type commander.

Nuclear Power and Weapons Assessments—There are a wide variety of inspections, assessments, and assist visits dealing with nu-clear-powered ships and submarines and nuclear weapons.

These are applicable to ships, submarines, and aircraft squadrons and are very complex and demanding. Most of the de-tails are classified, but it is important to remember that *any* evolu-tion dealing with nuclear power or nuclear weapons must be ap-proached with the utmost integrity, thoroughness, attention to detail, and honesty.

If you are involved in any aspect of such inspections—either in nuclear propulsion or in nuclear weapons—you must recognize the immense importance of these assessments and inspections.

Like the OPPE, CSA, and InSurv, these are shipwide evolu-tions and require a detailed POA&M and at least six months of dedicated effort for full readiness. It is also a program that must remain fully inspection-ready 365 days a year due to the sensitivity and importance of the subject.

Logistics Management Assessment/3M Inspection—The major sup-ply inspection is the logistics management inspection, and—as an integral part of that—the 3M inspection. Both are very demanding assessments that require shipwide involvement and thorough lengthy preparation.

The assessment, which will generally be proceeded by an assist visit, will consist of up to 30 inspectors for a destroyer-sized ship. They will examine every aspect of supply and logistics—including disbursing, ship's store and service structure, mess decks, ward-room, CPO mess, and supply support. Likewise, the 3M side of the assessment will examine every aspect of how maintenance is con-ducted and recorded on the ship—including observing many Planned Maintenance System (PMS) spot checks and entries into the Maintenance Data System (MDS).

The preparation for this inspection is generally split between the supply officer and the executive officer, with the XO focusing on 3M and the supply officer working on the logistics side of the assessment. It is very much a shipwide inspection requiring de-tailed preparation and a POA&M.

General Guidance for All Inspections

Aircraft squadrons, submarines, and coast guard ships all have basic variations on the fundamental inspections outlined here—corrosion control, weapons/combat, engineering, and so forth. The basic guidance applies in each case when approaching an external inspection:

• Find out who is in charge on the ship by checking with your department head.

• Read all references that pertain to your division.

• If you are so tasked, generate a POA&M; if you are not the primary drafter, obtain the POA&M.

• Execute all assigned duties on the POA&M; and based on your reading of the references, do all other tasks and keep the inspection/assessment manager informed of what you are doing and how it is going.

• Take the inspection and do great!

Plan of Action and Milestones (POA&M)

One of the best tools used in preparing for off-ship inspections like OPPE, LMA, CSA, or ARE is the Plan of Action and Milestones (POA&M). It is generated by the cognizant officer—usually a department head, but occasionally by a senior division officer—using all applicable references and checklists. It is best when kept simple and readable, generally including a list of references, a table of responsibilities, and due dates for completion.

It will be analyzed weekly by the cognizant officer and used to ensure that everyone is working toward the ultimate goal of inspection/assessment readiness. Any due items are reported as completed by the responsible officer or chief, and the POA&M is updated, normally on a weekly basis.

As the date of the assessment or inspection approaches, round-table reviews, chaired by the CO or XO, can be conducted. This gives everyone a chance to see how the pieces will fit together in the final few weeks and months.

An example of a POA&M is included in appendix B.

Dealing with Inspectors and Assessors

Personality should never have anything to do with inspections, but human nature has a way of injecting itself into every evolution—even in the Navy!

The best approach to take with any inspector or assessor is to be formal but friendly, professional, and calm. In every inspection, there will be moments when you think it is going great and other times when it looks like the sky is falling. Don't overreact in either direction. Keep your chain of command informed—immediately and privately—of any problems that surface after you conclude presenting any aspect of the program to the inspector. Don't try to make excuses and never, never mislead an inspector. If you don't know something, say so and go get your department head or XO to deal with the problem. Never get in an argument with an inspector about anything—just be noncommittal if you don't agree and let your chain of command know quickly about the problem.

Conversely, don't try to be overfriendly or ingratiating with inspectors—they see right through that act. Just be yourself and present your program confidently—after all, you've worked hard getting ready and should be proud of your work! If something is pointed out to you, take it on board in a constructive fashion, especially if it is offered in the category of advice. The inspectors see dozens of programs each year and probably have a far better idea than you do about what works and what doesn't!

Always approach inspections in a positive and upbeat way, particularly when discussing them with your sailors. They will take their cue from you. An inspection or assessment is your chance to show how hard you and your team are working—be proud, work hard to be ready, and you will do great!

8/Counseling and Welfare

> It is imperative for a naval officer to know sailors. Get to know them—know their strengths, their weaknesses, their skills, their wisdom.—*Admiral Arleigh Burke*

A key element in your job as a division officer is your ability to counsel your people. All of your ship, squadron, or submarine's capability—in the end—rests on the abilities and the morale of your sailors. They are the most complex challenge you will face—far more so than the AEGIS combat system, the F/A-18 Hornet, or the *Seawolf's* nuclear reactor. Taking care of your people also means taking care of their families—another demanding challenge.

You must be able to draw on the many resources available through the Navy's counseling, welfare, and family support systems. A good place to start this overview is to take a look at what you personally bring to the equation.

The Individual

Perhaps the easiest way to recognize the importance of each individual is first to consider yourself. You are the individual you know the most about. You probably react to each new situation in a way that is very similar to that of most others around you but at the same time is clearly your own. For instance, if you are from Florida, you may look forward to an at-sea training period that includes a visit to Mayport over a holiday weekend. The married persons on board might have preferred to be in home port during that time and will not share your enthusiasm over the Mayport visit. However, some of these sailors may be looking forward to the at-sea period because they will be involved in a missile shoot or a competitive gunnery exercise for which they've been training. Each person will see a situation in his or her own way based on background, experience, expectations, and personal prejudices and desires. You may be the type of individual who will do anything that is asked but reacts negatively to being ordered around with little apparent consideration. If this is the case (as it is with many people), you will probably be happier and more effective working for someone whose approach is, "Would you help me out by . . ." or "We need to dress up the bridge wings. Could you see that it gets taken care of for me?" Someone who simply told you, "Get the bridge wings painted out before liberty call," would probably rub you the wrong way.

Such differences in personality can result in harmony on the job or a morale problem that affects the quality of work. You know that the actions of others can cause you to react with enthusiasm or animosity. Obviously, you can affect others in much the same way. The way you affect those who work for you depends on how well you know them and how considerate you are in your approach. Clearly, you should never apologize because a job is too demanding. You might take the time, however, to let your crew members know you realize that doing their job requires a sacrifice from time to time. Tell them that although a particular job may be difficult or inconvenient, it must be done and done well. Whenever possible, take the time to explain why a job has to be done. A good time for this is at Quarters. Your sailors will appreciate knowing more about the reason for their work. Remember that someday you may have to ask them to risk their lives, and those situations don't usually allow time for explanations. If your people know that you have asked them to do jobs always with good reason, they will not hesitate to follow you when the going gets rough.

All people need to feel important. They want to know that they are making a worthwhile contribution. Unfortunately, not all of their duties may leave them with this impression. This is especially true of the more junior sailors. A feeling of personal worth, or a good self-image, is extremely important to an individual's happiness. People who feel that they have nothing to contribute probably will not do a good job at anything since they won't be interested in their work.

Our self-image comes mostly from the information provided by those around us. If our supervisors treat us as if we are important to them or to the accomplishment of vital functions, we feel better about ourselves. If they never acknowledge that we are needed, we could easily start to believe that we were unnecessary. As a division officer it is your responsibility to keep all of your people working to the best of their ability. As a leader, you can have a significant impact on the self-image of your subordinates. If you treat all of them with respect and dignity, they will feel that they are a valuable part of your division. Be sure that those standing watch not only know the technical information required to tune a radarscope, but also realize the importance of keeping that equipment in top operational condition at all times. Once they realize they are responsible for critical functions, even the routine jobs are less likely to seem boring, and they will perform those duties conscientiously.

The way sailors feel about their workload, themselves as individuals, and the division as a working group is termed *morale*. You are responsible for the quality of work, discipline, and morale in your division. These responsibilities are interrelated and must be considered together. By approaching each of these facets of leadership properly, you will be working on all three each time you work on one. Neglecting any of them will eventually degrade the others.

Personal Problems

When people feel that they are not important or that their importance is not recognized, they may try to change the situation by becoming braggarts, liars, bullies, or just loudmouths. Others become loners, antisocial, involved in drugs, or dependent on alcohol. All of this may reflect an attempt to get attention or to compensate for a poor self-image. As a division officer, you should know your sailors well enough to recognize these problems while they are developing and before they cause personal disasters or affect the quality of your division's work.

People who have special problems need advice and assistance, and should be encouraged to turn to their division officers. If they do not come to you voluntarily, reach out to them. A sailor may not get along with a shipmate or may feel picked on by a particular petty officer. The difficulty may be an alcoholic parent, an unfaithful spouse, or a sick child. Your people must know that whether their problems are trivial or serious, you are interested and will listen. One of your most demanding duties is that of counselor to your subordinates.

Counseling

There are no hard and fast rules about counseling, but you will be more effective if you realize the subjectivity of each situation. Remembering that each person is a unique individual will start you off right. What works in one counseling session may be wrong in the next. Only experience can prepare you for the myriad possibilities you will face when someone approaches you for help or you call someone aside to express your concern over a change in behavior. Understanding people and their backgrounds, feeling sympathy for the unfortunate, and using ingenuity in finding a solution are all parts of the wisdom an officer acquires. Above all, he or she must listen patiently; that in itself may be enough to help someone in trouble. Often the best medicine is for the person to talk it out and get it off his or her chest.

One thing to keep in mind is that unless there is an absolute emergency, always include your divisional chief or LPO in all counseling sessions. This is important, not only to be able to draw from their experience, but also to validate and document what the individual was counseled about. Before commencing a counseling session, always try to prepare for the individual problem and do your research, so as to lend credibility to your recommendations.

One essential technique in counseling is to be a good listener, a skill that must be cultivated to be effective. It is simply letting those individuals you are counseling know that you understand both their problems and their feelings. It is useful at times to paraphrase their words, adding statements about how you perceive their feelings. Most people are quite capable of solving their own problems, if they can find an attentive listener.

Your second most important skill as a sympathetic listener is the ability to recognize that the sailor, in this case a male, has a problem that exceeds your limitations. The best thing to do in this case is to help him get an appointment with a professional, such as a lawyer or psychiatrist. Do not give the impression that you are sending him on to someone else because you don't want to waste your time on him. Follow up on that appointment by consulting with both your sailor and the professional you referred him to. Make sure that he knows he has your support and concern while he is working out his problems. This may seem insignificant but it may motivate him to return more rapidly to his position as a contributing member of the team.

In combat, under the pressure of hard work and demanding conditions, or sometimes for no apparent reason at all, people sometimes lose their ability to get along with others and to do their work. They may complain of headaches, pains, sleeplessness, irritability, or depression, to mention a few of many symptoms. People who are sick should be sent to the doctor. Giving them a pep talk or trying to shame them are both useless. Others will respond to advice or perhaps just an old-fashioned "bracing up." Your instincts or prejudices may tell you a sailor is truly a malingerer, but think twice before acting on this instinct. A mistake in the case of a sincerely troubled person could prove traumatic or disastrous. If in doubt, have the person see a doctor.

The important point is to take all possible steps to salvage your casualties and return them to useful duty. Sick sailors are a military liability, whether they have pneumonia or a disordered mind.

If you have to call a person in because she has shirked her responsibilities, consider the situation closely before taking action. She may feel less threatened, and therefore more receptive to counseling, if you approach her less formally while speaking with her in your spaces. When you first broach the subject, whether on her territory (the working spaces) or yours (your stateroom), it may be helpful first to tell her how you feel about her past performance and to express your disappointment or annoyance, if appropriate, at the present turn of events. Let her know that her contribution is important and that you will not and cannot accept less than her best effort. She may open up to you and tell you what is bothering her. Don't accept excuses; if she can give you a reason for her poor performance, then you can work together to correct the situation. Don't accept protests that her work is good enough or that she is giving the same effort. Be firm and let her know you care. If you back down, she'll feel you only care about productivity. If you pursue the point of *her* performance, she'll know that it is she, personally, that you have noticed and care about. Nothing can substitute for sincerity in caring for your people and nothing can convince them that you do care if that is not the case.

There are also people who may need the services of a chaplain. A person may be grieved by the loss of a spouse or child. Another may have trouble with a spouse or relatives. Chaplains are experts in human problems. They have had special training, have developed special skills, and should be used freely as counselors, particularly in matters concerning death and grief. This is not to say that the division officer does not have an obligation to take appropriate action in helping someone in a stressful situation. Reassignment to more active working details, a brief leave, or special liberty could help, depending on the individual's personality.

Remember that as a division officer you are responsible for the well-being of your subordinates. Regardless of the demands of your other duties or personal matters, you must not slight the responsibility of ensuring that your personnel are well cared for.

As Admiral Arleigh Burke once pointed out:

> The average division officer, under these conditions (multiple duties), directs most of his attention and efforts to those tasks whose results are most immediately apparent to his seniors, or in other words, to those tasks which, if omitted or neglected, would cause immediate repercussions. In this process the supervision, guidance, knowledge, and understanding of the men of his division are often neglected.
>
> It is important to emphasize that only by knowing subordinates is it possible to evaluate their talents and limitations. Only by knowing men can they be properly placed. There must be continuous concern about men, and not concern just when they get into trouble or are about to ship over or go out.

The continuous concern that is the basis of a division officer's relationship with his or her subordinates is rooted in a moral charge to be responsible in the leadership of men and women.

Counseling Methods

There are many ways to approach a counseling session. If you provide the person to be counseled (the counselee) with information, answers to questions, and so on, you are doing directive counseling. If you help the person explore and try to understand his or her problem or alternatives by listening, questioning, and encouraging individual initiative and solution, then you are taking a nondirective approach.

In any event, there is a recommended sequence that may prove useful:

1. *Observe behavior*—People need specific, recent examples of what the performance problem looks like and why it's a problem.
2. *Document behavior*—Writing down the specifics of a problem has the value of letting the subordinate know the extent and seriousness of the problem; it also serves as a legal record, if that should ultimately be required.
3. *Initiate session*—The arrangement to meet with the counselee may come from the chief, the counselee, or the division officer.
4. *Create suitable conditions*—Given the constraints of space, the counselor should still try to find a private meeting area and arrange that there be no interruptions. The counselor's behavior should be open and relaxed, but with a professional tone in stating the problem that necessitated the meeting.
5. *Explore and understand the realities*—Counselors and counselees should come to an agreement of what the situation is *now.*
6. *Have counselee state his or her "ideal"*—Having acknowledged the problem, the counselee should set a goal for resolving it, and another goal for how he or she wants the situation to be in the future. (This goal and the session should both be documented, e.g., in the Division Officer's Notebook.)
7. *Monitor and follow-up*—The division officer should demonstrate

interest in the counselee's goal achievement by formal or informal monitoring and follow-up. Sincere effort on the part of the counselee should be recognized so that it will continue.

Navy Support

The Navy support system has many objectives:

1. Improved unit readiness and operational capability
2. Improved leadership and management of human resources at all levels in the chain of command
3. Improved personnel stability through the retention of top quality personnel in proper balance and to the required numbers
4. Improved communications at all levels in the chain of command
5. Improved image of the Navy as a professional organization that recognizes individual contribution and desire for respect by Navy personnel and the Navy's desire for recognition of the unique contributions provided by personnel of all grades, rates, creeds, and national origins
6. Greater career satisfaction, leading to increased recruitment, retention of capable and dedicated individuals, and development of a stable force of career personnel within the Navy
7. Demonstrated equal opportunity by the representative assignment of minority personnel throughout all grades, rates, and rating groups of the Navy
8. Guaranteed equality of promotional, administrative, and disciplinary practices and policies for all personnel, regardless of race, creed, religion, sex, or national origin
9. Increased overseas tour satisfaction and productivity, improved U.S. Navy image overseas through positive overseas diplomacy measures, and improved screening and preparation of personnel for overseas assignment
10. Identification and reduction of conditions and opportunities leading to drug and alcohol abuse, and willing acceptance and effective utilization of successfully recovered personnel upon return to duty with the command
11. Increased responsiveness to both command requirements and individual needs through the actions of the Command Train-

ing Team and the Command Assessor Team in the areas of resource management, equal opportunity/race relations, drug and alcohol abuse control

The Navy's support system is aimed at increasing awareness of and sensitivity to the problems of contemporary society as they exist in the Navy. It is a series of projects that assist the Navy with interpersonal and intercultural relations. The projects are two-pronged, usually including both a training phase to prevent problems from spreading and a remedial phase to help solve problems associated with drugs, alcohol, race relations, health, personal excellence, and career development. Many facilities and groups have been established to provide support to fleet units and shore stations. Division officers should know that almost any problem within their division may be handled by their becoming involved with and using the Navy support system or one of the organizations that traditionally have helped the Navy with long-standing problems. Educational programs can help division officers recognize and act on trouble areas with which they may have had no firsthand experience. The following brief descriptions of programs will give you a basic understanding of the scope of the support system.

Substance Abuse—Drug and alcohol abuse is expensive in terms of lost staff-hours and wasted paperwork. It hurts morale and esprit and undermines combat readiness, safety, discipline, and loyalty. The abuser is not alone in his or her misfortune; his or her shipmates suffer as well. The Navy's policy of *zero tolerance* indicates that drug abuse is incompatible with the Navy's mission in all its aspects. The following references are relevant: SECNAVINST 5300.28B and OPNAVINST 5350.4.

CHAMPUS—This is a program through which the government shares medical expenses incurred in civilian hospitals, and with civilian doctors, by Navy families. Division officers need not know all the details, but should be aware that the program exists and that the Health Benefits Advisor can help. The corpsman or command master chief will have information.

Family Service Centers—The Navy Family Service Center program was established by the CNO as an agency that could be used by service members, dependents, and retirees, to gain referrals for *any* personnel or family problem that can be encountered. Each Family Service Center is staffed by both military and civilian counselors with a goal of providing awareness of, and access to, reliable and useful information, resources, and services. Each center is also tailored to meet the needs of its unique geographic location. This agency does not provide direct financial support, but can refer personnel to other helping agencies that do. Every division officer should contact the local Family Service Center to identify the services offered by that particular office.

Health and Physical Readiness—All Navy personnel must be in good health and be physically fit in order to do their jobs well. It is now recognized that these are important factors in maintaining combat readiness. A program to promote good health is now part of the Navy's Personal Excellence program, which includes the following: weight/fat control, nutrition education, smoking prevention, high blood pressure identification, stress management, drug and alcohol control, low back injury prevention, and physical fitness/exercise. Physical readiness training is a complete conditioning program that develops and maintains the flexibility, cardiorespiratory and muscular strength, and endurance needed to perform Navy routine and emergency jobs. In addition it is important for division officers to stress AIDS and sexually transmitted disease prevention, particularly prior to deployment (OPNAVINST 6110.1 Refers).

Equal Opportunity—The policy of equal opportunity practiced by the Navy has its roots in the U.S. Constitution, which all U.S. Navy personnel are sworn "to support and defend," and in the moral concept of human dignity. It is the policy of the Department of the Navy that each person be fully informed of the intent of this instruction and be aware of the consequences of willfully disregarding its direction.

Problems with race and gender relations stem from intercultural prejudices, fostered by widespread misconceptions regarding the capabilities, dignity, and worth of individuals of another race, sex, creed, or national origin. These prejudices have always pervaded our society at one level or another. Today, we have new issues in male-female relations. It is indeed difficult to overcome the false beliefs of different segments of American culture, but if we fail to ensure the equality of all, both morally and under the law, we make a farce of the Constitution and of our profession. Each command is held responsible for its own equal opportunity posture. It accomplishes this through the Command Managed Equal Opportunity program (CMEO).

The CMEO program emphasizes the commanding officer's responsibility for creating and maintaining a positive equal opportunity (EO) climate within her or his command. OPNAVINST 5354.1 series contains specific information about the CMEO program and how it should function. Training responsibility, to assure that junior enlisted personnel receive the required Navy Rights and Responsibilities Training, is now the function of the Command Training Team (CTT). The evaluation of the command climate and the central group that advises the commanding officer on necessary action in this area is the Command Assessor Team (CAT). Every division officer must understand the relationships these groups have with the crew and how EO/RR matters are initially addressed.

Other Supports

As a division officer, you may find that your subordinates require several kinds of supports. The Navy has developed an extensive system of emergency assistance agencies, which operate in both official and semiofficial capacities. These services range from counseling, to financial assistance in time of personal crisis, to recreation designed to increase and maintain morale during times of separation and to increase group pride and identity. Some of these services are considered here in more detail.

Chaplains

Carriers, large amphibious ships, cruisers, tenders, repair ships, support ships, and major Coast Guard shore commands usually have chaplains. Carriers usually have both Catholic and Protestant chaplains. Major shore installations may have representatives of several religious denominations. Jewish chaplains are often available where fleet forces are concentrated. Many chaplains circuit-ride within organizations such as flotillas and squadrons. Chaplains stand ready to counsel sailors, regardless of organizational relationships, or to refer them to the appropriate chaplain.

Whether a chaplain is available or not, it is your duty as a division officer to offer what immediate help you can. This may mean reassuring a sailor of your continued interest, helping him find a new way to resolve a problem, or ensuring that he sees a chaplain as soon as possible. Whatever can be done to assist people who are in personal difficulty will help return them to their job.

The Command Master Chief (CMC)

The command master chief plays a vital role in the ship's routine. He or she is a handpicked chief petty officer (generally a master or senior chief) whose job is to provide advice to the commanding officer and the executive officer, representing the crew. He or she is concerned with welfare and morale issues and functions as an executive assistant to the executive officer. The CMC will normally attend Officer's Call in the morning, Eight O'clock Reports at sea, and usually has a small office on board. This person is an excellent source of information and advice for a division officer, since he or she has a good sense of the crew's feelings and reactions, has been a nonrated person, and has good access to the CO and XO. You should seek advice from the CMC on some of the tough management problems you may have. This is also a good person to send your chiefs to if they have a problem, as the CMC serves as the leader of the Chief's Mess.

Navy Relief and Red Cross

Every officer should be familiar with two semiofficial welfare agencies: the Navy Relief Society and the American Red Cross. When circumstances warrant, both will provide financial assistance and other services to Navy personnel and their dependents. The Red Cross, through its field representatives, also provides information for service personnel or their families during emergency situations. Detailed information on these two organizations is available in current directives and from the chaplain, the welfare and recreation officer, or the executive officer.

Complete information on the Navy Relief Society is contained in its publication "The Fundamentals of the Navy Relief Society." The Navy Relief Society is maintained and operated by Navy men and women for naval personnel. Its sole mission is to help naval personnel and their dependents by providing grants or loans. Division officers should familiarize themselves with the society's purpose, functions, and operations so that they can inform their subordinates of this service when the need arises. Many ships have an on-board representative of the Navy Relief Society, generally a volunteer chief. He or she can write a check immediately. Check with the executive officer or command master chief.

The American Red Cross is authorized to provide social welfare services, including financial assistance for naval personnel, medical and psychiatric casework, and recreational services for the hospitalized. The Red Cross is an authorized medium of communication between families of naval personnel and the Navy. In matters of emergency leave or the reported distress of distant families, the Red Cross will investigate and report the facts.

Another source of emergency financial aid is the ship's recreation fund, which can advance money to someone in need. This source is usually immediately available in an emergency, and it is the division officer's responsibility to know the ship's policy.

Officers and petty officers should avoid any personal financial dealings with their subordinates, even for the best of reasons.

Recreation

Recreation is an important part of the lives of young Americans. The division officer's job is to help the sailors take advantage of recreational facilities and, if those facilities are limited or do not exist, to help them improvise. In using leisure time creatively, money and elaborate facilities are not as important as imagination.

Your ship, squadron, or submarine will have a welfare and

recreation officer (either a junior officer or CPO collateral duty normally). The references for activities and fund management are BUPERINST 1710.11 series and OPNAVINST 1700.7 series. Both have detailed guidance and provide many good ideas.

Recreation does not mean only parties and social events, it means healthy and interesting activities. Many people on liberty in a foreign port will look for the nearest bar if nothing else occurs to them, but a little planning and initiative can make these port visits much more interesting. Sight-seeing tours, trips to resorts, or hunting and fishing parties can be arranged, and most sailors will prefer something of this nature.

A major point to remember concerning recreational activities is their enjoyment. Simply directing your people to go ashore and play ball is not enough. Recreation must be well planned and organized, and free of restrictions and formality.

A second major principle is that recreational activities must never be used as substitutes for good leadership. This means that a party may be an appropriate reward for good performance or may just be a good idea in itself. It should not serve to make up for poor organization and sloppy administration.

A third principle is not to overorganize your subordinates' activities. Do not attempt to schedule *all* their free time.

Recreational activities are too many and varied to be described in this chapter. Depending on the size and location of your outfit, and the time available, you can organize anything from a spearfishing party in a tropical lagoon to a river rafting trip. Information about activities will help you to evaluate the options.

Division parties can be excellent opportunities for the sailors to enjoy themselves. They also add to the esprit of a division; the men and women get to know each other better, and new personnel identify more quickly with the division. This division spirit is immensely important, and the right sort of party will add to it. While division parties are not official, they are an activity of a group for which you are responsible. If a division party gets out of hand, you will be held responsible by the commanding officer, who may also be embarrassed if the affair becomes widely known.

Be particularly careful during parties arranged overseas while deployed. It is just not smart for an officer to sanction a division party that will be open to criticism. A wise division officer will discourage parties that involve heavy drinking. Many of the younger personnel are not accustomed to hard liquor, and it is not sensible to further their education along these lines. Heavy drinking invariably leads to trouble—why stack the deck against yourself?

Information Contributes to Welfare

Many aspects of naval life, while not directly related to the activities of your division, are of intimate concern to your sailors. Among these are pay, allowances, travel of dependents, dependents' housing, the transportation of household effects, Navy Exchange activities, and medical care for dependents. If you are not married, most of these subjects will not interest you, but they are of interest to married personnel. While supply corps officers are the recognized authorities in supply matters, and the ship's doctor should have the latest word on dependents' medical care, you as a division officer must be reasonably familiar with all naval matters that are of real importance to your subordinates.

Welfare and Recreation Fund

Each ship and station maintains a unit recreation fund, the income of which is derived from ship's store or Navy Exchange profits. These funds support the unit's recreation program and cover such matters as athletics, dances, all-hands parties, games and associated equipment, hobby craft, and sight-seeing tours.

Expenditures are usually made as a result of recommendations of the unit's recreation committee—composed of enlisted personnel. The division officer can see that the needs and desires of subordinates are recognized by ensuring not only that the division's representative on the recreation committee fully understands his or her duties but also that the sailors of the division are aware of his or her appointment. The *Special Services Manual* requires that the recreation committee be kept fully informed about the condition of the fund and the reasons for any disapprovals.

Athletics

Athletics are the most popular and beneficial of leisure-time activities. Within reasonable limits, all types of active sports, particularly intramural games and competition, should be encouraged. But there is one yardstick that should be applied to all athletics: Does a large part of your division participate in and enjoy the game? There is little percentage in having a few stars who are excused from most of their work in order to attend practice on a "varsity" team. Their shipmates have to do their work, and the stars are a loss to their unit when it comes to military training and combat. Simpler team sports that all hands can play, such as softball, usually pay off best because more persons can take part at the same time.

The principle of maximum participation should be applied, however, with some judgment. If enough sailors enjoy watching the games or rooting for the team, then there is good reason to emphasize ship or squadron teams. Nothing is finer for the spirit of a unit than supporting its team. But the support must be voluntary and spontaneous; elaborate athletic programs set in motion by directives from above never accomplish anything unless they reflect the desires and capabilities of the sailors. Of course, most of this is beyond the control of the division officer. You can only inform your immediate superior if you feel that certain athletic requirements are interfering with work or training. Within the division, you should encourage athletics with vigor and ingenuity whenever your primary objective, training for combat, permits.

Other Recreation

In addition to athletics, other forms of outdoor activities such as hunting, fishing, and camping deserve support. Local sportsmen are usually glad to cooperate, and a small outlay in time and energy on the part of an officer will often pay large dividends. It is wise to supervise the preparations and to designate a competent officer or petty officer to be in charge of hunting, fishing, and camping trips. You should feel responsible for your division at all times.

Other important leisure-time activities are movies, books, and magazines. Most people enjoy films, and you should try to obtain good pictures and show them comfortably. Do *not* request the showing of training films just before the regular evening movie. There are times when this may be justified, but in general, sailors consider it an encroachment on their well-earned free time.

Books and magazines are of no value if they cannot be conveniently used. This requires a personal interest on your part, and appropriate action if so indicated. The ship's recreation committee is responsible for selecting the magazines the crew wants to read, since magazine subscriptions are paid for out of the ship's recreation fund.

It is important to look into the facilities available for reading, studying, and writing letters. A large ship should have a crew's lounge that is adequate. Every ship should have some space for these activities, with adequate lighting in each compartment. If you see your men and women writing letters and reading in dim corners, you know that some action is called for.

Like all other activities, those connected with recreation involve paperwork and planning. Officers who are custodians of recreational funds and equipment should consult the effective and pertinent directives in the *Special Services Manual,* NMPC publication 1710.11.

Coast Guard Supports

Every Coast Guard cutter has a designated senior enlisted advisor whose major role is to assist in communications between the crew members and their officers. Each Coast Guard district and major shore command has a command enlisted advisor, a civil rights officer, a drug and alcohol specialist, and access to a Navy chaplain.

Coast Guard personnel are eligible to use all Navy counseling and human resources and welfare programs with some minor exceptions. Coast Guard Mutual Assistance is the equivalent of Navy Relief. CG unit morale funds are also available for small, short-term loans. Other programs such as NASAP and family advocacy are used regularly by CG personnel when available.

9/Maintenance, Material, and Damage Control

All that equipment has to work the way it ought to or it is simply excess baggage.

Busted equipment won't help in battle. If your gear won't work, it's no good to anybody.—*Admiral Arleigh Burke*

So far this book has dealt primarily with people and their supervision. This should come as no surprise, since people are the most valuable resource of any efficient organization. Without a crew responsible for proper maintenance, a ship would be little more than a floating mass of steel, integrated with sophisticated engineering, electronic, and weaponry systems, but unable to defend herself even against the passage of time. As the division officer, you play a fundamental role in ensuring that the machinery, ordnance, compartments, and deck spaces for which you are responsible are kept in perfect order, with every piece of gear performing to its designed capability. Maintenance, material, and sound management go hand in hand, and always make the difference between a good ship and a great ship.

This chapter will focus primarily upon the Navy's 3M system: maintenance, material, and management. Closely related subjects such as damage control and supply matters will also be discussed.

People and material are not, of course, separate and distinct subjects. Properly motivated and managed bluejackets are needed to perform the upkeep and maintenance tasks for which a division is responsible. Division officers and their assistants must learn how to achieve this.

Although it is beyond the scope of this book to cover everything a division officer must know about the Navy's 3M system, this chapter should help you understand how the system works and give you new insights into the everyday problems you will face. Sources of additional information about the 3M system are cited throughout the chapter.

Efficient material maintenance depends on the form and effectiveness of organization within a ship, squadron, or station. Responsibility for the care of material is clearly defined in the *3M Manual.*

The maintenance information that follows, especially the description of the 3M system, applies to all division officers. In air squadrons, maintenance usually is concentrated in a separate department. Therefore, special features of maintenance in naval aviation are described separately.

A distinction must be made between highly technical knowledge of each piece of ordnance or machinery and the knowhow to see that this gear is maintained properly. It would be ideal to know more about the radars and aircraft engines than your highly trained petty officers do, but normally this is not possible. You should strive, instead, to be familiar enough with the gear to ensure that it is kept in excellent working condition. This involves extensive knowledge of maintenance procedures, particularly the checklists. It also means being able to judge when the machinery is operating at maximum efficiency—as in an air-search radar, which must be kept finely tuned to perform optimally. It is also your job to see that the technicians have an opportunity to read and study the technical bulletins, notices, and instructions promulgated by the technical commands. Finally, you must ensure that your subordinates continue to increase their technical knowledge by attending Navy schools, completing correspondence courses, or participating in other educational programs available to them.

Responsibility for Maintenance

As a division officer aboard ship, you will be responsible for the maintenance of certain spaces and machinery. If you have a deck division, the emphasis will be on spaces, although the assigned machinery must be maintained. You will probably have large deck areas, much of the exterior of the hull, as well as numerous passageways, and storerooms below decks. If you have the boiler division, for example, you will have more machinery to take care of than spaces. In the CE (electronics) division, you will have few spaces, but large quantities of complicated electronic equipment. In all cases, you will have two major responsibilities for material: its maintenance to ensure that it will operate reliably and effectively, and its appearance to ensure that it conforms with current military standards of cleanliness and preservation. These two requirements are complementary, not conflicting. If, in a rare instance, you must choose between the two, operating efficiency always should take precedence.

In the interests of conserving manpower and maintaining properly the increasingly complex machinery of our Navy, a systematic approach to maintenance and upkeep is mandatory. The key to success here is the careful and thorough assignment of each space and piece of equipment to one person, who must know that he or she alone is *responsible* for that space or that machine; others may assist in the work, but *he* or *she* is responsible. All assignments should be listed on the weekly and quarterly maintenance schedule. This may sound obvious and hardly worth emphasizing, but violation of this principle is the single largest cause of material failures and of ships that are below standard in appearance.

The Navy will always be short of skilled technicians and mechanics. This is why it is so important to organize and assist the many unskilled sailors who must be trained to maintain the machinery. They can do this job efficiently if they know their responsibilities and are provided with maintenance schedules and checklists. The few highly skilled personnel can then be used as troubleshooters and supervisors.

The same philosophy applies to the upkeep of spaces in which cleanliness and appearance are major considerations. Each passageway, compartment, or deck area must be assigned, in writing, to someone who will be held responsible for it.

The upkeep of passageways, deck areas, and spaces in general is largely a matter of attention to detail. Sailors will sweep down spaces and keep bulkheads reasonably clean without much supervision, but ladders, doors, scuttles, and hatches are difficult to take care of and thus likely to be ignored. These details are, of course, the very items that inspecting officers look at, and their cleanliness indicates immediately that the space is in good shape.

As a division officer, it is your responsibility to maintain all of your spaces and compartments in top material condition. Experienced division officers have found that a thorough weekly inspection of all compartments (this includes passageways and deck areas) is invaluable in determining if the cleanliness, preservation, and watertight integrity of each space has been maintained in top condition.

Cleanliness, or the lack of it, is not difficult to judge. See the procedure recommended in the chapter on inspections. Touch the horizontal surfaces of overhead beams in search of dust; check the covers, and behind and under furniture and machinery. Open drawers and cabinets. Dirt, trash, and dust have no place in the Navy; in some locations, such as in the back of electrical switchboards and in ventilation ducts, dirt is downright dangerous. Costly and damaging electrical fires result from an accumulation of dirt in places where short circuits are possible.

Preservation, as used here, means primarily freedom from corrosion. It also means the absence of any indication of extreme wear, such as frayed or worn electric cable insulation or loose pipe lagging. *Lagging* is a naval term for the canvas or sheet-metal covering for the insulation used around piping aboard ship. Worn threads, missing ladder pin chains, frayed lifelines or lifeline leathers are all included under the general term *preservation.* The most important aspect, however, is the one first mentioned, freedom from corrosion. Sometimes corrosion is not obvious and can lead to advanced decay under an apparently normal surface. The installation of fire-resistant linoleum tile over steel decks to improve habitability reintroduces an old problem of corrosion that can be well concealed.

Watertight integrity is another responsibility of the division officer. At first glance, you may be inclined to dismiss this responsibility, assuming that you really cannot determine watertightness without making an air test, so any visual inspection is of little value. Nothing could be farther from the truth. Regular and frequent visual inspection can determine whether anything has occurred that might imperil watertight integrity. Holes drilled in bulkheads are a too common example; these illegal perforations can be seen more readily if adjoining compartments are kept well lighted and the lights are momentarily turned off on your side of the bulkhead. Another important aspect of watertightness is the condition of knife edges and gaskets on doors, hatches, and scuttles. Greasing the knife edges to prevent corrosion promotes the deterioration of the gasket material, so grease must not be used. Instead, a light coat of silicone compound is applied to the gasket.

Navy Maintenance and Material Management System

The ship's 3M system was developed primarily for the purpose of managing maintenance and maintenance support to ensure maximum readiness. The intermediate objectives of the 3M system are:

1. Achievement of uniform maintenance standards and criteria
2. Effective use of available manpower and material
3. Documentation relating to maintenance
4. Improved maintainability and reliability of systems and equipment through analysis of documented maintenance information
5. Provision for reporting ship configuration changes
6. Identification and reduction of the cost of maintenance and maintenance support
7. Reduced cost of accidental material damage
8. Provision for scheduling and tracking maintenance
9. Gathering data on which to base improvements in equipment design

The 3M system can be divided as follows: the Planned Maintenance System (PMS), which is a series of *preventive* maintenance actions designed to keep the equipment operational, and the Maintenance Data System (MDS), which covers *corrective* maintenance when equipment must be repaired or altered. Chapter 5 of the 3M manual deals with PMS and Chapter 9 deals with MDS.

Planned Maintenance System (PMS)

The PMS has been developed to provide each ship, department, and supervisor with the tools to plan, schedule, and control planned maintenance effectively. It specifically provides:

1. Comprehensive procedures for planned maintenance
2. Minimum requirements for preventive maintenance
3. Scheduling and control in the performance of tasks
4. Description of the methods, materials, tools, and personnel needed for maintenance
5. Prevention or detection of impending malfunctions
6. Test procedures to determine material readiness

Equipment not covered by PMS should be maintained in accordance with existing procedures (manufacturer's and SYS-COM's technical manuals) until PMS is developed and installed.

The Planned Maintenance System includes a *Planned Maintenance System Manual,* Planned Maintenance System Schedules (cycle, quarterly, and weekly), and Maintenance Requirement Cards (MRCs).

A workcenter PMS manual contains the most recent List of Effective Pages (LOEP), which includes all the equipment in the workcenter included in PMS. Each piece of equipment has a Maintenance Index Page (MIP) number on the LOEP. All MIPs listed are also part of the PMS manual. They summarize all maintenance requirements, frequency at which work is to be done, and estimated staff-hours to do each check (see fig. 9-1). The work center PMS Manual is used to schedule all maintenance for the work center.

Actual scheduling is done by using the three interrelated PMS schedules—cycle, quarterly, and weekly. The cycle schedule, based on a ship overhaul cycle, lists the systems and subsystems in each maintenance group. Their annual, semiannual, and overhaul cycle maintenance requirements are fitted into a quarters-after-overhaul time frame. The cycle schedule is used by the department head in making out the quarterly schedule. Although this is the department head's responsibility, he or she depends on the division offi-

SHIP SYSTEM, SYSTEM, SUBSYSTEM, OR EQUIPMENT	REFERENCE PUBLICATIONS	DATE
Fire Control System Mk 99 Mods 1-4 4829	SE140-AG-AEG-000/T-1348/SPG SW279-CC-AEG-000/FCS CHAN SEL 6-0 SW279-CB-AEG-000/FCS SCC MK 12-0 SW279-CA-AEG-000/FCS DCC MK 15-0 SW273-AO-AEG-000/FCS DIR MK 81-0 SW262-AO-OPI-010/MK 666 Mod 0	October 1993

CONFIGURATION

ORDALTs: *20119, *20023, 20024, 20049, *20204, *30298				
48299	TV Camera TC 1005	4829914	Channel Selector Mk 6 Mod 0	
4829912	Data Converter Cabinet Mk 15 Mod 0	4829921 482992	Radar Transmitter T-1348/SPG Radar Set AN/SPG-62	
4829913	Switch Converter Mk 12 Mod 0	4829924	Guidance Director Group Mk 81 Mod 0	

T E S T	Q U B	SYSCOM MRC CONTROL NO.	MAINTENANCE REQUIREMENT DESCRIPTION	PERIO-DICITY CODE	RATES	MAN HOURS	RELATED MAINT-ENANCE
			NOTE: The following feedback reports/facsimile(s) have been incorporated: S-6507, S-5507 M-5 S-5976 2M-1 S-5863, S-5864 2M-2 S-5901, S-5975 Q-2R S-5926 Q-5 S-6480 S-1 S-6300 S-3 S-6232 S-4 S-5942 A-2 S-6232 A-6 S-5863 A-7R V-8998 A-10 S-6232 60M-1 S-6038, S-5862, S-6235, S-6382 R-4 S-6232 Retain all others. **NOTE:** Performance of FCS MRCs require the NECs 1106/1143. The NEC change is on this MIP. MRCs will include the NEC change as they are revised. No feedback report required. **NOTE:** Performance of MRCs R-3 thru R-8 require ensuring tightness of mechanical fasteners and couplings. Torque values will be specified only in cases where such torques are deemed critical. It is not intended that noncritical fastenings be loosened and retightened, rather, appropriate tools should be used to assure fasteners have not been left untightened as a result of corrective or preventive maintenance. Replace any missing hardware.				

DISTRIBUTION STATEMENT D
Distribution authorized to DOD components and DOD contractors only; critical technology; October 1993. Other requests for this document shall be referred to Naval Sea Systems Command (SEA 04TD). Destroy by any method that will prevent disclosure of contents or reconstruction of the document.

MAINTENANCE INDEX PAGE (MIP)
OPNAV 4790/85 (REV. 2-82)   PAGE 1 OF 9   SYSCOM MIP CONTROL NUMBER   **4829/001-A3**

Fig. 9-1. Maintenance Index Page

T E S T	Q B	SYSCOM MRC CONTROL NO.	MAINTENANCE REQUIREMENT DESCRIPTION	PERIODICITY CODE	RATES	MAN HOURS	RELATED MAINTENANCE
4		32 FJFT N	RADAR TRANSMITTER T-1348/SPG 1. Test external waveguide coolant loop fault reporting circuitry. 2. Test coolant loop fault reporting circuitry.	M-1	FC3 (1106/ 1143)	0.3	None
		99 FLPX N	TIME METER(S) READING 1. Read time meters and record on ships maintenance action form (OPNAV 4790/2K or /2Q).	M-2	FC3 (1106/ 1143)	0.6	None
		31 FMRJ N	RADAR TRANSMITTER T-1348/SPG 1. Perform AM and FM noise tests on channels 1, 4, and 7.	M-3	FC3 (1106/ 1143)	0.5	None
		92 FNHB N	RADAR TRANSMITTER T-1348/SPG 1. Perform AM and FM noise tests on channels 1, 4, and 7.	M-4	FC2 (1106/ 1143)	0.5	None
		A3 FQGR N	GUN AND GUIDED MISSILE DIRECTOR 1. Wash down antenna reflector, waveguide assemblies, and director. 2. Inspect antenna reflector and waveguide assemblies. **NOTE:** Accomplish M-5 only when ship is in calm water.	M-5	2FC3 (1106/ 1143)	2.0	None
		A3 FJFU N	GUN AND GUIDED MISSILE DIRECTOR MK 82 MOD 0 1. Clean and lubricate elevation stow pin, elevation shaft, antenna jacking screws, antenna yoke bolts, and camera base plate mount. 2. Inspect and lubricate elevation buffers. **NOTE:** Accomplish this MRC only when ship is in calm waters.	2M-1	2FC3 (1106/ 1143)	2.0	M-5
		A3 FQUM N	GUN AND GUIDED MISSILE DIRECTOR MK 82 MOD 0 1. Inspect director for corrosion. 2. Remove corrosion, repaint surface. **NOTE:** Schedule for accomplishment only when ship is in calm waters, outside temperature above 50°F and sunny skies. Safety harness is not required at director 4.	2M-2	2FC3 (1106/ 1143)	2.0	None
		13 FJFY N	EQUIPMENT CABINETS 1. Clean cabinet air filter. 2. Clean cabinet EMI Filters.	Q-1	FC3 (1106/ 1143)	0.3	None
4		A3 FJFZ N	RADAR TRANSMITTER T-1348/SPG 1. Test A2A1 control panel functions. **NOTE:** Perform quarterly or as required for operational checkout of transmitter during maintenance turn-on.	Q-2R	2FC3 (1106/ 1143)	1.0	None
		31 FJGA N	GUN AND GUIDED MISSILE DIRECTOR MK 82 MOD 0 1. Clean and inspect director blower air filter.	Q-3	FC3 (1106/ 1143)	0.5	None
		91 FMRK N	RADAR TRANSMITTER T-1348/SPG 1. Perform AM and FM noise tests. **NOTE:** Perform quarterly, within 72 hours of a scheduled missile firing on authorized channels or following removal/replacement of any major component of basic RF chain.	Q-4R	FC3 (1106/ 1143)	3.0	None

MAINTENANCE INDEX PAGE (MIP)
OPNAV 4790/85 (REV. 2-82)   PAGE 3 OF 9   SYSCOM MIP CONTROL NUMBER   4829/001-A3

Fig. 9-1. Maintenance Index Page (continued)

cers to supply information and proposed schedules for their divisions. The division officer must maintain and keep each schedule current.

From the cycle schedule a quarterly schedule is developed. Each quarterly board is divided into 13 weekly columns. Maintenance requirement codes are written into the column for the specific week in which the work is to be done. Unlike the cycle chart, the quarterly chart can reflect days the ship will be under way. This is important since some requirements can only be done at sea, (e.g., full-power runs for the engineering plant), while others can only be done in port (e.g., man aloft). Together the cycle and quarterly schedules give the overall planned maintenance program for the ship.

The weekly schedule, located in the work space, assigns individuals in the maintenance group area to specific tasks and is used by the working area supervisor to assign work and record its completion. To save time in making out a new weekly schedule, each week's permanent entries (daily and weekly requirements) are typed in and the board is laminated. Temporary entries, such as names of those having specific responsibilities, are written in grease pencil, and the division officer must sign the new weekly schedule in grease pencil.

The Maintenance Requirement Cards (MRCs) are the step-by-step instructions for doing each maintenance job. These cards (fig. 9-2) explicitly describe to the maintenance personnel what is to be done: the tools, the parts, and the material required, as well as safety precautions. The maintenance person must have the card in hand as the maintenance is done. A deck of MRCs in a metal container is in each maintenance group working area where it must be *readily accessible* to those doing maintenance work. Make sure that you have a complete and current deck of MRCs in each of your work areas. Duplicate cards are available from the CD-ROM held by the ship's 3M coordinator. Master LOEPs are held by the departmental 3M coordinator.

You must ensure that your maintenance is done in accordance with established procedures. Since you cannot personally super-

SHIP SYSTEM	SUBSYSTEM	MRC CODE	
Integrated Fire Control Systems 480	Fire Control System Mk 99 Mods 1-4 4829	4829	Q-2R

SYSTEM	EQUIPMENT	RATES 2FC3 (1106/ 1143)	M/H 1.0
Fire Control System, Missile 482	Radar Transmitter T-1348/SPG 4829921		

MAINTENANCE REQUIREMENT DESCRIPTION	TOTAL M/H
1. Test A2A1 control panel functions.	1.0
	ELAPSED TIME
	0.5

SAFETY PRECAUTIONS
1. Forces afloat comply with NAVOSH Program Manual for Forces Afloat, OPNAVINST 5100.19 series; shore activities comply with NAVOSH Program Manual, OPNAVINST 5100.23 series.
2. Voltage dangerous to life exists when equipment is open and energized. Do not work alone.

TOOLS, PARTS, MATERIALS, TEST EQUIPMENT
MATERIALS
1. [2366] Watch, wrist, No NSN -- W/C provide

NOTE: Numbers in brackets can be referenced to Standard PMS Materials Identification Guide (SPMIG) for stock number identification.

PROCEDURE
NOTE 1: Perform quarterly or as required for operational checkout of transmitter during maintenance turn-on.

WARNING: Voltage dangerous to life exists when equipment is open and energized. Do not work alone.

Preliminary
 a. Open and latch left and right cabinet doors.
 b. At A2A1 Control Panel, observe that PERM TO TEST indicator is lit.
 c. Press REMOTE/LOCAL pushbutton for LOCAL. Observe that LOCAL indicator is lit.
 d. If transmitter is in AIR READY (AIR READY indicator lit), press STANDBY. Observe that STANDBY indicator is lit green. Wait 5 seconds before proceeding to next step.
 e. Press SECURE pushbutton for SECURE mode. Observe that SECURE indicator is lit.
 f. At A2 Control Monitor, loosen captive hardware and slide assembly out to fully extended position.

LOCATION	DATE October 1993

PAGE 1 OF 4

A3

FJFZ

N

Fig. 9-2. Maintenance Requirement Card

g. Observe that DAC fan is operating momentarily placing a single sheet of paper on air intake filter.

h. Release A2 Control Monitor Assembly and slide it back into transmitter. Tighten 4 retaining screws.

1. **Test A2A1 Control Panel Functions.**

a. Set LOW VOLTAGE/CURRENT selector switch to A2PS1, A2PS2, A2PS3, and A2PS4; observe that LOW VOLTAGE/CURRENT meter indicates in banded region for each switch position.

b. At A2A1 Control Panel, press REMOTE/LOCAL pushbutton. Observe that REMOTE indicator lights and LOCAL indicator goes out. Press REMOTE/LOCAL again. Observe that REMOTE indicator goes out and LOCAL indicator lights.

NOTE 2: In step 1.b., during remote operation, transmitter will return to its original state. Ensure transmitter is in SECURE before continuing to next step.

c. Observe that DUMMY LOAD indicator is lit.

d. Observe that ELAPSED TIME HOURS-CABINET meter is running.

e. Press and hold LAMP TEST pushbutton and observe that all panel indicators are lit.

f. Release LAMP TEST pushbutton and observe that all indicators go out except DUMMY LOAD, PERM TO TEST, LOCAL, and SECURE.

g. Press STANDBY pushbutton. Observe that SECURE indicator goes out and STANDBY indicator lights white.

h. Wait 4 minutes and observe that STANDBY indicator lights green.

i. Set LOW VOLTAGE/CURRENT selector switch to A5PS3, A5PS1, A5PS2, and SOLENOID CURRENT positions, and observe that LOW VOLTAGE/CURRENT meter indicates in banded region for each switch position.

j. Set VOLTAGE selector switch to CROWBAR LV and CROWBAR HV positions; observe that VOLTAGE meter indicates in banded region for each switch position.

k. At A1A5 RF Power Monitor, set selector switch to -12V and +12V positions, and observe that power monitor meter indicates in banded region for each position.

l. At A2A1 Control Panel, observe that ELAPSED TIME HOURS-FILAMENT METER is running.

m. Press AIR READY pushbutton. Observe that AIR READY indicator lights white and STANDBY indicator goes out.

n. Wait 2 seconds and observe that AIR READY indicator lights green.

o. Press RADIATE pushbutton. Observe that RADIATE indicator lights white and AIR READY indicator goes out. Approximately 1 second later, RADIATE indicator lights green.

p. Set VOLTAGE selector switch to SCREEN PWR SPLY, REGULATOR ANODE, TWT COLLECTOR X1KV, and TWT CATHODE positions; observe that VOLTAGE meter indicates in banded region for each switch position except for TWT COLLECTOR X1KV which should read between 5.45 and 7.45 KV.

q. Press AIR READY indicator. Observe that AIR READY lights green and RADIATE indicator goes out.

r. Set VOLTAGE selector switch to OFF.

s. Set LOW VOLTAGE/CURRENT selector switch to BODY CURRENT X1mA. Observe that meter reads less than 1 milliampere.

SHIPINST 4790.1X

USS SHIP (DDG XX)
PMS SPOT CHECK REPORT FORM

FROM: (SPOT CHECKER)_____   DATE_____
TO: EXECUTIVE OFFICER
VIA: 3M COORDINATOR

W/C_____ MIP#_____ MRC CODE_____ WEEK MR ACCOMP_____
EQUIP NAME_____ MAINT MAN_____

SELECTING A MAINTENANCE ACTION (from the quarterly schedule Y   N   NA

1. Is this the MR in the accountability log?...............( ) ( ) ( )
2. Does date in accountability log correspond with the
    quarterly schedule?.....................................( ) ( ) ( )
3. Has the WC/DO updated the weekly/quarterly schedules?...( ) ( )
4. Did the maintenance man ensure the MRC was current?.....( ) ( )

    a. Does MRC control number match number on MIP?........( ) ( )
    b. Does MIP control number match number on LOEP?.......( ) ( )
    c. Is LOEP current with the latest SFR?................( ) ( )

5. Ask the maintenance man if he actually performed
    this MR..( ) ( ) ( )
6. Ask the maintenance man if there were any uncorrected
    discrepancies..( ) ( ) ( )
7. Is an EGL required?.....................................( ) ( )
8. Is the EGL attached to the MRC?.........................( ) ( ) ( )
9. If an EGL is applicable is it correct and
    comprehensive?...( ) ( ) ( )

PERFORMING THE MAINTENANCE ACTION

Instruct the maintenance man to perform the PMS check the same way that he did it
the last time it was performed or using the procedures in 4790.4B para 5-4.3.3.

SAFETY

1. Were the standard safety procedures followed?..........( ) ( )
2. WERE TAG-OUT PROCEDURES FOLLOWED IAW OPNAVINST
    3120.32B?..( ) ( ) ( )
3. Are portable tools (e.g. vacuum cleaner) safety
    checked?...( ) ( ) ( )
4. Were "R" checks done on safety equipment (rubber
    gloves/safety harness) immediately prior to each use?...( ) ( ) ( )
5. Is OPNAVINST 5100.19B on site, and is the MRC notated
    with applicable sections of the manual?................( ) ( )
6. If applicable, is maintenance man familiar with
    appropriate MSDS sheet(s) for any hazardous materials
    used to accomplish the MRC?............................( ) ( ) ( )
7. Were all required tools/materials available and IAW MRC?( ) ( )

EVALUATING THE MRC PROCEDURES

1. Are all blanks on the MRC filled in? (location,
    parts, procedures and etc.)............................( ) ( )
2. WERE ALL STEPS OF THE MRC COMPLETED STEP BY STEP?.......( ) ( )
3. Does the inspection show that the MRC was actually
    performed on the equipment?............................( ) ( ) ( )

Fig. 9-3. Spot Check Report Form

vise every job, you must spot-check. In accordance with OP-
NAVINST 4790.4 series you must check the maintenance requirement for each of your work centers weekly. The sailor responsible
for maintenance should actually do every step in the check in the
presence of the inspector if at all practicable. Questioning the

SHIPINST 4790.1X

4. Was mandatory related maintenance performed and
    recorded?...( ) ( ) ( )
5. Was the MR fully accomplished on all items on the EGL?..( ) ( ) ( )
6. Is the test equipment calibrated?........................( ) ( ) ( )
7. Was the maintenance man familiar with the equipment
    and MRC?...( ) ( )
8. Were all applicable deficiencies documented in the SWFL?( ) ( ) ( )

<u>GRADING THE MAINTENANCE ACTION</u>

1. Is this MR considered:

    ( ) SATISFACTORY (GOOD)
    ( ) UNSATISFACTORY ( ) PARTIAL ( ) NO-ACCOMP ( ) SAFETY
    ( ) GUNDECK ( ) OTHER

SEE THE SPACE BELOW FOR COMMENTS/REMARKS

_____   _____   _____
MAINTENANCE MAN   W/C SUPERVISOR   SPOT CHECKER

Remarks: _____

_____

_____

_____

_____

_____

_____

_____

_____

_____

_____

sailor about the check is not enough. She may know how the task is *supposed* to be done, but unless she actually does the work you cannot be sure that she can do it or has done it. This is particularly true whenever a tagout is required as part of the check. Often there are so many steps in tagging out a system that people get confused. PMS inspectors invariably want to see the complete check demonstrated; if your people have not actually done the work, your division will fail the inspection.

The following steps are recommended for your spot-checking:

1. Use the spot check form (see fig. 9-3).
2. Focus on safety, materials, and procedures.

PMS Feedback Report Procedures

The PMS Feedback Report (fig. 9-4) is a form used by fleet personnel to notify the systems command or the type command of apparent discrepancies, errors, or voids in some aspect of PMS. The report can also be used to request new or replacement PMS software or hardware. The PMS Feedback Report assists in timely and effective management and in improved planned maintenance. The report is a five-part form (original and four copies). Instructions for preparing and submitting the form are printed on the back of the last copy. These forms are obtainable through the Navy supply system.

Category A Feedback Reports are used only when an MRC cannot be found on the CD-ROM, which is very rare. Category B Feedback Reports are used mainly to request clarification or correction of an MRC.

Repair Categories for Ships

PMS is especially useful in identifying equipment in need of repair. These repairs fall into three basic categories: organizational maintenance (ship's force), intermediate maintenance (tender), and depot maintenance (shipyard) items.

Organizational maintenance items are those that are the responsibility of and performed by the ship's force without outside assistance.

Intermediate-level maintenance items are normally done by naval personnel on board tenders and repair ships, at Shore Intermediate Maintenance Activities (SIMAs), on board aircraft carriers, and at fleet support bases. Readiness Support Groups (RSGs) coordinate these repairs among fleet units.

Depot maintenance items are those requiring extensive work by a completely tooled facility capable of repairing, rebuilding, or overhauling equipment components and assemblies. These items make up the major portion of the shipyard work requests. They are compiled and submitted to the type commander before being

SEE INSTRUCTIONS ON BACK OF GREEN PAGE

FROM (SHIP NAME AND HULL NUMBER)	SERIAL #
	DATE

TO
- [ ] NAVAL SEA SUPPORT CENTER _____ (Category A)
- [ ] TYPE COMMANDER (Category B)

SUBJECT: PLANNED MAINTENANCE SYSTEM FEEDBACK REPORT

SYSTEM, SUB-SYSTEM, OR COMPONENT	APL/CID/AN NO./MK. MOD.
SYSCOM MIP CONTROL NUMBER	SYSCOM MRC CONTROL NUMBER

DESCRIPTION OF PROBLEM

CATEGORY A	CATEGORY B
[ ] MIP/MRC REPLACEMENT	[ ] TECHNICAL
	[ ] TYCOM ASSISTANCE
	[ ] OTHER (Specify)

REMARKS

ORIGINATOR & WORK CENTER CODE	DIV. OFFICER
DEPT. HEAD	3-M COORDINATOR

Originator do not write below. For TYCOM use only.

TYCOM [ ] CONCUR [ ] DO NOT CONCUR [ ] TAKES ACTION [ ] PASSES FOR ACTION

TYCOM REP SIGNATURE	DATE

OPNAV 4790/7B (Rev 9-89)   ACTION COPY   PAGE _____ OF _____
S/N 0107-LF-007-8000
Edition of 3-84 may be used until exhausted

Fig. 9-4. PMS Feedback Report

considered for approval at the arrival conference where the work to be done is defined.

Division Officer Responsibilities during Depot Maintenance

The inspection of work being done by a ship repair facility is the responsibility of the commanding officers of both the repair facility and the ship. The ship's commanding officer relies heavily upon his or her officers in determining if the work is progressing satisfactorily. As a division officer, you are responsible for checking and inspecting the portion of such work that relates to your division and for reporting the status to your department head. Those who operate and fight a ship must ensure that the repairs and alterations are made properly, and that all gear and machinery are working when the ship goes to sea. *Recreation or leave periods cannot interfere with this primary responsibility.*

In addition to following the progress of repairs and alterations, it is important to make certain that the work has been done correctly and completely before accepting a job as finished. Repair facilities have heavy workloads and other commitments; often they will exert pressure to get a job accepted. Ships' officers must resist any such pressure and be certain that everything is in order. In the rare instance of a serious difference of opinion, you should submit your views in writing to your department head.

In addition to inspecting the work done by repair facilities, a division officer has other special problems during a shipyard overhaul. One of these is the health and comfort of the division. Living spaces on board ship are apt to become noisy, overcrowded, dirty, and either too cold or too hot. Washroom facilities are usually reduced. If the crew is moved to a barracks temporarily, many staff-hours are lost in travel between ship and barracks, and it takes a great deal of administrative work to maintain the barracks. If possible, keep the crew on board ship and maintain the ship in as clean and orderly a manner as practicable. Trash accumulates quickly during an overhaul, and this presents two problems: fire hazard and the cost of removal. Shipyard laborers may remove the trash for a fee, thus reducing the amount of money that could have been spent for needed repairs and improvements. Smart division officers keep their spaces swept down and free of trash at all times. Workers usually work better in clean spaces and sometimes are encouraged to help out by keeping the area orderly.

An overhaul requires special precautions against fire, theft, and sabotage. The shipyard will assist, of course, but the ship has full responsibility for security.

The greatest continuous hazard during overhaul is fire. An overhaul often disrupts the ship's fire-fighting facilities, yet burning and welding usually go on every day. The ship must provide fire watches, and it is the division officer's job to ensure that the assigned fire watches are instructed in fire-fighting techniques, the location of the nearest shipyard fire alarm boxes, potential flammables in the area, and the wearing of protective gear (hard hat, steel-toe shoes, safety goggles).

Automated PMS Schedules

One new concept that is emerging in the fleet is an automated PMS system that uses a computer to generate the cycle, quarterly, and weekly boards (figs. 9-5, 9-6, and 9-7). This removes a great deal of the drudgery—as well as the clerical errors—of dealing with the PMS program.

Essentially, all the maintenance actions are entered in a database, along with pertinent information about periodicity, current quarter after overhaul, names of maintenance people, and so forth. The computer then generates the cycle, quarterly, and weekly boards, which are then signed by the appropriate officers.

The advantages of this system are extraordinary. First, the computer ensures that proper periodicity is maintained, that the boards are neat and perfectly printed, spacing is appropriate, and all the columns match up. Second, updates are done electronically and then simply printed out on a laser printer, ensuring that a neat, accurate set of boards is always available. All PMS cards are maintained on a CD-ROM and so are instantly available for re-

CYCLE PMS SCHEDULE (CONVENTIONAL)

SHIP	WORK CENTER	Sked Qtr After Overhaul				APPROVAL SIGNATURE
USS BARRY	CF02	1 13	2 14	3 15	4 16	DATE
		5 17	6 18	7 19	(8) 20	
MIP	COMPONENT	9 21	10 22	11 23	12 24	Each Quarter

MIP	COMPONENT					Each Quarter
3140/R51	400 HZ FWD	A-1,18M-1	18M-2,A-2	18M-1,A-3	A-4,18M-2	R-1,R-5,R-6,R-3,R-4,R-10(),Q-1 Q-4,R-2,R-7,R-8,M-2,M-3,R-9
	FIU EGL 1			A-6R		A-6R
	400 HZ AFT	A-4,18M-5	18M-2,A-2	18M-5,A-3	A-1,18M-2	R-1,R-5,R-6,R-3,R-4,R-10(),Q-1 Q-4,R-2,R-7,R-8,M-2,M-3,R-9
	FIU EGL 2			A-6R		A-6R
4121/012	UYK-44 ORTS				A-1	M-1,Q-1
	UYK-44 FCS#1			A-1		M-1,Q-1
	UYK-44 FCS#2		A-1			M-1,Q-1
	UYK-44 FCS#3	A-1				M-1,Q-1
	UYK-44 SGS				A-1	M-1,Q-1
	UYK-44 EAG				A-1	M-1,Q-1
4121/014	USH-26 FWD	S-2		A-1R,S-2		A-1R,R-1,M-1,Q-1
4121/R34	USH-26 AFT		S-2	A-1R	S-2	A-1R,R-1,M-1,Q-1
4361/051	ALARMS/WARNING		A-4			Q-2
4722/006	PCMS					M-1R,M-2R
4829/001	FCS MK 99 FCS#1					M-2
	TXMTR 1348 FCS#1	60M-5,S-1	60M-7,S-10R,S-5R S-3,60M-1	60M-4,S-1,A-20() A-10()	S-10R,S-5R,60M-3 60M-8,S-3	S-10R,Q-9R,S-5R,M-1,M-4,Q-2R Q-7,R-4,Q-11R
	MK 82 DIRECTOR FCS#1	S-9R(),2M-10,A-7R 2M-2	2M-10,A-5,A-12() 36M-1,2M-2	S-9R(),2M-10,2M-2	2M-10,2M-2	Q-3,R-1,S-9R(),2M-10,Q-8,R-6 Q-10,M-5,A-7R,2M-2
	MK 200 FCS#1	A-110,A-60	S-4		S-4	R-5,Q-5
	MK 15 FWD		A-8		A-9	Q-1,R-3
	FCS MK 99 FCS#2					M-2
	TXMTR 1348 FCS#2	60M-7,S-10R,S-5R S-3,60M-1	60M-5,S-1	S-10R,S-5R,60M-3 60M-8,S-3	60M-4,S-1,A-20() A-10()	S-10R,Q-9R,S-5R,M-1,M-4,Q-2R Q-7,R-4,Q-11R
	MK 82 DIRECTOR FCS#2	2M-10,A-5,A-120 2M-2	S-9R(),2M-10,A-7R 2M-2	2M-10,36M-1,2M-2	S-9R(),2M-10,2M-2	Q-3,R-1,S-9R(),2M-10,Q-8,R-6 Q-10,M-5,A-7R,2M-2
	MK 200 FCS#2	S-4	A-110,A-60	S-4		R-5,Q-5
	MK 15 AFT	A-8		A-9		Q-1,R-3
	FCS MK 99 FCS#3					M-2
	TXMTR 1348 FCS#3	60M-4,S-1	S-10R,S-5R,60M-3 60M-8,S-3,A-20() A-10()	60M-5,S-1,60M-1	60M-7,S-10R,S-5R S-3	S-10R,Q-9R,S-5R,M-1,M-4,Q-2R Q-7,R-4,Q-11R
	MK 82 DIRECTOR FCS#3	S-9R(),2M-10,2M-2	2M-10,A-120 36M-1,2M-2	S-9R(),2M-10,A-7R 2M-2	2M-10,A-5,2M-2	Q-3,R-1,S-9R(),2M-10,Q-8,R-6 Q-10,M-5,A-7R,2M-2
	MK 200 FCS#3	A-110,A-60	S-4		S-4	R-5,Q-5
4911/501	ORTS MK 7	S-1		S-1		M-1R,M-2,Q-1R,R-1
5832/005	LIFE SAVING EQPT EGL#1	S-2,S-1		S-2,A-10,S-1		R-1

Fig. 9-5. Cycle PMS Schedule

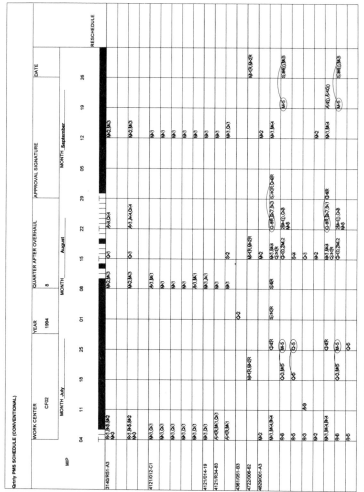

Fig. 9-6. Quarterly PMS Schedule

WEEKLY PMS SCHEDULE (CONVENTIONAL)

WORK CENTER CF02			PMS SCHEDULE FOR WEEK OF 04 - 10 July				APPROVAL SIGNATURE		
MIP	COMPONENT	MAINTENANCE RESPONSIBILITY	MONDAY	TUESDAY	WEDNESDAY	THURSDAY	FRIDAY	SAT-SUN	OUTSTANDING REPAIRS AND PM CHECKS DUE IN NEXT 4 WEEKS
3140R51	400 HZ FWD	SHIELDS				R-1,(R-5,W-1)#, M-2,M-3			R-1,R-5,R-6,R-3,R-4,R-100,W-1(#) R-2,R-7,R-8,R-9
	FIU EGL 1	SHIELDS							A-6R
	400 HZ AFT	SHIELDS				R-1,(R-5,W-1)#, M-2,M-3			R-1,R-5,R-6,R-3,R-4,R-100,W-1(#) R-2,R-7,R-8,R-9
	FIU EGL 2	SHIELDS							A-6R
4121/012	UYK-44 ORTS	SAWYER			M-1,Q-1				
	UYK-44 FCS#1	SAWYER			M-1,Q-1				
	UYK-44 FCS#2	SAWYER			M-1,Q-1				
	UYK-44 FCS#3	SAWYER			M-1,Q-1				
	UYK-44 SGS	SAWYER			M-1	Q-1			
4121/014	UYK-44 EAG	SAWYER			M-1	Q-1			
4121/R34	USH-26 FWD	ZORN		A-4R			M-1		A-1R,R-1
	USH-26 AFT	ZORN		A-4R			M-1		A-1R,R-1
4361/051	ALARMS/WARNING	ZORN						Q-1	Q-2
4722/006	POMS	MEEKER				M-2			M-1R,M-2R
4829/001	FCS MK 99 FCS#1	SHIELDS				M-1	R-4	M-4	S-10R,Q-9R,S-5R,Q-2R,R-4,Q-11R
	TXMTR 1348 FCS#1	SHIELDS		R-6					Q-3,R-1,S-9R0,R-6,M-5,A-7R
	MK 82 DIRECTOR FCS#1	McCLAIN				R-5			R-5,Q-5
	MK 200 FCS#1	SHIELDS		R-3					R-3,A-9
	MK 15 FWD	McCLAIN				M-2			
	FCS MK 99 FCS#2	SHIELDS				M-1,M-4	R-4		S-10R,Q-9R,S-5R,Q-2R,R-4,Q-11R
	TXMTR 1348 FCS#2	SHIELDS		R-6					Q-3,R-1,S-9R0,R-6,M-5,A-7R
	MK 82 DIRECTOR FCS#2	McCLAIN				R-5			R-5,Q-5
	MK 200 FCS#2	ZORN							

Fig. 9-7. Weekly PMS Schedule

placement if lost or damaged. Finally, the computer can vary the size of print so that entries fit in the appropriate spaces.

This is a great system and the sooner each work center and division switches over, the better. If your division isn't using automated PMS materials, check with your ship's 3M coordinator for assistance in making the conversion.

Quality Assurance (QA)

One increasingly important aspect of maintenance is proper quality assurance. After a series of incidents in the 1980s when major accidents were caused by improper use of materials and technique in repair work, the Navy instituted a Quality Assurance Program for surface ships. This mirrors more stringent QA programs already in place in the submarine and aviation forces.

While a complete discussion of QA is beyond the scope of this book, division officers should be aware of the importance of proper QA. This involves ensuring that the right materials are used, that a controlled work package is prepared for particularly sensitive systems (e.g., fuel, high pressure air), and that appropriate supervision and review is conducted for each job.

A QA officer is assigned in each ship, submarine, and squadron, and will provide specific training to the division officers involved in repair efforts. Two of the fundamental QA forms—the QA Planning Information Sheet (fig. 9-8) and the Miscellaneous Inspection Report (fig. 9-9)—are included for reference.

Maintenance Data System (MDS)

The Maintenance Data System, the second major subdivision of the 3M system, alerts the systems commands to basic problems concerning the performance, reliability, and maintainability of equipment in the fleet so that improvements can be made. These data also aid the CNO and type commands in determining the readiness of fleet units, overhaul and availability requirements, and personnel manning level requirements. The MDS is currently used to provide the following:

QUALITY ASSURANCE PLANNING INFORMATION SHEET								

SHIP | **JCN** | **DATE**

SYSTEM | **COMPONENT**

TASK DESCRIPTION

TECHNICAL DATA

PIPING | **OPERATING PRESSURE** | **OPERATING TEMP** | **SIZE**

DRAWING NO. | **ON BD** ☐ | **MATERIAL**

ISOLATION REQUIREMENTS

MECHANICAL | **TYPE EQUIPMENT**

DRAWING NO. | **ON BD** ☐ | **TECH DRAWING NO.** | **ON BD** ☐

APL NO. | **MANUFACTURER**

SYSTEM OPERATING PRESSURE | **OPERATING TEMP** | **SIZE** | **SYSTEM FLUID**

ELECTRIC MOTOR | **APL NO.** | **TECH MANUAL NO.** | **ON BD** ☐

MANUFACTURER | **I.D. NO.** | **MFR DRAWING NO.** | **ON BD** ☐

FRAME | **HORSEPOWER** | **SPEED** | **VOLTAGE** | **FREQ.** | **PHASE** | **AMPS** | **DUTY**

HULL (WELDING) | **TYPE STRUCTURE**

COMP. NO. | **FITTING NO. OR FRAME** | **EXACT LOCATION**

DRAWING NO. | **ON BD** ☐ | **MATERIAL**

REMARKS

PREPARED BY: | **APPROVED BY (DIVISION OFFICER OR HIGHER)**

SURFGEN QA 9090/13 (REV 7-85)
S/N 0116-LF-890-9106

Fig. 9-8. Quality Assurance Planning Information Sheet

MISCELLANEOUS INSPECTION REPORT OTHER THAN NDT OR HYDRO					
QA LOG NO.	**JCN**		**WORK CENTER**		**DATE**
SHIP		**SYSTEM**		**COMPONENT**	
JOB DESCRIPTION					
TYPE OF INSPECTION				**DWG. NO.**	
SKETCH					

REMARKS

FINAL DISPOSITION ACC./REJ.	**WORK CENTER QCI**	**DATE**

SURFGEN QA 9090/17 (REV 7-85)
S/N 0116-LF-890-9128

U.S. GPO:1988 - 505-007

Fig. 9-9. Miscellaneous Inspection Report

1. Automated Current Ship's Maintenance Project (CSMP) reports, which categorize and sequence deferred maintenance actions, as required by fleet managers
2. Computer-generated work requests from deferred maintenance actions for submission to tenders, shipyards, and ship repair facilities
3. Automated deficiency documents for use by the Board of Inspection and Survey (InSurv)
4. Effective management and control of Intermediate Maintenance Activity (IMA) workloads
5. Reports of fleet configuration, PMS, and Coordinated Shipboard Allowance List (COSAL) changes
6. Estimated and actual resource expenditures for depot-level maintenance
7. Automated input into the Ship's Force Overhaul Management System (SFOMS) for coordination and management of ship's force work during a shipyard overhaul
8. Analysis of supply support information necessary to improve reliability and maintainability
9. Computer-generated history of maintenance information

The purpose of MDS is to provide information about fleet maintenance and maintenance support for use by managers throughout the Navy, especially those at the shipboard level. Standard data elements allow for the use of automated data-processing equipment.

The basic flow pattern for MDS reporting is as follows:

1. Maintenance personnel
    (a) Prepare documents for own work
    (b) Initiate work request
    (c) Initiate supplemental data report
2. Supervisors
    (a) Screen for accuracy and completeness
    (b) Sign
    (c) Add comments: work request or supplemental data report
    (d) Assign maintenance control numbers

3. 3M coordinator
   (a) Screens for accuracy and completeness
   (b) Forwards to processing center via type commander
   (c) Generates Current Ship's Maintenance Project (CSMP) report
4. CSMP is continuously screened to appropriate maintenance activities—a shipyard, tender, or intermediate maintenance activity (IMA). The type commander sends a transaction summary showing where jobs are screened.
5. Naval Sea Logistics Center (NAVSEALOGCEN)
   (a) Processes data and serves as central data bank
   (b) Prepares reports to systems commands, CNO, and all levels of Navy management

As a division officer, you must understand all aspects of the Navy's 3M system, especially PMS scheduling and MDS reporting procedures. It is strongly recommended that you acquaint yourself with all sections of OPNAVINST 4790.4 series so that you can use the system fully. Computer printouts on a variety of topics contained in the 3M manual are available to all commands from the Navy Maintenance Support Offices.

The Shipboard Nontactical ADP Program (SNAP II/III) computer system includes a Maintenance Data Management Subsystem. The database contains the COSAL, the Ship's Equipment File, and all ship's maintenance files. Within this system, division officers and work center supervisors can generate Ship's Force Work Lists to document own ship's work and Deferred Maintenance/Material History Reports (OPNAV 4790/2K). The system also permits creation of Configuration Change Reports (OPNAV 4790/CK) to document the addition, removal, or change to equipment or equipage. This particular system can communicate directly with shore-facility maintenance computer systems without the use of outside data-processing facilities.

Alterations and Equipment Changes

Division officers often submit alteration requests. Before doing this, you should study the *Fleet Modernization Instruction*. No alterations may be made without proper authority.

Fleet modernization means improvements or alterations that enhance the military and operational characteristics of ships. Directives from OPNAV, material commands, and fleet commanders authorize these ship alterations (SHIPALTS), ordnance alterations (ORDALTS), and equipment changes.

The Fleet Modernization Program (FMP) is intended for alterations in active and reserve fleet ships, and encompasses the budget year and four additional years. The FMP consists of two basic administrative plans, the Military Improvement Plan (MIP) and the Technical Improvement Plan (TIP). Planning procedures for the FMP are described in OPNAVINST 4720.2 series.

SHIPALTS

Approval of a proposed ship alteration is granted by the signature of the systems command manager on NAVSEA form 4790/4, or the ship alteration record, and on the SHIPALT. These forms are issued for all approved ship alterations, whether or not they affect military characteristics. SHIPALTS are actually planning documents and do not in themselves constitute authorization to make an alteration. Policies and procedures regarding SHIPALTS are in NAVSEAINST 4720.4. There are three basic SHIPALTS:

1. Title D ship alterations are authorized for accomplishment by type commanders, and the installation cost is funded under Operations and Maintenance, Navy (O&MN) as operating expenses.
2. Title F is assigned to alterations that are capable of being accomplished by forces afloat and do not require Special Program Material. Title F ship alterations are authorized by type commanders. No depot-level maintenance assistance is required.
3. Title K is assigned to all other type ship alterations authorized by

NAVSEA as specified within the FMP. Program and installation cost is funded by the CNO under the O&MN account.

Alterations Requests

Commanding officers are responsible for initiating alteration requests when the proposed change satisfies one or more of the following criteria:

1. Increases the offensive power of the ship
2. Increases the ship's ability to survive the forms of attack or other hazards to which it might be exposed
3. Increases the radius of action under war conditions
4. Significantly simplifies or increases the reliability of an equipment installation
5. Reduces personnel manning requirements
6. Significantly benefits personnel safety, health, and morale
7. Is necessary to the safety of the ship or its equipment
8. Increases the military effectiveness of the ship
9. Significantly improves maintainability

Because of the long lead time required from initiating an alteration request to approval and final authorization, action must be taken as soon as possible after the need becomes apparent.

Each alteration request is made by letter. For alterations affecting military characteristics, the letter is addressed to CNO via type commander, fleet commander, and the cognizant systems command. For alterations not affecting military characteristics, the letter is addressed to the cognizant systems command via type commander. The description of the requested alteration should cover all facets of the problem.

Alteration Equivalent to a Repair (AER)

An alteration is considered equivalent to a repair when it involves:

1. The use of different materials approved for a similar use, and such materials are available from standard stock
2. The replacement of worn or damaged parts, assemblies, or

equipment to implement a later and more efficient design approved by the systems commands concerned

3. The strengthening of parts that require repair or replacement, in order to improve reliability of the parts and of the unit, provided no other change in design is involved
4. Minor modifications involving no significant changes in design or functioning of equipment, but considered essential to prevent recurrence of unsatisfactory conditions
5. The replacement of parts or equipment with like items of more efficient design when the cost of installation and maintenance of the new is less than the cost of maintenance of the old

Only the Systems Command having technical control over the article shall designate an alteration as equivalent to a repair and approve it.

Class A changes are authorized automatically and are to be made by forces afloat at the earliest opportunity.

Class C changes are authorized and funded by NAVSEA as part of the Fleet Modernization Program and are usually issued as SHIPALTS.

Completion of electronic field changes should be reported within three days.

Ordnance Alterations (ORDALTS)

ORDALTS cover nonexpendable ordnance equipment under the technical cognizance of NAVSEA. Policies and procedures regarding them are in NAVSEAINST 4720.4. Material should be obtained through normal supply channels unless otherwise directed.

Electronic Field Changes

Electronic field changes cover electronic equipment under the technical cognizance of NAVELEX. Policies and procedures regarding electronic field changes are contained in *NavSea Technical Manual,* and in applicable electronics installation and maintenance books.

Materials for electronic field changes are furnished in kit

form. The kits are identified by change number, parent-equipment nomenclature, and by type and class designations that indicate responsibility for funding and making the change and describe the contents of the kit.

Documentation of Maintenance

To keep track of all maintenance within the work center, the supervisor maintains a copy of the CSMP. The TYCOM continuously screens the work for scheduling availabilities with IMAs and shipyards. The division officer should review each CSMP weekly to verify its accuracy.

The Shipboard Nontactical ADP Program (SNAP II/III) computer system maintains the JSN log, SWFL, and CSMP within its database and is updated automatically through user input. Additionally, the COSAL is updated automatically through the use of magnetic tapes, and it interfaces with the shore-based ship's equipment and weapons systems files. The system can also generate work package processing for availabilities and overhauls. It can generate numerous management reports concerning all areas of shipboard maintenance.

Material History

For every item of machinery, a record is kept of its origin and any casualties, repairs, or alterations reported by fleet personnel through SMAFs, OPNAV 4790/2K, or 1250-1s. This material history information is processed into the 3M system's Central Parts Control Center (Navy Maintenance Support Office Department) (SPCC [NAMSO]) in Mechanicsburg, Pennsylvania.

Requests for material history reports may be submitted directly to SPCC (NAMSO). Address and format information are found in OPNAVINST 4790.4 series.

Naval Aviation Maintenance

The above discussion of maintenance, especially the 3M system, applies generally to an aviation division officer. In an aircraft squadron or wing, however, a separate department is responsible for maintenance. The department usually has the following divisions: quality assurance, data analysis, aircraft, avionics/armament, and line. A separate direction in five volumes (OPNAVINST 4790 series) governs aviation maintenance.

Aviation junior officers should refer to the *Naval Aviation Guide* (Naval Institute Press) for a detailed explanation of aviation maintenance.

Coast Guard 3M System

The Coast Guard also uses the PMS system, but it has been modified slightly to account for differences in the two services. Each particular piece of equipment on board the ship or station will have a PMS card describing the maintenance to be accomplished and its periodicity. These cards are generally grouped by type (electrical, main propulsion, etc.) and bound in notebooks. The division officer is responsible for ensuring that all required work is accomplished by trained technicians and is properly recorded in the PMS record. A great deal of the paperwork that the Navy uses for the PMS program has been deleted by the CG, thereby reducing the amount of safety checks in the system and making the division officer's supervision critical.

Maintenance requirements and procedures are found in the Naval Engineering Manual, Commandant Instruction 19000.6A and Commandant Instruction 4790.1B, Naval Engineering PMS. The *Electronics Maintenance Manual,* Commandant Inst.M10550.14 is used with the *Electronics Manual*—Administration and Supply, Commandant Inst.M10550.13. Ordnance and antisubmarine warfare (ASW) weapons on Coast Guard cutters are supplied by the Navy and come under the Navy PMS. CG 272, the *Ordnance Manual,* section 2600, ComdtInst.7100.4, and OPNAVINST 4790.4 series are the references. As a gunnery or ASW officer, you are responsible for maintenance but may obtain assistance from the warrant gunner on the engineering staff in each CG district.

While the Coast Guard has not fully adopted the 3M system of the U.S. Navy, many of the same procedures are used. Each division should have a worklist prepared assigning the repairs to be accomplished each week. Long-term and shipyard projects are scheduled by preparing a Current Ship's Maintenance Project (CSMP) form and submitting it to the type desk for your region. SHIPALTS, ORDALTS, and electronic alterations must be approved by the appropriate authority for your cutter.

Supply Matters

Under the Naval Material Command the Navy Department, the Sea System Command, and the Naval Air System Command combine with the Naval Supply Systems Command to support the operating forces with all needed material, including spare parts. Inventory Control Points, staffed by supply and line officers, are responsible for supplying all repair parts necessary for the operation and maintenance of equipment.

In order to direct the work of your division, you must have essential materials readily available. Although the Supply Corps is responsible for the procurement, stowage, and issuing of materials, the division officer must identify the needed materials. A supply officer can obtain the desired item only if it is properly identified and described. The most reliable means of identification is a stock number.

Most materials used in the Navy are identified by thirteen-digit National Stock Numbers. Supply Department personnel use these numbers to locate items in supply catalogs. With new equipment being introduced into the fleet almost daily, it is virtually impossible to keep these up-to-date. Sometimes you may have to use technical publications, drawings, and instruction books to identify new items. When the stock number is known, the part can be ordered by the repair parts petty officer (RPPO) or division supply petty officer using a NAVSUP form 1250-1 requisition document.

To find the stock number of the repair part, the RPPO uses the Coordinated Shipboard Allowance List (COSAL). The COSAL is both a technical and supply management document designed to enable ships to operate for a maximum period of 90 days independent of logistics. Items listed in the COSAL include: repair parts; special tools and equipage items required for operation and repair of ships' equipment; and items and consumables required for the safety, care, and upkeep of the ship itself. The COSAL does not include food, medical supplies, ammunition, fuel, or charts. Each ship has its own hull-tailored COSAL.

Contained in the COSAL is a listing of all Allowance Parts Lists (APLs) and Allowance Equipage Lists (AELs) applicable for each ship. An APL is simply a complete listing of all repair parts associated with a particular piece of equipment, including stock numbers and important supply information.

The AEL specifies requirements for shipboard equipage and lists miscellaneous material requirements for mechanical, electrical, ordnance, or electronics systems. Normally, items of AELs are carried in operating spaces aboard ship rather than in the storeroom. AELs are coded to indicate operating-space items and storeroom items.

The SNSL (Stock Number Sequence List) is another section of the COSAL. The SNSL lists all stock numbers in order of NIIN (National Item Identification Number), for which the ship has an allowance to carry the part on board. Those items for which the ship does not have an allowance are not listed. This section is particularly important to the supply officer since this is what instructs him or her in how many of each part he or she should keep in his or her storerooms.

For more in-depth instructions on using the various sections of the COSAL, and the interpretation of the codes, consult the *COSAL Use and Maintenance Manual* SPCCINST 4441.170A.

Both the maintenance and supply personnel are responsible for ensuring that the COSAL is up-to-date. Since the maintenance personnel are most likely to discover inaccuracies in the COSAL, they should be familiar with procedures for making changes. With an accurate COSAL, the division officer can be assured of better supply support and ultimately less downtime for equipment.

The following three documents are used to change the COSAL:

1. Configuration Change form (OPNAV 4790/CK)—Used whenever the maintenance results in the

(a) Addition or installation of any new equipment
(b) Deletion, removal, or turn-in of any installed equipment
(c) Replacement or exchange of any equipment
(d) Modification of any installed equipment
(e) Relocation of any equipment

(See OPNAVINST 4790.4 series for instructions on completing a 4790/CK form.)

2. Allowance Change Request (ACR) NAVSUP 1220-2—Used to request a change for either a repair part allowance for equipments/components or equipage.

(See the *COSAL Use and Maintenance Manual* for instructions on completing an ACR.)

3. Fleet COSAL Feedback Report (FCFBR) NAVSUP Form 1371— Used to report technical deficiencies found on APL/AELs not covered by a 4790/CK or ACR (e.g., misprint of a stock number).

(See the *COSAL Use and Maintenance Manual* for examples and circumstances under which they are submitted.)

Since the COSAL is maintained within the Shipboard Nontactical ADP System (SNAP II/III), stock numbers can be located easily and requisitions for parts generated quickly. Once generated, these requisitions are sent up the chain of command electronically for approval. The system allows users to stock-check the shipboard supply spaces for the part without leaving the computer terminal. If approved, a NAVSUP Form 1250-1 is generated with budget reports, supply stock inventory, and storage records updated almost automatically.

Supply Issues for Division Officers

As a division officer, there are a few key things you should know about the supply system.

First, you must think of yourself as a fiscal conservative. You are in control of taxpayer monies, and it is important that you work to conserve them all the time. Don't let your people waste anything—paint, office supplies, tools, computer paper, photocopy paper, or any other consumable supply! Develop a reputation for conserving what is issued to you.

Second, you are responsible to your department head for spending operating funds, which are the budgeted monies you receive to run the division. Called OPTAR, these funds come in two basic varieties: EMRM and other. Emergent Repair Monies (EMRM) make up the portion of the operating funds that is used for repair parts. In fact, EMRM funds are often referred to as "repair money." This is the portion of your budget used when you draw repair parts from supply to fix your equipment. The other portion of OPTAR is other funds, often called "consumable" money. This is used to buy consumable supplies such as paint, toilet paper, office supplies, and hand tools.

Depending on your job, you may manage a great deal of OPTAR—as first lieutenant, for example. The deck division generally buys all the ship's paint, toilet paper, and foul weather clothing—a very expensive proposition. Or, you may have a division like CIC that receives very little—because the operations specialists don't require much in the way of funding to run their division.

Another supply term you may encounter is Maintenance Assisted Module (MAM). If you run a division with a great deal of expensive electronic or engineering equipment, you may be responsible for some MAMs. These are supply parts stored in your spaces that are used for troubleshooting your equipment—an example would be circuit cards. Be thorough, and ensure that they are inventoried frequently and stored properly.

You may also be responsible for some "controlled equipage." These are highly desirable items such as binoculars, foul weather jackets, night-vision devices, and computers. They have to be issued under a specified signature, generally the cognizant division officer. If you are "signed" for controlled equipage, you must ensure that it is secure and won't be stolen. Making frequent inventories and keeping it locked up when not in use is the best policy.

Feel free to discuss supply matters with your ship or squadron supply officer. Few division officers do so, and the supply officer will be impressed that you are interested and concerned. You owe it to yourself—and the taxpayers!

Naval Aviation Supply

The Inventory Control Point (ICP) for naval aviation is the Aviation Supply Office, which is under the technical control of the Naval Air System Command and is managed by the Naval Supply Systems Command. The Aviation Supply Office is responsible for the parts and supplies required by naval aircraft even though some of the material may be located at other naval inventory control points, in Department of Defense depots, or in U.S. Air Force logistics centers. Most supplies of aviation material are located at the major industrial air stations, such as the Norfolk Naval Air Station, or at operating air stations such as the one at Miramar. A ship carrying aircraft has a special unit under the ship's supply officer to ensure its logistics. For a detailed explanation of aviation supply, see the *Naval Aviation Guide* (Naval Institute Press).

Coast Guard Supply

The Coast Guard does not have a supply corps as such. Supply departments aboard ship generally consist of one or two enlisted personnel, while some large cutters have a warrant officer as the supply officer. Since the latter cannot control the inventory for each division, the division officer must act as a supply officer. Most cutters are supported with repair parts by the Ship's Inventory Control Point (SICP). Here critical parts are stockpiled. Commandant Instruction M4410.4 gives the descriptive Coast Guard stock list. See also Commandant Instruction M4441.100.

Control of Material

Whether or not your department has a strict budget, there will be constant emphasis on the wise use of funds. There is a natural tendency to stockpile materials, especially those made available through the excess material redistribution program, but you should resist the urge to accumulate such a hoard. The Supply Department stocks items that are needed regularly, and keeps track of usage to assure a continuing supply. If material is used from the unofficial stocks held by the division, the actual ship's usage will not be recorded, so the Supply Department may not have an adequate supply of the item when you try to obtain it there.

The foregoing points up the necessity for the closest liaison between supply personnel and division officers. Only through an easy flow of information between the two can changing requirements be met.

Learn all you can about the intricacies of supply documentation. All too often, the parts center receives incomprehensible or illegible paperwork from the divisional work centers, mostly due to ignorance or carelessness. Divisional work centers that turn in consistently correct requisition forms inevitably get better supply service than those whose supervisors leave it to the supply personnel to untangle their documentation errors.

Conservation of Material and Man-Hours

The tremendous size and costs of the armed forces have resulted in taxpayer pressure for economy and conservation of material. This is a natural concern for those who pay for our military strength. We in the Navy are more than the custodians of military strength; we are the trustees of a huge investment. Remember that we all pay the taxes that support the Navy. The income taxes alone paid by a ship's company are about equivalent to the ship's annual allotment for upkeep. Looking at it this way, the crew of a ship pays for its own ship's upkeep. This is a good point to get across to your crew.

Conservation does not mean hoarding materials or refusing to use them in the quantities needed; it means using the least to do the most at the lowest cost possible. It can just as well be called maximum utilization. Conservation is really maintaining combat readiness and effectiveness by the most economical expenditure of manpower, material, and time.

A piece of equipment should be carefully used and conscientiously maintained to ensure a maximum length of service. Even then, before being scrapped, it should be overhauled, repaired, or cannibalized for parts, if this is functionally possible or economically feasible. When deemed no longer of service, it can be disposed of as scrap.

Scrap is an important source of metal, but not so important as to cut the service life of products fabricated from metals. Before a piece of equipment is relegated to the scrap pile, uses other than its original one should be considered. This practice can reduce the need for new equipment.

Conservation goes beyond saving money and material; it involves man-hours too. This is more difficult to appreciate because Navy personnel are not paid by the hour, but wasted man-hours are too common. Work must be organized and supervised, and this is where you come in. Be alert for opportunities to avoid fruitless standing around and waiting, which is wasted work time. When you know the crew will be idle, use the time for training.

If your division work never seems to get done, make a survey of actual man-hours on the job. You may have enough hands, but inadequate supervision. If many of your people are off on personal business or in sick bay, you cannot expect much useful work to be done. Be money conscious, material conscious, and man-hour conscious.

Damage Control

The control of damage due to enemy action or shipboard casualty has long been considered an "all-hands" evolution. Damage control does not, however, begin with enemy action or a casualty, but is an ongoing day-to-day concern. As a result, the division officer plays an important role as manager and leader in determining whether a ship can survive.

Shipboard damage control has three basic objectives:

1. To take preventive measures before damage occurs, principally by preserving watertight integrity, removing fire hazards, and maintaining and distributing damage-control equipment
2. To combat damage as it occurs, by means of fire fighting, flood-

ing control, preserving stability and buoyancy, and providing first aid treatment
3. To make emergency repairs to restore maximum fighting effectiveness

The third objective is somewhat beyond the scope of this text since it is performed mostly by specialists and does not always involve the division officer.

Preventive Measures

> A division officer shall ensure that all damage-control equipment, fittings, and checkoff lists in his assigned spaces are maintained in proper working condition and are properly labeled.— *Standard Organization and Regulations of the U.S. Navy.*

All division officers who are responsible for personnel and equipment have damage-control duties. These duties include damage-control training, maintenance of damage-control equipment and fittings, and general good housekeeping in all spaces assigned to their divisions.

To help in preserving watertight integrity, a compartment check-off list (CCOL) is posted in each compartment. These lists indicate the location of all classified fittings and other equipment useful in damage control and thus are quick references for those responsible for setting material conditions. "Classified" here means a lettered fitting that is kept open or shut in accordance with the material condition prescribed for the ship as a whole. Examples of the items listed on the compartment check-off lists are:

1. Doors, hatches, scuttles, manholes, air ports, windows, and hoist covers
2. Ventilation controllers and closures
3. Valves of the firemain, oil, sprinklers, compressed air, and drainage systems
4. Air-test fittings and sounding-tube caps
5. Portable damage-control equipment such as carbon dioxide extinguishers, PKP extinguishers, battle lanterns, and fire stations.

At this point you may be wondering how this affects you as a division officer. The compartment check-off lists in your assigned spaces are your responsibility. Not only must they be absolutely accurate and complete, but in many cases opening and closing the listed fittings will be the responsibility of your subordinates. The importance of these check-off lists can hardly be exaggerated; they are the basis for effective damage control. During operational readiness inspections and refresher training evolutions, a single error will earn a compartment an unsatisfactory mark in damage control. Two or more unsatisfactory compartments are enough to give a ship an overall mark of unsatisfactory.

Material conditions, referred to above, should also be defined. Material condition means that certain fittings are either open or shut depending on a ship's activities at the time and her location. If all are closed (Condition Zebra), maximum watertight integrity is achieved. Since this would be most inconvenient for the crew, Condition Z is assumed only when the ship is at General Quarters (battle stations) or when the ship is entering or leaving port during wartime. When Material Condition Z is set, all fittings with a Z, Y, or X classification are shut and properly secured.

In contrast, Condition Yoke is set for normal, peacetime cruising, when the ship is leaving or entering port during peacetime, and after normal working hours when in a protected harbor. This material condition permits a maximum amount of access about the ship while preserving a reasonable degree of watertight integrity. All fittings with a Y and X classification will be secured while Material Condition Y is in effect.

Material Condition X-Ray provides the minimum amount of watertight integrity and is set only during normal working hours while berthed in a protected port. When in Material Condition X, only those fittings with an X classification are required to be secured.

There are a few special classifications that might be found on watertight fittings. For example, the capital letter D enclosing a red Z means that this particular fitting must be secured during darken-ship conditions; a circle enclosing a W, X, Y, or red Z signifies that this fitting can be open under certain conditions. It should be noted that circle Z can only be open by permission of the commanding officer.

All fittings in your compartments will have a classification. Those fittings and their classifications will be noted on the compartment check-off list for that compartment. Unless someone else is specifically assigned to open or shut the fittings in your spaces, it is your responsibility to see that your people take proper action when the word is passed directing a certain material condition to be set. It should be apparent how important compartment check-off lists are. A single error, a single vent left open, for example, could result in progressive flooding in the event of damage.

Each division officer is responsible for the damage-control equipment located within his or her spaces and compartments. According to the *Standard Organization and Regulations of the U.S. Navy,* each division officer will assign a divisional damage-control petty officer (DCPO). It is your responsibility as a division officer to acquaint your DCPO with all the phases of the ship's damage-control organization and procedures. You may want him or her to help you instruct division personnel in damage control, fire fighting, and chemical, biological, and radiological (CBR) defense procedures. In assigning a divisional DCPO, remember that you are not assigning responsibility; that rests with you as the division officer. It is highly recommended that a responsible first-class petty officer be assigned as the DCPO.

Your divisional DCPO will set the specified material condition within your divisional spaces and make the proper reports. However, you should check the setting of the material condition occasionally to ensure that your DCPO is faithfully carrying out his or her assigned duties. In addition to setting material conditions, your DCPO will also be charged with performing PMS on equipment related to damage control that is found in your spaces. The DCPO will weigh all portable CO_2 bottles, inspect and test damage-control and fire-fighting equipment, and ensure that all battle lanterns, dog wrenches, and spanners are in place and in usable condition in all divisional spaces.

Remember that as the division officer you are responsible "through frequent inspections to ensure that the spaces, equipment, and supplies assigned to [your] division are maintained in a satisfactory state of cleanliness and preservation." Each division officer is responsible for conducting damage control, safety, and watertight inspections in the spaces assigned. You must inspect assigned spaces for cleanliness, state of preservation, watertight integrity, and the proper operation of safety devices.

If these routine inspections are to be effective in identifying deficiencies in the ship's material condition, the following principles must be observed:

1. A systematic approach must be adopted to ensure thorough inspection of all spaces.
2. Inspection of assigned spaces must note more than just general appearance of the compartment. For example, inspection for the state of preservation must include an examination for hidden corrosion underneath, behind, and at foundation joints or welds of fixed equipment. Inspection for watertight integrity must include all piping, cable stuffing tubes, ventilation ducts, watertight doors and hatches, and associated gaskets and fittings.

Fighting Fire and Flooding

> The importance of efficient damage control cannot be overemphasized, and the desired state of readiness can only be achieved by a firm program stimulated by effective and dynamic leadership and executed by enthusiastic, well-trained, and determined officers and crew from all departments aboard each ship.—*Surface Ship Damage Control* (NWP 62-1)

The preventive measures discussed earlier in this section will play a large part in determining a ship's ability to survive damage and to continue her mission. The second factor that will determine survival is the ability of the ship's crew to combat the damage. Although the damage-control organization (repair parties) will be expected to fight the fires and control flooding, every member of the ship's crew must be prepared to step in to assist or even take over depending on the circumstances. Training and leadership is the key to an effective and organized damage-control effort.

As a division officer, you will be charged with the supervision and training of the personnel assigned to your division. A good divisional training plan will not only contain those topics that are required for job performance, but will also include topics of a more general nature, including damage control. All personnel assigned to surface ships are required to complete Basic Damage Control PQS within six months of reporting on board. The Basic Damage Control PQS is designed to give a good basis and understanding of damage control and of the ship to which you are assigned. By ensuring that you and all of your personnel have completed the PQS, you have taken a big step in improving damage-control readiness on board your ship.

All your people should also demonstrate on a monthly basis the ability to use an Emergency Egress Breathing Device (EEBD) and don an oxygen breathing apparatus (OBA). Every three months, they should practice escaping from their berthing area and primary work space while blindfolded.

Many of the personnel in your division may be assigned to a damage-control team. This could mean that they are each a member of one of the repair parties that are formed when the ship goes to General Quarters at sea, or they could be members of the in-port emergency team, the main damage-control team when the ship is in port. Regardless of the team to which they are assigned, they will have PQS to complete in order to qualify for the position that they are filling on that team. Your job as a division officer is to ensure that the personnel that you assign to the damage-control teams are qualified for their position and that they continue progress toward further qualification and responsibility.

All the training conceivable cannot save a ship if there is no leadership to direct the efforts of the damage-control teams. Past experiences have clearly illustrated that fact. Had it not been for the knowledge and the leadership displayed by many members of the crew, the USS *Princeton* could have been lost after she hit an Iranian mine in the Persian Gulf in 1991. The damage-control organization in the *Princeton* did, in fact, fight the effects of flooding and save a very badly damaged ship in a superb all-hands evolution.

Leadership comes, in part, from knowledge. Knowing damage-control systems, their capabilities and their limitations, makes it possible for the division officer to make an informed decision. Knowledge of fire-fighting procedures, the dangers of flooding, the basics of stability, the defenses employed in a chemical, biological, or radiological environment all will aid you in assuming a role of leadership during a massive conflagration on board your ship. Unfortunately, space does not permit an in-depth discussion of those systems and procedures in this text. There are, however, volumes of information available to the division officer on board ship that should be reviewed on a regular basis.

Damage control cannot be taken lightly. The very survival of your crew, your ship, and your life depends heavily on your ability as a division officer to train and lead your crew in times of peace and war. Regardless of whether it is preventive measures or the actual control of damage, the division officer plays an active role in damage control every day.

Watertight Integrity

Piping, wiring, air-conditioning systems, shafting, and access openings installed in ships must function properly for optimal damage control. In order to function, they must pierce watertight bulkheads or decks, but in doing so, they create a potential hazard to the ship's essential watertight integrity. Without the necessary precautions to minimize this danger, an otherwise sound damage-control program may not save the ship.

Every naval vessel is subdivided by decks and bulkheads, both above and below the waterline, into as many watertight compartments as are compatible with the ship's mission. In general, the more minute this subdivision, the greater the ship's resistance to sinking from damage. A modern, nuclear-powered aircraft carrier has well over 1,500 watertight compartments. The condition of this subdivision (the watertight integrity) is crucial and must be maintained precisely as specified.

The watertight integrity of boundaries to watertight compartments must be rigidly maintained. The Naval Sea Systems Command has devised methods to test watertight integrity periodically. Although this procedure involves additional work for the forces afloat, this vigilance in watertight inspections must not cease.

Loss of watertight integrity may result from:

1. Corrosion
2. Holes in, or improper fit of joints of, structural members
3. Loosening of boundaries or joints
4. Defective closures or fittings at bulkheads or decks
5. Defective piping, tubing, ventilation ducts, and similar installations
6. Carelessness in making alterations

Corrosion or rusting is oxidation of metal caused by the action of air and moisture or by electrolysis. Corrosion is accelerated by the presence of salt, and has a tendency to be increased when one metal is placed in contact with a dissimilar one. Corrosion weakens structures, boundaries, joints, piping, and ventilation ducts. It hampers the operation of, and causes defects in, fittings. Because it reduces structural strength and attacks watertight integrity, corrosion must be kept under control.

The quantities of fuel, water (including required ballast), provisions, stores, and ammunition carried must not exceed the amounts permitted by directives from the systems commands of the Navy Department, except as ordered for a specific operation by an operational commander. Division officers are responsible for reporting their loading requirements and must ensure that they are satisfactory in all respects.

Material deficiencies discovered during inspections should be corrected by the ship's force if possible. Deficiencies that are not corrected immediately by the ship's force must be reported and made part of the deferred-action work list.

Weight and Stability Control

Ships tend to gain weight and lose stability, with corresponding loss of reserve buoyancy, because of the large number of relatively small items that are brought on board. Loss of stability is caused by the fact that these items usually are located high in the ship. Drastic measures have sometimes been necessary to avoid compromising the ship's survival with these small unauthorized weight additions. Division officers must check their spaces for these types of items.

The following measures will help to prevent overloading:

1. Prohibiting unauthorized alterations
2. Identifying unnecessary equipment, structures, fittings, and stores and recommending the removal or reduction of these items
3. Recommending the installation of items that can be made lighter

A ship's ability to survive damage is closely related to its loading. If the liquid loading prescribed for torpedo and mine protection and ballast is maintained, survival capability generally increases as the displacement decreases. Limiting displacements are established for all ship types.

Ten Commandments of Damage Control

1. Keep your ship watertight.
2. Do not violate material conditions.
3. Be confident in your ship's ability to withstand heavy damage.
4. Know your way around—even in the dark!
5. Know how to use and maintain damage-control equipment.
6. Report damage to the nearest damage-control station.
7. Keep personal articles properly secured at all times.
8. Practice personal damage control. Protect yourself so you can protect your ship.
9. Take every possible step to save the ship as long as a bit of hope remains.
10. Keep cool; **DON'T GIVE UP THE SHIP!**

10/Correspondence

Beneath the rule of men entirely great,
The pen is mightier than the sword.
—*Edward Bulwer Lytton*

The ability to communicate clearly in writing is a decided asset that can distinguish a division officer from his or her peers. Its importance is illustrated by the following true incident.

As is customary, a newly commissioned ensign, orders to his first ship in hand, wrote an introductory letter to his first commanding officer. He had a form letter commonly used for this purpose, but, exercising his initiative, he elaborated on his background and preferences for initial assignment. His letter was not long but it did reveal a person with a genuine point of view and an ability to communicate. When the ensign reported on board, the executive officer greeted him with "So you're the new ensign who knows how to write a letter." Until he left the ship two years later, the ensign enjoyed a close working relationship with his commanding officer. His writing ability enhanced his overall professional performance and development.

Those who read a good deal and have done well in English and literature at school probably write with reasonable ease. Others, whose major interests may be science or math, may not be as well read and may find concrete facts and figures more appealing than the abstractions of literature. For those in this second group, writing can be difficult.

As officers, all of you face certain obligations, whether pleasant or not. Writing memos, official letters, and reports is a duty that increases in frequency and importance as you advance in rank. The ability to write is a distinct professional advantage and one that is highly prized by your superiors.

References

Many writing guides and textbooks have been published. The very best for a division officer is the *Guide to Naval Writing* by Robert Shenk, published by the U.S. Naval Institute. All division officers should have a copy of this fine work.

A Some Basic Rules

Before describing the common forms of naval correspondence, it may be useful to outline the basic rules of good writing. Writing is essentially the transfer of facts and ideas from an author to the reader. The objective is to do this simply and clearly. Thus, good writing is a tool as well as a communications system.

Brevity, simplicity, and *clarity* are the marks of good writing. Never say "effect the unloading" when you mean "unload." Avoid adjectives unless they are vital to the meaning of a sentence. When you can say "flood" avoid "inundate," when you mean "unusual" why use "esoteric." Do not use words that will make the reader refer to a dictionary. Use short sentences.

The basic building block of all writing is the sentence. The sentence should be effective as a unit in itself and as a contributing part to the paragraph. You must have a firm grasp of the concept of a complete sentence. Incomplete and run-on sentences indicate a lack of maturity as a writer. To be an effective writer you must frame your thoughts using correct sentence structure.

Paragraphs are recognized as divisions of your overall idea. The paragraph should clearly reflect the central thought that is usually stated in the topic sentence. All sentences in the paragraph should contribute something to that central point. Inexperienced writers commonly underestimate the importance of this relationship between the parts and the whole and have problems with transitions. You do not want to insult your reader's intelligence by overstatement, but you do want to provide the necessary transition from one idea to another. The text referred to above can help you in this all-important area.

The yeoman who types your letter or report should know how to punctuate and spell, but since you will sign the letter or report, you should be sure it is right. If you use a technical or nautical term, be sure you are using it accurately. The Naval Institute Press, the publisher of this volume, also publishes the *Naval Terms Dictionary*. There should be a copy in your ship or station library.

Anything longer than a message or a simple notice should be based on an outline. This helps you organize your thoughts, ideas, and facts, and enables you to present them logically. Start your outline early so that you have a framework on which to hang your ideas. It may sound strange, but your subconscious mind often works on while you sleep or work and you may develop ideas and crystallize thoughts without a conscious effort. So if you have something important to write, it pays to let it simmer on the back burner.

Getting started on any writing project is probably the hardest part of the task. It even becomes difficult to put the outline on paper. Instead of staring at a blank piece of paper and getting discouraged, let your mind run freely. Jot down your ideas in sentence form or as an outline without regard to order, grammar, punctuation, or syntax. Keep writing as long as the ideas keep coming. Once you have done that, you can reread, review, and reorganize your thoughts into a clear, concise, and readable form.

Every letter or report should have an introduction. Most of the time only a sentence or two is needed to give the reader an idea of what follows. Many busy people may pick up your letter or report. You should capture their interest and get their attention on track. Start off with a clear statement such as, "This letter (report, etc.) describes a series of problems the USS *Barry* has suffered with the vapor compressor distillers, analyzes the probable causes, and makes recommendations." This sort of introduction ensures that your paper is routed to the right people immediately and does not get hung up on the desk of someone who has no real interest in, or responsibility for, the subject.

Regardless of the subject or type of correspondence, a well-organized written communication should do the following:

1. State the purpose—*introduction*
2. Discuss and prove the findings—*body*
3. Present conclusions or recommendations—*findings*
4. Include the pertinent details—*appendix/enclosures*

If your correspondence includes this material, it should provide your reader with the desired information. The main differences between one form of correspondence and another concern format and procedures. If you can write a good, clear letter, you should be able to duplicate your success in a well-written report.

Naval Correspondence

There is little difference between naval correspondence and any other written correspondence, except for certain format and procedural considerations. These exceptions improve naval correspondence through standardization, which facilitates preparation, reading, comprehension, filing, research, retrieval, job orientation, and performance. Standardization is particularly beneficial in situations where personnel rotate frequently.

It is beyond the scope of this chapter to present all of the types of naval correspondence that you are likely to encounter. All naval correspondence follows the same basic principles of brevity, simplicity, and clarity emphasized earlier.

Special Types of Naval Correspondence

Standard Naval Letter

The usual purpose of a naval letter is to provide concisely stated information about a single subject. Standard formats and styles can expedite reading as well as writing because your reader knows where to look for what he needs.

Each letter should focus on a single subject. You do not save time or paper by accumulating problems, comments, and requests and then presenting them in one long, confusing letter. Remember, brevity, simplicity, and clarity are your goals.

The organization of a naval letter is quite simple. The first paragraph should tell your reader what the letter is about; the next paragraph(s) should explain circumstances and present your conclusions or recommendations—that is, give orders, make requests, give consent, refuse permission. Enclosures should provide pertinent details; references should tell the reader where to find information not included in the letter.

Some writers become so accustomed to a list of references at the top of a Navy letter that they list references out of habit. Unless you direct attention to a reference in your letter, don't list it. List references in the order of usage. If you list a reference, then say enough about it in your letter to indicate what the reference is about. For example:

> 1. Reference (a) requested information about the allowance lists for the next 3 fiscal years. Reference (b) pointed out that such information is available for only 2 years in advance and that figures for those 2 years were not yet ready. The figures are now available for fiscal 1995 and 1996 and they are as follows.

As with references, enclosures should not be used just to make the correspondence look official. Enclosures should provide necessary information or assistance to the reader.

After you write a letter or report, sit back and try to read it with another's eyes. Is it clear and to the point? Is it complete? Is it exactly what you really mean to say?

Now is the time to condense, cut, and simplify. Cross out every adjective, modifying clause, and phrase that is not needed. Excess words are a waste. Substitute simple, short words for long ones unless the longer word is more precise.

Check your letter for coherence. Do thoughts, ideas, conclusions, and recommendations follow logically? They will if you made a good outline. Have any important addresses been omitted? Are references and enclosures complete but not redundant? Do all your addresses have copies of the references? If not, change the reference to an enclosure. Are your references up-to-date? Again, put yourself in the reader's position. Would you be content to receive this letter?

The Department of the Navy uses two basic formats for all correspondence. The regular business letter is used in writing officially to addressees outside the Department of Defense. It is sometimes used internally for informal correspondence instead of a memorandum. The naval letter is used in writing to addressees within the Department of Defense and may be used when writing to addressees outside the department who are accustomed to receiving such letters.

With slight variations, the format of a naval letter serves as the format for the memorandum and for special types of naval correspondence like the message. Finally, there is considerable similarity between the naval letter and the Department of the Navy's formal directives system (instructions and notices), which will be discussed later in this chapter.

Since the style of the naval letter sets the pattern for all types of correspondence, it is logical to start with it. Figure 10-1 shows the form and style of an unclassified naval letter.

The first page of a naval letter is typed on the letterhead of the activity. Second and successive pages are typed on plain bond paper, similar to the letterhead in size, color, and quality.

Note that no salutation or complimentary close appears on a naval letter. The letter is prepared in block style, that is, without indenting, except for the first lines of subparagraphs or for extensive quotations. Each paragraph is numbered flush at the left margin with an arabic numeral. All paragraphs are single spaced, with double spacing between paragraphs. The date, which is typed or stamped, is the date the correspondence was signed. Finally, the correct classification for the naval letter—top secret, secret, confidential, or unclassified—must be assigned by the originator.

Memorandum

Another form of naval correspondence is the memorandum or memo. As a division officer you will become familiar with this form of naval correspondence. It is a quick and simple way to communicate with others in your ship. It is generally used for informal communication between subordinates, usually within the same activity. The "From–To" memorandum may be typed on plain bond paper,

DEPARTMENT OF THE NAVY
USS BARRY (DDG 52)
FLEET POST OFFICE
AE 09565-1270

IN REPLY REFER TO

5000
06 Feb 95

From: Commanding Officer, USS BARRY (DDG 52)
To: LCDR Benjamin J. Goslin, Jr., USN, 434-84-5883/1110

Subj: AUTHORIZATION TO SIGN "BY DIRECTION"

Ref: (a) SECNAVINST 5216.5C
       (b) NMP 5030100

1. In accordance with the provisions contained in references (a) and (b), you are authorized to sign "By direction" correspondence of a routine administrative nature required in the performance of your duties as Executive Officer, USS BARRY (DDG 52).

2. This authorization does not constitute authority to establish command policy.

3. This authorization shall be cancelled upon transfer from this command.

Jim Stavridis

J. STAVRIDIS

Fig. 10-1. Unclassified Naval Letter

or on the Department of the Navy memorandum form (OPNAV 5216/144). Informal communications within your division may be handwritten on the OPNAV form. Memorandums may also be written by using the Shipboard Nontactical ADP Program (SNAP II/III) computer system's word processor. Copies of a memorandum dealing with a short-lived or inconsequential subject are not required. A complimentary close is not desired or required; however, as a junior officer you will sign correspondence "very respectfully" when submitting to a senior officer, and "respectfully" if you are sending correspondence to subordinates. All other guidelines and format considerations are identical to those discussed for a naval letter. Figure 10-2 shows a typical "From–To" memorandum.

Often the subject matter of a memorandum is to remind others of such things as upcoming deadlines, meetings, or to request action on matters of low priority. On matters such as these, the

3 March 1995

```
From:   Engineer Officer
To:     Commanding Officer
Via:    Executive Officer
```

Subj: FULL POWER TRIAL

1. Captain, I'd like to propose we conduct a pre-OPPE full power trial during our underway in April for TSTA I. That should ensure that we have everything ready to go as we begin serious preparations in May.

2. With your concurrence, I will make the necessary arrangements with the Operations Officer.

J. Syvertsen

```
Copy to:
MPA
OPS
```

Fig. 10-2. A Typical "From–To" Memorandum

SNAP II/III Mail System allows authorized users to send electronic mail to a variety of destinations, whether it be a single individual or the entire command. These messages are transmitted electronically and displayed on the computer terminal when the desired recipient signs on to any terminal. The message may then be reviewed, retained, or deleted by the recipient.

Message

A message is used only when information must be transmitted rapidly, or when communication by any other means is infeasible. Do not use a message if the information can reach its destination in time for proper action when transmitted by naval letter. Messages are prepared according to instructions issued by the chief of naval operations.

In the message, specified abbreviated titles of the command or activity are used in the "FM," "TO," and "INFO" lines. These short titles are listed in NTP-3, Supp. I, the *Plain Language Address Dictionary*. For brevity and security, the number of addressees should be limited to those who need to know. Messages should be concise and should use standard abbreviations such as IAW (in accordance with), IRT (in response to), and UNODIR (unless otherwise directed). The latter is useful in that it relieves your superior of the need to reply, often influences him or her to do nothing, and lets you do as you wish. It shows initiative on your part and is usually the mark of a good officer. In naval correspondence and in your day-to-day relations with your superiors, never ask permission or instructions if you can use UNODIR instead.

Unclassified Naval Messages can be produced in a format nearly completely ready for direct transmission through the use of the Shipboard Nontactical ADP Program (SNAP II/III) computer system. The database contains a vast number of addressees that can be inserted as ACTION or INFO addressees. The system also allows you to build and save frequently used message headers, greatly reducing the time required to produce the message since only the text needs to be written to obtain a complete message. The final draft of the message may also be printed out using the system's papertape punch/reader, reducing the workload and message processing time in radio central.

Joint Interoperability of Tactical Command and Control Systems (JINTACCS)

With more emphasis being placed on interservice operations, the need for the compatibility and interoperability of tactical command and control systems became evident. JINTACCS was developed to fill that need. JINTACCS is a standardized system of equipment, procedures, and message formats that allows fast and understandable communications between services. Many intraservice reports have also been changed to use JINTACCS. Figure 10-3 is an example of a JINTACCS message.

Other Naval Correspondence

There are several types of naval correspondence that you should be aware of, although it is unlikely that you will initiate them. The *Department of the Navy Correspondence Manual* describes these types of correspondence in detail.

```
UUUUUUUUUUUUUUUUUUUUUUUUUUUUUUUUUUUUUUU
U     UNCLASSIFIED      U
UUUUUUUUUUUUUUUUUUUUUUUUUUUUUUUUUUUUUUU
```

```
PTTUZYUW RULYSGG2826 0371650-UUUU--RHNVBBZ.
ZNR UUUUU
P 061650Z FEB 95   ZYB PSN 530489N29
FM USS BARRY
TO RUEACNP/BUPERS REENL MGMT WASHINGTON DC//PERS254//
BT
UNCLAS  //N01080//
MSGID/GENADMIN/BARRY//
SUBJ/ENCORE REQUEST ICO CHRISTOPHER M. ALLEN 230-37-9391//
REF/A/DOC/DMRSMAN/94MAR01/1080  //
AMPN/REF A IS DIARY MESSAGE REPORTING SYSTEMS USERS MANUAL//
RMKS/1. THE FOLLOWING SUBMITTED VIA MSG DUE TO THE USE OF SOURCE
DATA SYSTEM BY THIS COMMAND.
2.RS1,230379391,ALLEN,Y,4,Y,Y,Y,BOOOO,N,NA,N,950203,21660/
  RS2,230379391,ALLEN,N,N,P18,N,N,N,Y,IS,NA,NA,21660/
  RS3,230379391,ALLEN,N,NA,NA,NA,N,NA,NA,NA,Y,21660/
  RS4,230379391,ALLEN,9,9,9,9,9,9,9,9,9,A,A,A,A,9,21660/
  RS5,230379391,ALLEN,A,A,A,A,A,A,A,A,A,A,A,A,21660/
  RS6,230379391,ALLEN,9,9,9,9,9,9,9,9,9,9,9,9,A,9,21660/
  RS7,230379391,ALLEN,21660,1,CO RECOMMENDS APPROVAL FOR/
  RS7,230379391,ALLEN,21660,2,SCORE CONVERSION TO IS RATING/
  RS7,230379391,ALLEN,21660,3,SBI AND DD398 SUBMITTED VIA FAX//
PAGE 02 RULYSGG2826 UNCLAS
  RS7,230379391,ALLEN,21660,4,APPRECIATE ASSISTANCE.//
BT
#2826
NNNN
DLVR:USS BARRY(1)...ORIG
RTD:000-000/COPIES:
```

*** MDU office codes that have received this message: ***

CICO	CMC	CO	COMMO	MDUOPR
NAV/ADM	NC1	OPS	RMC	XO

1 OF 1

```
UUUUUUUUUUUUUUUUUUUUUUUUUUUUUUUUUUUUUUU
U     UNCLASSIFIED      U
UUUUUUUUUUUUUUUUUUUUUUUUUUUUUUUUUUUUUUU
```

Fig. 10-3. A JINTACCS Message

Unit Directives System

It is important for you to understand the Navy directives system. As a division officer, you will be called upon to write a ship's bill or instruction. This will test your ability to write well and to follow complex format guidelines. A sample directive is provided in figure 10-4.

Commands use directives to communicate plans and policies to subordinates. To understand the purpose of directives, you must know the definitions of policies, procedures, orders, instructions, and regulations (see chapter 4, "Administration").

A *directive* is an order or instruction that prescribes policy, organization, conduct, procedures, or methods. Two types of directives that you as a division officer will be concerned with are instructions and notices. An *instruction* contains authority or information of continuing reference value or requiring continuing action. It remains in effect until superseded or canceled. A *notice* is a directive of a one-time or brief nature with a self-canceling provision. It has the same force and effect as an instruction. Usually it remains in effect for less than six months but no longer than a year.

The purpose of the Navy directives system is to establish a simple and uniform way of issuing, maintaining, filing, locating, and referring to directives. A directive system must provide for wide dissemination of the command's policies. It must also provide a way for subordinates to amplify and supplement instructions in order to put those policies in effect. Finally, it must permit integration of unit directives with those received from outside the unit, thus ensuring that the unit's policies and procedures are continually in keeping with the plans and policies of the Navy Department and of fleet and type commanders.

In addition to the directives mentioned above, there are others that are not included under the Navy directives system. The most important ship's directives are Plan of the Day, Captain's Night Order Book, Engineer Officer's Night Order Book, and Officer of the Deck Standing Order Book.

You may not be required to initiate any of these shipboard directives, but you should be aware of what each contains. Ship-

DEPARTMENT OF THE NAVY
USS BARRY (DDG 52)
FLEET POST OFFICE
AE 09565-1270

IN REPLY REFER TO
Canc frp: Jan 95

BARRYNOTE 5214

<u>USS BARRY (DDG 52) NOTICE 5214</u>

Subj: RECURRING REPORTS TICKLER

Ref: (a) BARRYINST 3120.1 Series

Encl: (1) Recurring Reports Tickler

1. <u>Background</u>. Reference (a) requires review of the ship's
Recurring Reports Tickler at each meeting of the Planning Board
for Training. Enclosure (1) establishes BARRY's Recurring
Reports Tickler.

2. <u>Action</u>

    a. The Executive Officer is responsible for keeping this
notice current and for coordinating preparation of all material
and events noted in enclosure (1) in time to reach the ultimate
reviewing authority by the required date.

    b. Department heads and cognizant ship's force personnel are
responsible for completing the tasks assigned in enclosure (1) in
time to permit Commanding Officer review prior to transmission of
the report off ship or, in cases where the report will not leave
the ship, to reach the Commanding Officer on the date indicated
in enclosure (1). Department heads and cognizant ship's force
personnel will also submit recommended changes to enclosure (1)
to the Executive Officer.

    c. This notice will be updated as required but on an
interval not to exceed one year.

J. STAVRIDIS

<u>Distribution</u>:   (BARRYINST 5216.1)
List I (Case A)

Fig. 10-4. Sample Navy Directive

board directives are discussed in the *Standard Organization and Regulations Manual of the U.S. Navy.*

Bills

As a division officer, you will be responsible for updating and keeping current those ship's bills that affect you and your division (see chapter 3). For a complete discussion of the types of bills that you will find on your ship, read chapter 6 of the *Standard Organization and Regulations Manual of the U.S. Navy*. All ship's bills follow the same general format.

A ship's bill sets forth policy for assigning personnel to duties or stations to execute specific evolutions or accomplish certain functions.

Reports

The final area of naval correspondence that you will be interested in as a division officer is report writing. A long report may take weeks or months to prepare. It is hoped that this chapter has given you new ideas as well as insights that will help you prepare well-written reports. Since reports can vary from a one-page tabulation of figures to a one hundred-page document on engineering capabilities, the discussion that follows is confined to brief general statements.

A common error in report writing, as in any writing, is to write from the standpoint of what you, the author, want to say on the subject. Such an approach often results in a rambling discussion or an essay on generalities—leaving your reader hoping for an answer to his or her questions. A report should be written from the reader's standpoint: What does he or she need or want to know about a subject? Modern practice puts the conclusions and recommendations at the beginning.

In some instances, your reader is already familiar with the subject and is looking for figures or a list of procedures. Or he may want to know how you arrived at your conclusions or recommendations; if so, then a word about method and sources should appear near the beginning of the report.

Some officers find it difficult to focus on the conclusions and recommendations. They want to prepare the reader by giving all the facts and discussion before springing the answers on her. Or they insist on showing the reader how the answers were obtained. If you fit into this category, don't feel alone. You should realize that most readers of reports turn directly to the recommendations, whether they appear at the beginning or at the end of the report. Usually the people who asked for the report agree with many of your conclusions. For areas they are unsure of, or in disagreement with, they will check your method of compiling the information, which should be described in the body of the report.

The guiding principle of report writing is to cast your final draft in a form that immediately shows your reader the sought-after information. Reports may be written and organized in several ways, but regardless of their form, they should be written clearly and concisely.

Completed Staff Work

Since much of your initial writing will entail preparing drafts for seniors in the chain of command (department head, executive officer, commanding officer), it is appropriate to mention the idea of completed staff work. This concept often is a source of frustration for a junior officer, who wonders, "What's the use of learning to write better, when the commanding officer or XO rewrites my stuff anyway?" The answer is twofold: (1) constructive criticism improves your writing skills, and (2) when you become the boss you will have to supervise the writing efforts of your subordinates.

In many cases you will be asked to write a particular piece of correspondence because you are the expert on the subject. As the first lieutenant, for example, you would understand the requirements for an accommodation ladder and therefore would be the logical one to initiate correspondence for the commanding officer's signature requesting shipyard alterations.

You must expect your drafts to be modified and edited by your superiors, but this does not relieve you of the responsibility for trying to submit a flawless piece of work. If your work turns out to be perfect, you will have received your reward. If it was not completely acceptable, find out what was wrong so that you know how to improve your work, remembering that each individual you will write for will be a little bit different from the other.

Letter to a New Command

You will only have one chance to make a first impression, and very often a new command's sense of your professionalism—to say nothing of your writing skills—will be a direct reflection of the first letter you write them.

First of all, your letter should be directed to the commanding officer of the ship, squadron, submarine, or shore station to which you will be reporting.

Second, make your letter simple, brief, and direct in both tone and content. Begin by saying you have received orders to the command and are very happy with your assignment. Let the new command know a little about your background—qualifications, family status, and hometown.

Finally, include your travel plans and arrival desires—ensuring that you indicate your flexibility based on the needs of your new command. It is also perfectly acceptable to mention your desires for a given position within the command, for example, "I have greatly enjoyed studying electrical engineering at Annapolis, and I hope to start out in the engineering department."

Two good examples of letters to a new command—one from a USNA graduate reporting to her first ship and the other from a LTJG moving to his second—are included as figures 10-5 and 10-6.

Note for the Plan of the Day (POD Note)

One thing you will be expected to write quickly and often is a note for the Plan of the Day, generally referred to as a POD note. These are short, concise announcements that are typed up and included in the command's daily plan, which is distributed first thing in the morning or very late the previous night.

Think of writing a POD note as you would the lead paragraph in an article in a newspaper. You need to pack all the relevant information into a very brief space. Always tell who, what, when, where, and how—the basic questions—and add a headline. Copy it onto a disk and take the disk to the administrative office for down loading into its file—it makes it far easier on the office. Clearly annotate how long you want to run the note. In most commands, the review of the POD is done by the executive officer just before signature, so there shouldn't normally be a need to have it chopped before submitting it to the administrative office.

36th Company
U.S. Naval Academy
Annapolis, MD 21412
14 March 1994

Commander James Smith, USN
Commanding Officer
USS BARRY (DDG-52)
FPO AE 09565-1270

Dear Commander Smith,

I recently chose USS BARRY (DDG-52) during service selection. I am looking forward to serving on what I feel is the best ship in the Navy.

Upon graduation on 25 May 1994, I will be assigned to the Naval Academy complex for TAD until my SWOS reporting date of 23 September 1994. While at the Academy, I have been active in Varsity Track, Mids-n-Kids, Conditioning Squad, CPR training, and Officer's Christian Fellowship. I had summer training on USS Shenandoah (AD-44) and USS Fox (CG-33). I was also on the plebe detail for two years.

On 26 May 1994, I will be getting married to 2d Lieutenant Bill Jones, USMC. He is planning to go to TBS in Quantico in August 1994. We enjoy hiking, camping, biking, and many other activities.

I understand that the billet I will hold on the ship is based on availability and need. However, if given the choice, I would prefer to work with some area of combat systems.

I received your letters, the photos, and information concerning BARRY. I thank you for so quickly extending a welcome to me. I am already excited about joining the crew.

I would like to take up your offer to visit BARRY. I will try to schedule a weekend this semester to come to Norfolk. I will call ahead of time to work out the details.

I am looking forward to future communications with you and to working with the wardroom and crew.

Very respectfully,

Jane Taylor
Midshipman First Class, U.S. Navy

Fig. 10-5. Letter to a New Command (First Ship)

LTJG Scott Barnes
USS Milwaukee (AOR-2)
FPO AE 09578-3024
November 10, 1993

Commanding Officer
USS BARRY (DDG-52)
FPO AE 09565-1270

Dear Commander Smith,

   Last month I received orders to BARRY, and I am very
much looking forward to serving aboard.
   Currently, I am serving as the Main Propulsion
Assistant on board USS Milwaukee, a position I have
held for the last year. I have stood the majority of
my watches on the bridge, and have completed three
Caribbean Drug Operation cruises and a Mediterranean
deployment. To date, I have completed my Surface Warfare
Officer and EOOW qualifications.
   I will be detaching from Milwaukee in December and
will proceed directly to my assigned schools. My intentions are to report to BARRY on 15 April, unless you
would like me to arrive at a different date. In case you
need to contact me, I can always be reached through my
parents at 1111 Willis Drive, Norfolk, Virginia, 23452.
The phone number there is (804) 432-1770.
   I am originally from North Carolina, and I graduated
from NC State with a BS in chemistry and a commission
via the NROTC Program.
   In closing, I would again like to mention how happy
I am to be assigned to BARRY. I greatly look forward to
checking aboard.

                    Very respectfully,

                    Scott A. Barnes
                    LTJG, U.S. Navy

Fig. 10-6. Letter to a New Command (Second Ship)

Here is an example of a good, concise, informative POD note:

> XX. **Gunshoot Procedures.** At 0800 today, the crew members listed below need to assemble on the fantail for transportation to the gunfire qualification range at Camp Pendleton. The uniform is dungarees with long-sleeved shirts and steel-toed shoes. Qualification will take approximately two hours, and all shooters will be returned to the ship at 1130. Weapons and ammunition will be provided at the range.
>
> | | |
> |---|---|
> | SN Smith, OD Division | FA Jones, MP Division |
> | SM3 Barnes, OC Division | GSM2 Taylor, MP Division |
> | EM3 Woods, E Division | EN2 Watson, A Division |

Awards and Evaluations

While the subject of making awards and evaluations is too broad to cover completely in this small chapter, a few basic points should be kept in mind. A thorough treatment of both awards and evaluations is included in the *Guide to Naval Writing*, published by the Naval Institute, as well as in the references annotated at the conclusion of this chapter.

• *Be on time.* Nothing will make you stand out more to the executive officer than timeliness in the submission of awards and evaluations. Most commands request them, typically, 60 days before a transfer for an end-of-tour evaluation and 30 days before the end of the reporting period for periodic evaluations. Get yours in early or on time—never late.

• *For awards, submit the right level.* The hierarchy of awards runs from medals (Navy Commendation, Navy Achievement) down to Flag Letters of Commendation (which provide advancement points) and lesser awards, such as Commanding Officer Letters of Commendation and Letters of Appreciation. Each command and community in the Navy has slightly different approaches to who should get what award for which task—so ask your department head for advice. Generally, you'll receive some guidance before the fact, but if you have an individual preparing for transfer, talk to your department head about what award—if any—would be appropriate. Don't forget that awards don't have to be given only at the end of a tour—they should be a constantly used tool to motivate and reward top performers. On a good ship, with a motivated and hardworking division, about a fourth to a half of the people in it should receive some kind of commendation in a year's time.

• *Submit neat, double-spaced roughs.* Use clean folders, clearly mark the chop chain on the front of each, and include the computer disk for all awards and evaluations submitted. Mark the name of the individual on the folder.

• *Be specific.* Don't lapse into generalities. A few superlatives at the beginning and the close are fine, but get to the facts early. "Petty Officer Smith brilliantly controlled 150 F-14 aircraft intercepts in a 20-day period during high-tempo operations in the Adriatic Sea," as opposed to "Petty Officer Smith is an excellent air controller."

• *Use white space and graphics.* Don't cram every inch of the page with writing. Use big headline-style grabbers at the top, like "EM3 Jones is ranked #1 of 21 E-4s in Engineering!" Have a space between paragraphs, use just a little boldface and underlining to really emphasize the highlights.

• *Tell it like it is!* Don't leave the reader to guess at your meaning. If someone is getting an award, it ought to be for truly superb performance; and an evaluation should be—above all—honest. Don't go for subtle innuendo—say what you mean. And make sure the words and marks match. For example, if someone is a 3.6 performer, he or she clearly isn't "outstanding."

• *Bullets in the middle, sentences at top and bottom.* Bullets are great, but crisp, clear, complete sentences have a power all their own. Openings and closing should be complete, stand-alone sentences with powerful images and good specifics.

• *Grammar, spelling, and punctuation.* Be perfect. Show your evaluations to another division officer, and review theirs in return. When you turn in an award or evaluation—and you will do hundreds during your first tour—you are not only showing your chain of command something about the person being reviewed, but about yourself as well. Make your awards and evaluations a pleasure to read—and you will get the results you desire, both for the subject and for yourself!

11 /Career Planning

> To become successful, a naval officer must devote himself
> entirely to his career—not just for short periods of time—
> nor only to selected aspects of his duties. He must devote
> his life—and his lifetime—to become as highly skilled in his
> profession as he possibly can.—*Admiral Arleigh Burke*

How the System Works

From the moment young officers step into a ship or squadron,
they must begin career planning. In order to do so, they must have
a basic understanding of the way a career in the Navy is structured.
While there are obvious differences between all the warfare communities, many basic aspects of career planning are the same, particularly early in a career.

After an officer checks aboard a ship or squadron, he or she
begins working on initial qualification. This varies widely in the different communities, but in each specialty the initial set of qualifications opens the door for future assignment. The art of negotiating
a new set of orders requires the division officer to have an understanding of two key players in the detailing system: the detailer
and the placement officer, both of whom work at the "bureau."

The Bureau

The entire process of officer detailing is carried out in Washington, D.C., at the Navy Annex. This is a large complex of brick
buildings situated on a small rise overlooking the Pentagon. The
command responsible for officer detailing (along with all of the
Navy's personnel management) is the Bureau of Naval Personnel.
This is often shortened to simply "the bureau." The bureau controls all officer personnel functions, and firmly holds the reins on
detailing, placement, and the generation of all officer orders.
While other branches of the Department of the Navy frequently

try to (and occasionally do) influence the order-writing process, the bureau has a strong record in maintaining a relatively unbiased, honest-broker record in detailing. When you call or visit your detailer, you will find him or her in an office with other detailers in the annex. If you are in the Washington area, it's an excellent idea to stop by and see your detailer, if only to put a face with the name for both of you. Call first, since detailers are frequently involved in boards or on travel.

Detailer

The detailer is your representative and is generally familiar with the background, performance, and personal situation of the officers he or she is detailing. Each detailer keeps track of a pool of officers with similar year groups and communities. Detailing is done by community. The system has grown fairly sophisticated over the years, and when an officer calls the bureau, the detailer can instantly call up the preference card and performance record of an individual on the desktop computer.

Detailers deal with preference cards, which are forms that all officers should fill out early in a tour. Their job is to match an officer with a position that makes sense both for the Navy and for the individual, trying to fit people into jobs they both want and are qualified to perform. As a division officer, you should fill out a preference card after about a year in your first tour. About 12 months before your projected rotation date (PRD), you should send in an updated preference card and call your detailer.

Calling a detailer is an art. First of all, use the autovon system or a Navy-funded commercial system. As a last resort, call collect. Never use your own money to call a detailer. All of the telephone numbers are listed in the monthly magazine *Perspective,* which also includes a great deal of vital information about career planning. Second, get organized *before* you call. Have copies of your most recent preference card in front of you. Make up a list of questions you want answered. Take notes on the conversation and write a follow-up letter to the detailer after the call to confirm any comments either of you made.

It is far better to call a detailer with a plan or a specific proposal than to call up and say, "I'm coming up for orders next summer. Do you have any ideas about what I should do?" At best, you'll get the standard answer for your year group, and at worst you'll suddenly fill the bill for a "challenging set of orders" to Saudi Arabia or Adak that he's trying to fill. Far better to call up and say, "This is LTJG Chadwick on USS *Barry*. I'm rolling next summer, and I'm very interested in shore duty in Washington, D.C., specifically on the OPNAV staff. Do you have my current preference card?" By making a specific request you accomplish two things: First, you demonstrate that you've done the basic research to have an intelligent conversation that will affect two to three years of your life. Second, you place the detailer in a position of working toward your negotiating position.

The detailer will be scanning your record and making a quick judgment about you while you make your opening comment. He or she will probably respond with something like, "Well, Rob, I see you've completed your surface warfare officer qualification and you have your engineer officer of the watch letter. You're off to a good start. Would you be interested in going directly to Department Head school and going to sea again?" This is the critical juncture in the conversation. If he makes a suggestion that is unacceptable to you, be firm and honest. Tell him what you want to do: "No, I've thought about going straight to sea, but I think my long-term career interests and my personal situation would be better served by a shore tour right now. I'm planning to get my master's degree in the evenings in D.C., and I'm really set on going there. What are my chances?" If you have a good record, he'll probably respond with something like: "Let me look at some of the openings in D.C. You've got the record to support it. I'll take a look at your preference card and you can call me in a couple of weeks." He might try to continue to talk about other options, but normally won't push you, assuming you have a firm plan in mind and reflect it in your preference card and conversation with him. After the conversation, write the detailer a letter and confirm what you've agreed upon.

A couple of other points on the art of talking to detailers:

—Be honest about your desires. The worst they can do is say no.

—Don't threaten a detailer with a resignation or a phone call from your CO or a flag officer. Detailers, like most people, don't respond well to threats.

—Keep your preference card updated as your desires change. Not having one on file essentially tells the detailer you'll go *anywhere!*

—Recognize your limitations. If your record doesn't support you for a certain job, a detailer can't help out.

—Remember, detailers are sharp officers with good records. That's why they have the job. In general, they will give intelligent career advice that you should temper with information received from other sources.

Placement Officer

You have virtually nothing to do directly with placement officers. They represent the Navy (specifically the interested commands) in the officer order-writing process. The detailer "proposes" you to the placement officer. Placement will turn around and ensure that you meet all the qualifications for a certain job and will then tell the detailer that you are a "sell" in a specific job. You hope it's one you want. The detailer will then return to you and make sure you are willing to accept the orders. Naturally, there is a good deal of proposal/counterproposal in all of this, but the system works surprisingly smoothly. Don't call a placement officer. You will politely and firmly be sent back to the detailer. His job is to deal with COs and XOs about their needs in filling jobs, not to negotiate jobs with individuals.

Career Advice

Obviously, a young division officer will need some career advice. There is a wide variety of sources for advice on career planning.

Commanding Officers—The CO of a ship or squadron, along with the XO, should spend a good deal of time working on career planning for their officers. This generally includes casual conversation, formal presentations in the wardroom, calling detailers' bosses and placement officers on your behalf, writing recommendations and endorsements, and setting you up with other people who can talk to you about an idea you have developed. Your CO and XO should be the prime movers in your career-planning process. After all, they have clearly done some successful career planning in your community to get to their present positions.

Peers—In this category include your immediate boss, a department head, and the officers on board who have a couple of tours under their belts. While there is a certain amount of hearsay that floats through any wardroom, these officers' info on recent calls with detailers can give you a key heads up to the current approach at the bureau. Listen to them as they relate their experiences in negotiating orders before you do your own negotiating.

Publications—As mentioned above, the magazine *Perspective* is a fine source of information on soon-to-open jobs, current trends, outlooks for all the major warfare communities, and other tidbits. It is published by the bureau, and has a wealth of good information. The *Naval Officers Guide* also has a section on career planning that is helpful.

Common Sense—Use your head. Taking back-to-back shore tours doesn't make sense for most naval officers, and neither does staying at sea for ten years. Try to maintain a balance in your career pattern, and make sure you take jobs that you want. Taking a hot job that you know you won't enjoy doing isn't going to get you ahead. More likely, it'll make you miserable and you'll do poorly. Take challenging jobs, get lots of sea duty, earn a master's degree, and face up to a Washington tour early in your career, and you'll be on the right track at the division officer and department head level.

Screening Boards—For some types of early assignments, a screening board is required. Even at the division officer level, looking ahead to your next tour, there are several screening boards of interest to you. These include boards for Department Head School and Postgraduate School. A screening board generally consists of a group of officers in Washington who review records and select candidates for whatever is being screened. The process is not as formal as a promotion board, but it is imperative to have your service record fully up-to-date when a board affecting you is coming up. In order to do so, write to the bureau and request a microfiche copy of your record. Do this at least 90 days before a screening (or promotion) board. When you get the fiche, check that all your qualifications are entered, all FITREPS are in place, the photo is up-to-date and clear, and that the record is generally in order. If you do this early, you will have ample time to get anything added that should be in the record. If time is short, send the material directly to your detailer, with a copy to the records office, by registered mail, return receipt requested. Overnight mail, while expensive, can be a lifesaver. You can also fax information to your detailer. Just call and ask for a phone number. Make sure your record is squared away—it reflects on your attention to detail more than anything else. And the board has nothing to judge you by save your written record.

FITREPS

There is a great deal of mythology surrounding the entire Report on Fitness of Officers (FITREP) system. Very simply, and quoting from the Navy instruction, "fitness reports are the principal documents used in the career management of officers in the U.S. Navy. They are maintained in the records of each officer at the Naval Military Personnel Command and are the primary tool used for comparing officers and arriving at career decisions with respect to relative merit for promotion, assignment, retention, selection for command, selection for subspecialty, term of service, and other career actions as required." Basically, they are the report cards that serve to record an officer's relative standing in the Navy so that decisions can be fairly made. While a knowledge of FITREPs is important for career planning, one basic piece of advice is not to focus on them. Focus entirely on doing your job to the best of your ability, and good FITREPs will follow.

A basic FITREP consists of identifying data, numerical grades for certain aspects of performance and qualities, a rating among peers, and a one-page written assessment of the officer's performance over a given period in time. The front side contains the numerical grades, signatures of the officer and the evaluator, and all pertinent data on the officers. The reverse side contains a one-page, generally bullet-format description of the officer. From a career-planning standpoint, think of FITREPs as report cards. They are the tickets you need to work your way into the very best jobs. One of the hardest things for a young officer to do is evaluate his or her own FITREP. There are several ways to do this:

1. Listen to the counseling you receive along with the FITREP. Your CO, XO, or department head (normally the CO) will sit down and discuss the FITREP with you. Ask questions when you are counseled initially.
2. Ask questions later. Don't be afraid to go back to your department head and ask about a particular mark. It's perfectly acceptable to say, "I received a 'B' in personal behavior, and I'd like to know what I can do to improve," for example. It's worth bearing in mind that your department head only provides an input, so you might want to consider showing him or her the final product and asking for advice on it.
3. Talk to your detailer, who sees hundreds of FITREPs weekly and knows exactly how your reports compare with your peers'. He or she will be very honest and frank with you, particularly on promotion and assignment issues.
4. Evaluate your FITREPs against each other. Naturally, you have a limited number of FITREPs (normally just your own) that you see. You can still compare them with each other and discern important trends (hopefully up) and key strengths and weaknesses.

Some of the questions you might want to ask on your FITREPs include:

    —Did your rank change relative to your peer group?

    —Were you recommended for early promotion? How many times?

    —What is the period of your best reports? End of tour (often called a "kiss goodbye") or regular term (competitive with other peers)?

—What are your marks in key areas: watch standing, airmanship, seamanship (as applicable), judgment, military bearing, response in stressful situations?

—What does the write-up say and how does it compare to early/later FITREPs?

—Is the trend steadily upward?

Promotion and Your Record

Your promotions will be based almost entirely on your FITREPs and the contents of your service record (medals, letters of commendation, photograph, and so forth). Along with the cold, hard facts in the service jacket, however, is another intangible in the promotion process that is called "service reputation." This is the opinion of all who work with you (peers, juniors, and seniors) that eventually works its way around the fleet. As a young division officer, this won't yet be formed on you. As you advance throughout your career, and numbers of officers get smaller, the book on a given officer grows. People sitting on promotion boards often have a hint about an individual's service reputation, and it does play a part in promotion.

For the most part, promotion is based on your proven ability in the jobs you have held, as documented in your FITREPs. Boards consider a large number of officers for a limited number of openings, either in promotion, selection to command, or subspecialization. They look for tie breakers because there are often many superlative records before them. Be sure your record is up-to-date, that your picture is recent and sharp, that all required forms are entered, and that the entire package is squared away. To ensure that this is so, request a copy from the bureau well before your promotion board meets by writing to:

Bureau of Naval Personnel (Pers-312), Washington, D.C. 20370.

You can also review your record personally in Washington, D.C., at the Navy Annex in the Officer Record Review Room (Room 3036).

Finally, if you feel there is information that should be changed in your record, you should consult the *Military Personnel Manual* for the proper way to do so.

Medals, Letters of Commendation, Letters of Appreciation

Medals and other awards, like FITREPs, are something that you shouldn't worry about. If you are to be awarded one, your chain-of-command will take care of it. Don't ask about how to get one or discuss it at all. If you are fortunate (and hardworking) enough to receive one, great! If not, just keeping working hard, and sooner or later you'll be recognized. Policies on medals vary widely from command to command and community to community.

As a division officer, you might receive a letter of commendation or appreciation for a job you did particularly well, either from your own CO or someone higher in the chain of command. There are always a few Navy Achievement Medals given after a major deployment or for individual jobs of a superb nature. Finally, at the end of your tour, you may be awarded either a Navy Achievement Medal, or in some rare cases, the higher Navy Commendation Medal.

Receiving a medal might help your record and your chances for promotion, selection for specific programs, or early selection, but not receiving one won't damage your hopes or chances.

Deep Selection

"Getting picked up early" is an expression that means an officer is selected for advancement to the next rank a year or two early. It is a very rare honor, and is a result of a super record with many recommendations for accelerated promotion. There is very little you can do to point yourself in this direction. At the LCDR level, for example, there are always a wide variety of career patterns among the early selectees. Some have stayed at sea exclusively, others have been aides, some have undertaken especially challenging jobs and done well, others have been to graduate school. There is no one set pattern for success, and the deep selection process recognizes that fact just like all other selection processes in the Navy.

Initial Career Steps

Records

As a division officer starting out, you need to establish a series of personal files that can be maintained as your career progresses. These files should generally be kept aboard ship with you, although it isn't a bad idea to have copies at home as well. Each can be kept in a manila file folder, although another option is keeping everything in a single large binder.

The first file should contain all of your personal copies of Fitness Reports. These are your report cards and give you a very clear idea of your progress in your career. You will refer to them a surprising number of times, both while on the ship or at home working on personal correspondence. Keep a copy of all of them in files at both locations.

Another important file to keep is of all your disbursing records. These should be retained for about two years, then discarded. Taken together, they are a permanent record of your accumulated sea duty, leave on the books, pay accounts, and allotments. A single set of these is normally sufficient in a single file on board your ship.

A third file should contain official correspondence. This should include letters of commendation and appreciation, award nominations, letters certifying completion of various warfare qualifications, and so on. The file is a backup to your service record and will be very handy when working on correspondence. In this file, keep all your PQS qualifications as well.

Finally, keep a career-planning file with clippings from magazines like *Perspective, Navy Times,* and the U.S. Naval Institute *Proceedings* about items pertaining to career paths, jobs, qualifications, trends in the career system, and so forth.

Establish Career Goals

Each warfare community has a fairly orderly progression for the young division officer. In the surface line, for example, an officer checks aboard and is briefed on all his or her goals over the next three years (at a good command with an active officer-training program). He or she will be told to qualify in general damage control, maintenance, as an officer of the deck, a surface warfare officer, and as an engineering officer of the watch, all in three years. You should strive mightily to complete all of these qualifications as rapidly and professionally as you can. While the goals assigned vary from community to community and command to command, they are the basics. They outline your program of professional growth.

Beyond these formally assigned career goals, you should mentally (and perhaps even jot down) your personal career goals for your first tour. They might be something like this:

Assigned: Damage Control
3M Maintenance
Officer of the Deck (In port)
CIC Watch Officer
Officer of the Deck (Under way)
Surface Warfare Officer
Engineering Officer of the Watch

Personal: Top 1% Fitness Reports with all As and Bs
Scoring excellent—outstanding on the PT test every 6 months
Screen for Postgraduate School
Screen for Department Head School
Serve in at least two departments with good results

Qualification

In the surface and submarine community, and to some degree in other warfare communities, division officers have a very structured path toward full qualification. The normal means of qualifying is via a series of Personnel Qualification Standards, written tests, and oral boards. Generally, a division officer will be given an interview with the training officer of the command upon arrival. If he or she doesn't approach you within a week, go and see him or her. He or she should counsel you on the goals for qualification, and will generally assign some time frames to meet.

It is important to move forward steadily toward qualification. If you are given two years to qualify as a surface warfare officer (SWO), for example, set out to do it sooner. Steady progress is the key. Try to set aside an hour each day to work on your qualifications. Additionally, standing watch is a good time to obtain qualifying signatures for individual watch stations, if doing so won't detract from the quality of your watch standing. Often, simply performing the watch will earn you qualifying signatures, although you'll have to hunt down the officer you stood the watch with and have him or her sign your books.

Once you've obtained all the signatures and performed all the basic tasks associated with qualifying, you'll need to see the ship's training officer again and arrange to take the written test and/or oral board. Study for these evolutions, again trying to set aside an hour or two each day to prepare. Remember, qualification is a big part of your job during your first tour. You are not taking time away from your division officer job, because qualification is part of it. To practice for an oral board, have a group of your peers give you a "mock board."

Fitting In

Joining a wardroom or ready room as a young division officer can be a very intimidating experience. This is especially true if your commissioning source did not include midshipmen cruises, which give at least an overview of life in a naval organization operating at sea. Some time-honored approaches for a division officer just starting out include:

1. Relax and be yourself. Don't try to put on an act.
2. Stop, look, and listen. When you are starting out, no one expects you to know everything. You can learn the most when you quietly listen to those with more experience, especially when you go slowly.
3. Listen to your chief petty officer, who has probably been around and has good instincts.
4. When you don't know the answer, try to find it out on your own (unless time is of the essence). If you still don't understand, ask.
5. Work hard to learn your job, especially the technical aspects of your equipment and the details about your troops.

Wrapping Up the First Job

As you move through your first tour as a division officer, you will probably do very well. You should complete your basic package of qualifications by the two-year point and begin to function as a very valuable asset to your command. It is hoped that in addition to qualifying, you've completed or made good progress on all your other personal career goals. Assuming all is going well, you need to start thinking seriously about a very important set of orders—your second assignment. At this point, you need to understand the way the detailing system works as you prepare for that initial round of discussions with your detailer.

Surface Line

Career planning at the division-officer level in the surface line revolves around rapid qualification as a surface warfare officer (SWO) and selection to Department Head School. After checking aboard, the new division officer should have an interview with the ship's training officer (normally the operations officer). The OPS officer will probably validate a great deal of the basic SWO PQS that is based on successful completion of Surface Warfare Officer School (SWOS). It is then up to you to move rapidly and complete all the various component books in the overall SWO PQS.

SWO qualification varies from ship to ship. Most have a system that revolves around signing off the PQS while standing a variety of under-instruction and junior-level watches—such as junior officer of the deck (JOOD), junior officer of the watch (JOOW), CIC watch officer (CICWO), and junior engineering officer of the watch (JEOOW). Some ships have elaborate lecture programs that make signatures fairly easy to obtain, while others simply have the officers demonstrate their drive and initiative in tracking down the requisite signature authority.

All ships should have a list of authorized PQS qualifiers who can sign off the SWO PQS. The authorized signers are often the line (SWO) officers in the wardroom. Don't be afraid to be aggressive in pursuing signatures. Take your books with you on watch and get the signature immediately after you complete the task.

Your first sea tour is generally 30–36 months. You will usually serve in two different departments, rotating at the 18-month point. Naturally, this is dependent on the ship's overall officer-manning plan, your performance and desires, and many other factors. During the 30-month tour, you should complete SWO qualification, and hopefully complete an engineering officer of the watch qualification as well. Eventually all surface officers must qualify as EOOWs, and the sooner you get it out of the way the better. As you complete qualifications, send copies of the letters to your detailer, and he will enter it in your record. After you SWO qualify, you'll be screened by the Department Head Screening Board. When you have completed both major milestones, you have several options open to you at the division officer level: split touring to a sequential sea tour, going ashore, or going straight to Department Head School and back to the fleet as a department head.

Sequential Sea Tours

The big advantage of a sequential sea tour is the additional experience it will offer you going into the critical department head tour. Especially if you move into an area you haven't seen before, you will vastly broaden your capabilities and knowledge about all facets of surface warfare. Some of the programs include:

1. Carrier Readiness Improvement Program: A very selective program that sends a limited number of truly outstanding performers into engineering jobs on aircraft carriers. The work and the hours are very hard, and the challenges immense. A young LTJG can expect to serve as boilers or main engines officer, for example, with over 150 men, a dozen chiefs, and two officers working for him or her. This tour carries a set of guaranteed orders from the bureau and normally ensures an outstanding initial department head tour coming out of Department Head School. It will also earn the young officer an EOOW letter on a very complex plant at an early point in his or her career.
2. Precommissioning: Going to PRECOM normally provides a break, as the PRECOM period is often less demanding than sea duty. It will put a division officer in an interesting and unique situation as he or she commissions a new ship. If you are so fortunate as to go to an Aegis destroyer, you'll also be working with

front-line technology and superb systems. They also take a long time, typically another 30–36 months following the initial sea tour.

3. Post-Division Officer Job: Positions available include Aegis cruiser and destroyers, large amphibious ships like LHAs and LHDs, or afloat staffs. These are interesting, challenging, and fairly short (18-month) tours that can pay high dividends in broadening experience. Particularly on cruisers, these are superb positions.

Shore Duty

Going straight to shore duty from your initial division officer tour has some real benefits. It gives you a break from the rigors of sea duty and provides an opportunity to spend some time with your friends and family. Further, if carefully planned, a shore tour can accomplish two important goals, even very early in a career:

1. You can earn a master's degree: The Navy places a very high value on postgraduate education. During the initial shore tour, an officer can get a master's either at Navy expense or during off-duty hours. At the Navy's postgraduate school in Monterey, California, many academic programs are offered. This is an excellent and career-enhancing course of action at the immediate post-division-officer level. An officer can also obtain a master's at many off-duty programs, especially in Washington, D.C.

2. You can begin developing a subspecialty: by working in a given shore-duty job, you begin to develop your subspecialty, which will be very important later on. Some examples include working at BUPERS and beginning to gain an expertise in personnel management; working on a joint staff, taking a job at NAVSEA in engineering or procurement; and so on. When combined with accomplishing a master's degree on the side, this sort of tour completes many objectives at once.

Other options ashore include teaching at SWOS, Fleet Combat Center, Fleet ASW Center, the Naval Academy, and many other schools; going to overseas duty, generally preceded by some language training; working in Washington in many different fields; serving as an aide to a flag officer; and many others. Do research on jobs that appeal to you by talking to those who have served there before. Discuss them with your CO/XO/department head, talk it over with your family, call your detailer, and read about the different jobs in *Perspective* and other Navy publications. Pick what you want and talk to your detailer.

Back to Department Head School

Another exciting option is to push straight back to Department Head School and come charging out as a young (LT) department head. This is a "fast track" approach with the advantage of having everything fresh in your mind, moving you very quickly through important career milestones, and opening room in your career path for many different options later on. The problems include possible family burn out from too much straight sea duty and separation, the relatively less challenging billets available to very junior Department Head School graduates, and your own relative youth and inexperience in competing with other, more senior department heads. While not for everyone, it is an option that receives strong endorsement from many detailers, who are trying to reduce grade creep in sea billets.

Aviation Officers

As a division officer in an aircraft squadron, you will find your career planning is relatively simple. You will be assigned a variety of jobs, rotating through the major departments. The key, of course, is to do well in all your squadron jobs while performing well in the cockpit. The initial squadron tour lasts about three years. Hopefully, you will have a chance to serve in two or more of the four major departments: operations, maintenance, safety, and administration.

Toward the end of your second year in the squadron, you should start thinking about your first shore tour. Researching your next assignment should include all the ideas mentioned above, and the same basic set of opportunities are available to aviators as they are to surface warriors. One major source of shore-duty jobs is in the Fleet Readiness Squadron or "RAG" (Replacement Air Group), which requires a large number of pilots and NFOs for instructors. The big advantage, of course, is the additional flight time accrued in the RAG. Additionally, many aviators have the opportunity to attend PG school or serve in any of the shore-duty billets discussed above.

Submarine Warfare Officers

On a submarine, there is a heightened emphasis on engineering qualification. Most junior officers are initially assigned to the engineering department, for example, to begin to qualify as EOOWs. At the same time, you will begin work on the 12–15 month process that leads to qualification in submarine warfare and earning your coveted "dolphins." The first at-sea tour is normally 36 months. Some split tours are available, wherein a young division officer spends two years operational and two years in a PRECOM setting on a new SSN or SSBN. Prior to the first shore tour, the division officer must complete both EOOW and SS qualifications, which will take most of the three-year tour.

Shore duty can commence as early as the two-year point for a few selected officers who will rotate ashore to teach at prototype. For the rest, shore duty will come at the three-year point, and all the same jobs indicated for surface line officers are available to submariners. The shore tours are two years, as for all the line communities, and are followed by Department Head School and DH tours.

Coast Guard

While basically similar to Navy Surface Line career planning, the Coast Guard places a heavy emphasis on command early in the career. This is due to the great number of smaller ships in the Coast Guard. Command is the best duty, and the best route to command is XO duty, followed by sequential command tours.

As in the Navy, it is important to learn the basics of the Officer Evaluation Report (OER) system. You should ask for specific recommendations for downstream jobs you want.

Finally, the Coast Guard places a strong emphasis on operational skills. As with the Navy, service at sea is at the heart of a professional career. Graduate education and the development of a shore specialty are important, but the key to promotion is to have a good number of maritime operations in your record.

Conclusions and Looking Ahead

While you certainly don't need to plan every step of your 20–30 year career as a division officer, there are a few important points to keep in mind as you do some basic career planning. In addition to the specifics discussed above for your first and second tours (the division officer level), you should think in terms of the long haul. Some of the downstream career issues to keep in mind include:

1. Subspecialization: As you grow in your Navy career, you will need to develop a subspecialty. Your specialty, of course, is your primary warfare area. A subspecialty is generally oriented toward what types of jobs you undertake when ashore. You will develop a subspecialty either by going to postgraduate school and studying some specific area (political-military planning, electrical engineer, management, personnel) or by on-the-job training in a given area. Early on, you should talk to more senior folks and find out about the various subspecialties available. Try to pick out one that interests you, and push for either postgraduate school in that area or a shore tour that complements it.

2. Postgraduate School: Both in the Navy and after you eventually retire and start a second career, a postgraduate school is a huge plus. There are a wide variety of ways to obtain an advanced degree. The first is through dedicated study at the Naval Postgraduate School in Monterey, California. This is an all-expense-paid, full-time billet. Another route is the Advanced Education program, which offers an officer time off, with full pay and allowances, but requires the officer to pay tuition costs. A third means of obtaining a postgraduate degree is to win a scholarship, grant, or fellowship. The Navy will permit you to take the time off to complete the degree. Finally, you can obtain the de-

gree at your own time and expense during your off-duty hours while stationed ashore. The appropriate instructions describing all of these programs are available through your ship's office.

3. Service college: A little later in your career, you may want to attend a service college, such as the Naval War College, the Army War College, the National Defense University (Industrial College of the Armed Forces and National War College), foreign war colleges, and so on. These are generally one-year tours, and are very career-enhancing. You can also complete the Naval War College curriculum via correspondence by writing to the Center for Continuing Education, U.S. Naval War College, Newport, Rhode Island 02840.

4. Washington tour: Into most successful careers, a little Washington must fall. A tour in Washington, where major decisions are made, is very valuable for any officer. Generally, the earlier a Washington tour, the better. Time spent in D.C. can give an officer a perspective that is difficult to obtain in any other way. Generally, the best jobs are on the CNO's staff (i.e., in OPNAV), although most other assignments in D.C. are also very competitive.

5. Aide: Many people advocate tours as aides to flag officers or civilian officials, citing the access to a very senior person and the benefits of seeing the decision process at a personal level.

6. Detailer: Serving as a detailer gives an officer a unique perspective on the personnel process.

7. Teaching: Teaching, especially in a strong tactical environment, has the advantage of keeping an officer current in his/her warfare areas. There are many superb training commands in virtually every Navy home port.

8. Joint assignment: Tours with joint commands, such as on the Joint Staff in Washington or a unified command (CINCPAC, CINCLANT, etc.) are generally career enhancing.

12/Conclusion

The effectiveness of a Navy is dependent on many factors and the most important factor of all is the quality of its officer corps. There is no profession as demanding as the Navy.
—*Admiral Arleigh Burke*

People and Leadership

Your sailors are the most important assets you have; they are the one common denominator in all naval activities. Machinery can be repaired, and compartments repainted with routine ease, but tired, disheartened, or demoralized sailors cannot be restored to fresh energy and spirit without the employment of much time and skill. Burned out motors or bearings are not difficult to replace, but someone deeply hurt and embittered may never again become fully useful to an organization. People are profoundly vulnerable emotionally, yet they can also be inspired to prodigious labor and self-sacrifice. The greatest resource you have as a division officer lies in your sailors. To release this latent energy takes wisdom and skill in human relations, but the rewards can be almost immeasurable. People will perform more efficiently and will make more sacrifices for a leader they respect and trust, than for one who merely drives them along with the force of his or her impersonal and delegated authority.

Comprehending these truths provides a firm base on which officers can build their professional skill and develop their professional knowledge. Most officers deal with people all their lives, so the measure of their success with people is a measure of their success in their profession. It is not difficult to see how this idea applies to your daily tasks as a division officer. While you must accept and operate the weapons and machinery furnished to you, you do not have to accept the performance of your sailors in using the weapons or in running the machinery. There are almost no limits to the proficiency you can develop in your sailors. No matter how sophisticated the equipment you are provided with, you still have to select and train people to operate it. The fingers that designed, assembled, and programmed the SPY-ID AEGIS radar are the same human mechanisms that released the English arrows at the Battle of Crécy.

Customs, Traditions, and Manners

Naval customs, traditions, and manners have evolved over a period of nearly two hundred years, during which time they have been tested and proven through usage. In fact, they are sometimes recognized in legal proceedings as almost having the force of law.

Every naval officer should endeavor to know, understand, and follow naval customs, traditions, and manners, realizing that they derive from the experience in peace and in war of generations of our worthy predecessors. They should be departed from only after the most careful thought and consideration.

Young officers, new to the service and unaccustomed to life on board ship, sometimes offend by an apparent lack of manners or respect for certain Navy customs. Senior officers, with whom they work and live in close contact, have acquired a deep respect for the traditions and customs of the Navy. As a result, these officers may be sensitive to behaviors of which new officers may not even be aware. Crowded living conditions make it particularly important for all officers to recognize those conventions of shipboard behavior and those vital traditions whose observance and recognition distinguish officers and gentlemen.

Junior officers are prone to treat the wardroom of a ship as if it were the lounge of their fraternity or sorority house at college. This behavior is understandable, but is not well received by those who have learned that consideration for their fellow officers can make crowded ships livable and comfortable. Do not leave books, papers, charts, caps, jackets, and rain clothes in the wardroom. Do not remove wardroom magazines or rest your feet on coffee tables. Return empty coffee cups to the sideboard. Don't smoke. Leave the best seats at wardroom movies vacant for your seniors. Never place your cap on wardroom mess tables, sideboards, or buffets. These all seem to be small and obvious points, yet collectively they are important. As a junior officer, you should be prompt for meals, especially when guests are present. When you have guests of your own, introduce them to your shipmates, particularly to the senior officer, who is normally the command duty officer.

In leaving the ship, junior officers always enter a boat first. It may seem natural to step back and let your seniors precede you, but naval customs and tradition require you to enter a boat or automobile first. In a boat, move well forward unless the only shelter is forward; in that event, take the most exposed seat in the boat, leaving the sheltered seats for your seniors. In returning to the ship, the senior officers are the first to debark and the first to go up the accommodation ladder or brow.

The Navy draws a firm line between official or shipboard relations and social relations. On board ship there must be a certain formality and dignity, particularly on the bridge, on the quarter-deck, or in the presence of a group of sailors. Officers of about the same rank with the same job interests tend to group together. Ashore, at a party, or at someone's house, a more informal atmosphere is appropriate. Officers' spouses often make close friendships among themselves with little regard for seniority, and a first-name basis is quite normal for officers on the golf course or on the tennis court despite a disparity in rank. You can never go far wrong in being perfectly natural and friendly ashore, while observing a certain formality and reticence on board ship until you get to know your seniors.

Institutional Aspects of the Navy

In the chapter on discipline, the point was made that a division should be run in a regulation manner. In this chapter, the importance of naval customs and traditions has been stressed. There are some excellent reasons for these important points. The Navy, like any other institution, owes much of its strength and vigor to well-established procedures and ceremonies. Over a period of centuries, men and women living in groups have been conditioned to react to certain fixed symbols and formalities. The study of humans in their environment (sociology) has a direct military application. Officers who are too individual, who run things their own way, who do not stress the normal, regulation way of doing things, create a difficult situation for anyone who succeeds them. Strong individualists must recognize their role as that of only one officer in a long line of officers.

It is in this context that the official formalities of Navy life should be considered. Morning Quarters, colors, and the ceremony of the quarterdeck are all important in that they demonstrate the permanent spirit and tradition of the Navy. The wearing of the uniform, the manner of saluting, and correct military behavior in speech and in correspondence all must be recognized, observed, and enforced by junior officers. New sailors and officers, fresh from civilian life, are often prone to discount and ignore Navy rules of behavior. The services, to be strong and effective, must be authoritative in nature. No officer, however humanitarian or idealistic his or her views, should feel apologetic in observing the military rules and traditions of his or her profession. Furthermore, an officer without real pride in the service and without a sense of obligation and duty cannot hope to achieve success in the Navy.

The petty annoyances that are bound to occur—the last-minute schedule change that upsets your weekend plans, the hurry-up-and-wait of a fueling evolution, perhaps even an unmerited harsh word—must be taken in their proper context. The Navy, whether you are in it for a career or a short period of volunteer service, is a large and complex operation run by fallible human beings. There will always be mistakes in judgment or casualties to equipment, though perhaps to a lesser degree than in any other organization of comparable size. These must not become a preoccupation. "Keep your eyes beyond the beam of your ship," as a venerable salt once advised, and appreciate instead the power and importance of naval tradition.

Navy People

Just as all commands incorporate informal organizations that differ from the formal, official ones found in those units' organization manuals, so the Navy as a whole contains an informal organization. It might appear to you as a newly commissioned officer that the rank structure represents a constant and fixed set of values, but this is far from true. For example, the Navy warrant officers, while technically junior to ensigns and junior lieutenants, actually represent a group of seasoned, responsible, and skillful officers who exert a much greater influence than their broken stripes would indicate. Warrant officers are exceptionally able people who have a detailed knowledge of their specialty and a wealth of experience in the Navy. A newly commissioned ensign or junior lieutenant should tread very lightly in dealing with these wise old-timers, and should solicit their advice on technical matters and their guidance in dealing with naval problems. Warrant officers, proud of their special skills and long service, are always glad to help a young officer get squared away in a new job.

Some ensigns and lieutenants have also had many years of service, gained as they worked up through enlisted and warrant status. The point is that rank does not always indicate length of service or degree of skill and background. Do not judge people solely by their rank; check into their background and experience.

It is important that you establish a good working relationship with your senior petty officers, who, in most cases, will be chief petty officers. The chiefs have traditionally been referred to as the "backbone of the Navy," and think of themselves as such. They are the ones through whom you must translate orders into action, theory into practice. They stand at the top of their careers, have proved themselves through years of experience, and stay with their "gang" while division officers come and go.

Your tacit acknowledgment of these facts will almost always result in the wholehearted cooperation of your senior petty officers. They will be eager to share with you their hard-won knowledge of the Navy and of their specialties, and will take pride in knowing that they have had a part in your development as a professional naval officer.

How to Estimate Your Success as a Division Officer

As a division officer, you may very well wonder how to judge your effectiveness. There is no simple rule of thumb, but there are several questions you can ask yourself. The first is: Do I run my division in an atmosphere of approval? If you like and respect most of your subordinates, if there is very little bitterness and recrimination noticeable in the daily routine, if your subordinates like to talk things over with you, the answer is probably affirmative. While a certain amount of stress is inevitable in running any military outfit, there is no excuse for the excess of emotion that so frequently accompanies the handling of people. It is a sign of instability and immaturity on the part of the officer in charge. Complications, problems, and mistakes are all part of the normal daily routine and should not be considered by any officer as a personal affront. People usually perform their routine tasks more efficiently when not distracted by displays of temperament.

Standards of Discipline

Another criterion of efficient division leadership is standards of discipline. A well-led outfit has few mast cases, few absent without authority, and a minimum number of small incidents of bad behavior. The sailors should conform to regulations and meet the standards of appearance, performance, and behavior that have been established. They should do so because they have accepted those standards as the standards of their group. The appearance of your subordinates, while working and when ashore, will reveal to a critical observer a great deal about the discipline of your division. Their performance can be estimated by the comments made during formal inspections. All these matters are relative, of course, and it is not reasonable to expect perfection. Compare your division with other divisions when making such a judgment.

Team Spirit

An important criterion of a division's leadership is team or group spirit. Are the men and women interested in the various forms of competition? Do they generate ideas and enthusiasm over a group activity such as a baseball game or a picnic? Do they really work hard before an inspection, or do they just go through the motions? A highly motivated group will voluntarily work many hours overtime, if they must, to prepare properly for an inspection. There are dozens of other indications of team spirit—or the lack of it—in a division. Of course, factors beyond your control may dampen the spirits of your sailors, but in general you should be able to judge their spirit in comparison to that of other divisions.

Being alert to these matters may assist you in uncovering sources of irritation or confusion that would not normally be brought to your attention. For example, a leading petty officer may be going stale through overwork or may have personal problems that are reflected in his being a little rough on his subordinates. You may first become aware of this by observing the sailors in their daily tasks.

Relations with Seniors

It may have occurred to you that a junior officer not only has to be a good leader; he or she also must be an accomplished follower. All of us work for someone in the Navy and cannot be successful unless we please our seniors. As you will discover, this can be difficult until you learn a few basic principles and techniques. In a military organization, you cannot choose your immediate superior, yet your first duty is to carry out his or her orders.

A dual relationship usually develops between you as a division officer, and, let us say, your department head. You may even become close friends and play golf together. The important feeling, of course, is one of mutual respect; friendship can be a bonus. It is wise to keep these relationships separate. Enjoy the friendship ashore but be careful to treat him or her as your superior officer on board.

If you find yourself in strong disagreement with your senior on some professional question, do not fight the problem. Do it his or her way—then suggest changes if you still want them. When you present new ideas or new ways of doing things to your senior, try to do it in a modest, quiet manner so as not to arouse a natural opposition to change.

The most important thing you can do for your seniors is to take action on their orders. Take notes to be sure you are responsive to *all* of their ideas. Some officers rarely give a firm, clear order; they suggest or imply—it is up to you to act.

Remember the value of completed staff work. Wrap up a project if possible and present it in a positive manner. Ask as few questions as possible. It is better to say, "Unless you direct otherwise I propose to. . . ." Then all you need is a nod and you can go ahead. But remember that your superior must answer to *his* boss. Keep him informed so that he is not embarrassed, for example, by the commanding officer asking questions that he cannot answer.

Retention

One of the most serious problems the Navy has had to solve in recent years has been that of retaining trained personnel. New ships have been built and advanced detection, weapons, and propulsion systems have been developed, but the most sophisticated hardware in the world is only as good as those who maintain and operate it. This means the Navy has to retain qualified people if it is to make effective use of the ships and equipment provided.

The reasons people give for not reenlisting are many and varied. Some of them are real and valid, many are imaginary. The unhappy fact is that the Navy has lost many valuable trained sailors, and this has adversely affected its condition of readiness and professional standards of performance. For each person so lost the cash investment in training alone runs to thousands of dollars.

Over a period of years, the Navy has developed many ways to improve personnel retention. The system for advancement in rating is fair and objective. It rewards sailors who study hard by allowing them to compete with their contemporaries on an equal basis through standard exams. Cash payments for reenlistment have, for some highly technical ratings, amounted to thousands of dollars. Career-counseling programs instituted in all ships and shore activities are designed to inform sailors of the advantages of a Navy career plus the opportunities open to them. These programs have had some, but not enough, effect on retention.

The problems of reenlistment and retention can be partially solved at the Navy Department and at the political level, but probably even more significantly at the levels of the division and ship. As a division officer you play a vital role in this program, on which the very effectiveness of the fleet depends. First, as you learn to become a leader whom your sailors can respect and look up to, you must become familiar with all the actual benefits and advantages enjoyed by a career person. Many data of this sort are available in the fleet reenlistment manuals and from career counselors.

Second, you must show your dedication to the Navy by your attitude. Never, under any circumstances, talk the Navy down. As rigorous and demanding as the Navy can be, there are rewards in feelings of accomplishment and pride that no civilian can comprehend, much less measure. Talk up and stress the aspects of naval life that appeal to all. Those leaving the Navy look back with pleasure and satisfaction upon the experiences of travel and foreign cruises. Similarly, they cherish the memories of friends and shipmates, of danger and hardship faced together. Yet too many of us shy away from even mentioning these really important aspects of life.

Many worthwhile people decide not to reenlist because their Navy pay would be lower than what they could earn on the outside. They will reenlist only when they are convinced—by the example, attention, and interest of their leaders—that what we do in the Navy is tremendously more important than how much we get paid for doing it. No worthwhile persons will turn permanently to the Navy for a career unless they are convinced that the Navy not only needs them, but will make the most of their individual abilities. Your part is to convince them of that.

Three key points to emphasize with your people are:

• The Navy offers the chance to work with the best people in the world, under challenging circumstances that bring people together.

• In the Navy, you are constantly challenged with new jobs that improve your talents and abilities, moving you forward in your profession.

• There is a good retirement system that provides the basis for excellent lifetime financial security.

The Meaning of a Commission

Note the wording of an officer's commission: "Reposing special trust and confidence in the patriotism, valor, fidelity and abilities . . . I do appoint . . . by and with the advice and consent of the Senate." *Special trust and confidence* is more than a polite phrase; it means just that. A commissioned officer is assumed to be a man or woman of honor and integrity.

It is true, of course, that in this era of huge armed forces, it is not always administratively feasible to accept an officer's word at face value. National security often requires that an officer provide proof of his or her actions or identity. Despite this, an officer in uniform is recognized as the custodian of the country's honor and safety.

With the war in Vietnam fading into history, the nation's attitude toward the military has reverted to more traditional respect for the armed forces. The history of the United States shows that the military is most respected when it is most needed. An officer must appreciate his or her appointed position of special trust and confidence and must earn public respect by maintaining traditional standards of honor and devotion to duty.

Remember that an officer who takes an oath of commission is obligated to support and preserve the Constitution. Since the Constitution defines the great moral and judicial principles upon which our republic is founded, it follows that an officer is, by the oath of office alone, committed to the exercise of moral leadership.

By extension, an officer must present a moral example to his or her sailors. This means applying such basic life principles as not lying, cheating, or stealing; trying to be a good example to others in the chain of command in every way; and maintaining a positive attitude around the command and in public on liberty.

Patriotism

In this age of conflict, ideological as well as military, all officers should recall the oath they took upon receiving their commissions. Our enemies attack us with ideas that are designed to destroy our faith. This must stimulate us to affirm our faith and our pride in our country, and all that she stands for. We cannot afford to be complacent about our freedom and prosperity.

Attitude surveys of enlisted personnel reveal many who do not know why large military forces are needed by the free world. Many of us assume that young people in the services are aware of their responsibilities as American citizens to defend the United States. This is not necessarily true, and no officer should hesitate to counter the apparent cynicism of youth in regard to patriotism.

Remember, your sailors are not just employees and your role is not simply that of a manager. You and your division represent the United States in a manner in which very few are privileged to represent her. You are her strength, her commitment, and her guarantee to the world. You, and others like you, must meet the task or the whole world pays the price. Every ship that cannot meet her commitments, every plane that is grounded, weakens our position. Each of us plays an important role in the maintenance of our strength. Few have a role as important as the division officer. Naval officers find themselves charged with this responsibility very early in their careers. Too often that portion of their career is over before they realize its true importance.

The quality of your leadership and performance is the measure of America's future. Seize this opportunity before it escapes you. It can bring rewards and knowledge you will treasure for a lifetime.

Deterring confrontation, providing forward presence, controlling free passage of the world's sea lanes, exercising American sea power, and being fully prepared to project power ashore from the sea are *your* missions. These roles embody the missions of the Navy. Whether through might or mere show of force, our naval power is the key to our success. You hold the key to keeping our naval power at its peak.

As an officer whose obligation and privilege it may be to lead your men in war, you should seize every opportunity to encourage and inspire loyalty toward, respect for, and devotion to, our country. People have always fought more effectively when fighting for something they believed in. The barbarians did not overrun Rome until her freemen had lost their faith and vigor.

War and Peace

As a division officer, you should realize early on that all the demands imposed upon the division and division personnel can never be completely satisfied. Rarely will there be perfect appearance of personnel and materiel and at the same time complete preparation in all respects for wartime operations. The emphasis on spit and polish sometimes tempts young officers to believe that appearance and smartness are the most important considerations in apportioning their time. It is a grave mistake, however, to believe seriously that any responsible senior is more interested in appearance than in combat efficiency. Ships that are outstanding in appearance may win the battle efficiency awards, but in most cases the same ships are outstanding in fighting potential too.

Never forget that you and your sailors have one primary mission: to prepare for and to conduct wartime operations. All duties and activities should lead by some means to this end.

Appendix A:
Suggested Reading

Here are a few titles to stock a small seagoing library. They include both fiction and nonfiction, and represent many classic professional and maritime works. How will you find time to read at sea? Eventually, as you become more experienced and your division runs more smoothly, you will find time to do a little reading—and probably watch a movie or two as well!

Naval Classics

(Published in the series Classics of Naval Literature by the Naval Institute Press)

Autobiography of George Dewey, Admiral of the Navy George Dewey

Bluejacket: An Autobiography, Fred J. Buenzle with A. Grove Day

The Caine Mutiny, Herman Wouk

The Commodores, Leonard F. Guttridge and Jay D. Smith

The Cruel Sea, Nicholas Monsarrat

Delilah, Marcus Goodrich

Journal of a Cruise made to the Pacific Ocean . . ., Capt. David Porter

Man-of-War Life, Charles Nordhoff

My Fifty Years in the Navy, Adm. Charles E. Clark, USN

Ned Myers; or, A Life Before the Mast, James Fenimore Cooper

The Quiet Warrior: A Biography of Admiral Raymond A. Spruance, Thomas B. Buell

Recollections of a Naval Officer, 1841–1865, Capt. William
    Harwar Parker
Run Silent, Run Deep, Edward L. Beach
Sailing Alone Around the World, Joshua Slocum
The Sand Pebbles, Richard McKenna
The Sinking of the Merrimac, Richard Pearson Hobson
Two Years on the Alabama, Arthur W. Sinclair
The Victory at Sea, Rear Adm. William S. Sims, USN, and Burton J.
    Hendrick
White-Jacket, Herman Melville
With the Battle Cruisers, Filson Young

Professional Works

Dutton's Navigation and Piloting, Elbert S. Maloney
Farwell's Rules of the Nautical Road, Capt. Richard A. Smith, RN
    (Ret.)
Fleet Tactics, Capt. Wayne P. Hughes, Jr., USN (Ret.)
Guide to Naval Writing, Robert Shenk
International Law for Seagoing Officers, Burdick H. Brittin
Knight's Modern Seamanship, John V. Noel, Jr.
Moods of the Sea, edited by George C. Solley and Eric Steinbaugh
Naval Shiphandling, Capt. R. S. Crenshaw, Jr., USN (Ret.)
Short Stories of the Sea, edited by George C. Solley, Eric Steinbaugh,
    and David O. Tomlinson
Watch Officer's Guide, Comdr. James Stavridis, USN
Weather for the Mariner, Rear Adm. William J. Kotsch, USN (Ret.)

CNO Reading List

All Quiet on the Western Front, Erich M. Remarque
American Caesar: Douglas MacArthur 1880–1964,
    William Manchester
The Art of War, Sun Tzu
Assignment—Pentagon: The Insider's Guide to the Potomac Puzzle,
    Perry M. Smith
Admiral Arleigh Burke, E. B. Potter
Bull Halsey, E. B. Potter

Command of the Seas, John F. Lehman

Democracy in America, Alexis de Tocqueville

Eisenhower: At War, 1943–1945, David Eisenhower

The Face of Battle, John Keegan

First to Fight: An Inside View of the U.S. Marine Corps, Victor H. Krulak

Flight of the Intruder, Stephen Coonts

The Geopolitics of Superpowers, Colin S. Gray

The Guns of August, Barbara Tuchman

The Hunt for Red October, Tom Clancy

The Influence of Sea Power Upon History, Alfred Thayer Mahan

The Killer Angels, Michael Shaara

The Last Lion: Winston Spencer Churchill, William Manchester

The Mask of Command, John Keegan

Military Strategy, Joseph C. Wylie

Modern Times: The World from the Twenties to the Nineties, Paul Johnson

Nimitz, E. B. Potter

On War, Carl von Clausewitz

Out of the Crisis, W. Edwards Deming

The Price of Admiralty: The Evolution of Naval Warfare, John Keegan

The Red Badge of Courage, Stephen Crane

The Right Stuff, Tom Wolfe

Sea Power: A Naval History, E. B. Potter

Seapower and Strategy, edited by Colin Gray and Roger Barnett

Two-Ocean War, Samuel E. Morison

Vietnam: A History, Stanley Karnow

War and Remembrance, Herman Wouk

The White House Years, Henry Kissinger

The Winds of War, Herman Wouk

Appendix B: Sample Plan of Action and Milestones (POA&M)

12 Jul 95

From: Commanding Officer, USS DESTROYER (DDG XX)
To: All Officers and Chiefs

Subj: LOGISTICS MANAGEMENT ASSESSMENT

Encl: (1) Supply POA&M
        (2) 3M POA&M

1. DESTROYER will have its first LMA in December 1995. Although it is five months away, it is imperative that we start preparing now. In order to prepare for the inspection, a POA&M has been developed.

2. The best way to approach this task is step by step. The LMA checklist promulgated by COMNAVSURFXXXX is comprehensive. If it's in the checklist, then prepare to be inspected on it. Set the standards for your people and take a steady strain. Every day is an opportunity to prepare for the LMA and prevent crisis managment. We all receive the benefits of good material readiness.

3. Sound operating procedures and a strong training program are key to a successful inspection. We have built a solid foundation, but there is still considerable room for improvement. Let's use this inspection to improve customer service and show the fleet that DESTROYER is a legitimate BLUE E contender. If you have any questions or need assistance, don't hesitate to contact the Supply Officer, Disbursing Officer, or 3M Coordinator.

4. LMA is an all-hands evolution!

    J. P. JONES

USS *DESTROYER* (DDG XX)
LOGISTICS MANAGEMENT ASSESSMENT (LMA)
PLAN OF ACTION AND MILESTONES

DUE DATE	*COG*	*ACTION*
15 Jun 95	Dept Heads	Conduct internal Material Obligation Validation (MOV).
20 Jun 95	Disbo	Distribute LMA checklist to Supply CPOs.
30 Jun 95	Disbo	Conduct inventory of ship's store and vending machines.
30 Jun 95	HM1	Conduct sanitation inspection of Supply Department spaces.
08 Jul 95	Supply CPOs	Return LMA checklist to Disbo.
10 Jul 95	Suppo	Submit quarterly Food Service returns.
11 Jul 95	Disbo	Discuss LMA areas of concern with Suppo.
15 Jul 95	Dept Heads	Conduct internal Material Obligation Validation (MOV).
15 Jul 95	HM1	Conduct sanitation inspection of Food Service spaces.
31 Jul 95	Disbo	Conduct inventory of Ship's Store and vending machines.
31 Jul 95	HM1	Conduct sanitation inspection of S-2 and S-3 spaces.
09 Aug 95	Supply CPOs	Inspect all Supply Department spaces for material discrepancies.
15 Aug 95	Dept Heads	Conduct internal Material Obligation Validation (MOV).
15 Aug 95	HM1	Conduct sanitation inspection of Food Service spaces.
22 Aug 95	Disbo	Distribute customer survey forms for Food Service and Ship's Store.
29 Aug 95	Suppo	Plan meeting to discuss LMA procedures and areas of concern with Disbo and Supply CPOs.

31 Aug 95	Disbo	Conduct inventory of Ship's Store and vending machines.
31 Aug 95	HM1	Conduct sanitation inspection of S-2 and S-3 spaces.
12 Sep 95	Suppo	Conduct assessment of Supply Department training programs with Disbo.
12 Sep 95	Disbo	Inspect all Supply Department spaces with LCPOs and LPOs.
15 Sep 95	Dept Heads	Conduct internal Material Obligation Validation (MOV).
15 Sep 95	HM1	Conduct sanitation inspection of Food Service spaces.
19 Sep 95	Disbo	Distribute customer survey forms for Food Service and Ship's Store.
30 Sep 95	Disbo	Conduct end of the accounting period inventory for the Ship's Store and vending machines.
30 Sep 95	HM1	Conduct sanitation inspection of S-2 and S-3 spaces.
05 Oct 95	Suppo	Inspect all Supply Department spaces with Disbo.
10 Oct 95	Suppo	Submit quarterly Food Service returns.
12 Oct 95	Suppo	Conduct wall to wall inventory of GSK and storerooms 3 & 4.
15 Oct 95	Dept Heads	Conduct internal Material Obligation Validation (MOV).
15 Oct 95	Disbo	Submit end of the accounting period Ship's Store returns.
15 Oct 95	HM1	Conduct sanitation inspection of Food Service spaces.
20 Oct 95	Suppo	Conduct assessment of Supply Department training programs with Disbo.
24 Oct 95	Supply CPOs	Complete LMA checklist and develop a discrepancy list with a plan to correct areas of concern.

25 Oct 95	Suppo	Discuss status on Supply Department equipment with Cheng, Auxo, Electo, and Disbo in the Wardroom.
25 Oct 95	Supply CPOs	Provide Suppo with a list of out of commission (OOC) equipment and material discrepancies.
25 Oct 95	Disbo	Distribute customer survey forms for Food Service and Ship's Store.
26 Oct 95	Disbo	Inspect all divisional spaces.
30 Oct 95	Disbo	Conduct inventory of Ship's Store and vending machines.
31 Oct 95	HM1	Conduct sanitation inspection of S-2 and S-3 spaces.
08 Nov 95	Suppo	Conduct Maintenance Assistance Module (MAM) inventory.
10 Nov 95	Suppo MS3 Moore	Conduct wall to wall inventory of Food Service storerooms.
15 Nov 95	Dept Heads	Conduct internal Material Obligation Validation (MOV).
16 Nov 95	HM1	Conduct sanitation inspection of food service spaces.
21 Nov 95	Supply CPOs	Provide Suppo with a list of out of commission (OOC) equipment and material discrepancies.
21 Nov 95	Supply CPOs	Complete LMA checklist and develop a discrepancy list with a plan to correct areas of concern.
21 Nov 95	Disbo	Distribute customer survey forms for Food Service and Ship's Store.
22 Nov 95	Suppo	Discuss status on Supply Dept equipment with Cheng, Auxo, Electo, and Disbo in the Wardroom.
23 Nov 95	HM1	Conduct sanitation inspection of Food Service spaces.
29 Nov 95	Disbo SHC	Take retained Ship's Store returns to NEXCOM for review.

30 Nov 95	Disbo	Conduct inventory of Ship's Store and vending machines.
30 Nov 95	HM1	Conduct sanitation inspection of S-2 and S-3 spaces.
05 Dec 95	Disbo	Conduct wall to wall inventory of the bulk storeroom.
06 Dec 95	Supply CPOs	Field day all Supply Dept spaces.
06 Dec 95	Suppo	Obtain LMA Inspection Team roster.
07 Dec 95	HM1	Conduct sanitation inspection of all Supply Department spaces.
08 Dec 95	Disbo	Submit welcome aboard package to suppo, XO, and CO.
08 Dec 95	Suppo	Inspect all Supply Department spaces with Disbo and Supply CPOs.
09 Dec 95	Disbo	Conduct price line inventory in the ship's store.
09 Dec 95	1st LT	Make RSG parking signs.
11 Dec 95	1st LT	Place RSG parking signs on the pier.
12 Dec 95	Suppo	Welcome aboard meeting in the Wardroom with CO, XO, Suppo, Disbo, Supply CPOs/LPOs, Cheng, ENC, and EMC.

Appendix C: Personnel Administration Reference Index

FIRST AID TRAINING	MILPERSMAN	6610160
FITNESS REPORTS	MILPERSMAN	3410100
	MILPERSMAN	3410115
	BUPERSINST	1611.17
FLEET RESERVE		
Applications for transfer to	MILPERSMAN	3855180
Active service required for	MILPERSMAN	3855180
Release from active duty	MILPERSMAN	3855240
Physical examinations	MILPERSMAN	3855260
	MILPERSMAN	3860160
Material available to members	MILPERSMAN	6220120
Preseparation ceremony	MILPERSMAN	3810200
Retainer pay	MILPERSMAN	2630100
Separation Leave	MILPERSMAN	3020250
Travel or residence outside CONUS	MILPERSMAN	3855280
FLEET TRAINING ASSESSMENT		
PROGRAM (FLETAP)	CINCLANTFLTINST	1541.4
	CINCPACFLTINST	1541.4
FLIGHT PAY	MILPERSMAN	2620150
	MILPERSMAN	2620300
FLIGHT TRAINING	MILPERSMAN	1820240
	MILPERSMAN	2620300
FOOD MANAGEMENT TEAM PROGRAM	ENLTRANSMAN	9.05
FOREIGN LEAVE TRAVEL	MILPERSMAN	1810280
	MILPERSMAN	3020520
FOREIGN SHORE DUTY	MILPERSMAN	1810580
	MILPERSMAN	1820180
	MILPERSMAN	2620110
	ENLTRANSMAN	4
	*NAVPERS	15980
FRATERNIZATION	OPNAVINST	5370.2A
FREEDOM OF INFORMATION ACT (FOIA)	SECNAVINST	5720.42E
FROCKING POLICY	MILPERSMAN	2230130
FULLY FUNDED GRADUATE EDUCATION		
PROGRAMS (OFFICERS)	OPNAVNOTE	1520
FUND RAISING	SECNAVINST	5340.2C
GARNISHMENT OF MILITARY PAY	MILPERSMAN	6210140
For child support / alimony	MILPERSMAN	6210120
GENERAL EDUCATION DEVELOPMENT	MILPERSMAN	5030280
GENERAL MILITARY TRAINING (GMT)	OPNAVINST	1500.22D
GENEVA CONVENTION CARD	MILPERSMAN	4620100
GI BILL - Vietnam Era	CNETINST	1560.3D
	*NAVPERS	15878
GI BILL - of 1984	OPNAVINST	1780.3
GIFTS	SECNAVINST	4001.2F
GOOD CONDUCT MEDAL	SECNAVINST	1650.1F
Required marks for	MILPERSMAN	3410150
Graduate Education	OPNAVINST	1520.23B
	OPNAVNOTE	1520
GRADUATE EDUCATION (OFFICER)	OPNAVINST	1520.23B
	OPNAVNOTE	1520
GUARANTEED ASSIGNMENT RETENTION		
DETAILING (GUARD) III PROGRAM	ENLTRANSMAN	8.01
	*NAVPERS	15878

Appendix D: Division in the Spotlight Instruction

USS SHIP *(DDG XX) INSTRUCTION 4790.1A*

Subj: COMMAND QUALITY PROGRAM

Ref: (a) U.S. Navy Regulations, 1973
      (b) OPNAVINST 3120.23B
      (c) SHIPINST 3120
      (d) OPNAVINST 4790.4B

Encl: (1) Standard Divisional Quality Agenda
      (2) Divisional Quality Program

1. *Purpose.* To promulgate procedures for the conduct of the Commanding Officer's Divisional Quality Program.

2. *Background.* References (a) through (d) and other directives require the conduct of various regular assessments within each ship including zone inspections, personnel inspections, 3M inspections, etc. This instruction provides the procedures for integrating many different required assessments into a single, CO's quality review process with the twin objectives of:

    a. Simplifying the assessment program, and

    b. Improving the value of such a quality review by focusing them on one division at a time.

3. *Policy.* The Command Quality Program is the principal assessment and quality process review program conducted within the ship. Elements of the program include:

    a. The conduct of a Commanding Officer's Zone and Personnel Inspection with each division.

Note: Two divisions may be reviewed together if their size and interrelationship make that appropriate. Conversely, a very large division may, when necessary, be reviewed in two increments.

b. The assessment of selected aspects of the division's operations in (3M, PQS, CSMP, etc.) will occur in the week designated by specially designated officers, chief petty officers, or petty officers from the command quality team.

c. The conduct, on the day of the quality review and following the zone inspection, of a quality review conference to SHIP-INST 4790.1A review all other pertinent aspects of the division's operations, to receive the critiques of the various separate inspectors, and to evaluate (and redirect as necessary) the division's managers up through the department head and down through the senior E5 level.

d. Follow up by the normal processes of the chain of command, and for material discrepancies, by use of the SFWL/CSMP to document maintenance tasks and scheduling.

e. The meeting of the Command Quality Team and Divisional Quality Team to process suggestions and ideas for improvement.

3. *Procedure and Responsibilities.* Enclosure (1) provides an outline checklist for the conduct of each Commanding Officer's Divisional Quality Review. In addition to the use of that guide:

a. The Executive Officer will designate individuals to conduct the various component reviews and to join the review party for the critique. Because those duties are normally consistent with the individual regular responsibilities, such designations will be informally promulgated.

b. The Executive Officer will promulgate, through the Planning Board for Training, both a cycle schedule (update as necessary to keep the division informed of the week during which their next inspection is scheduled, and the detailed schedule (through the Plan of the Week/Day) as required.

c. In connection with the development of each new quarter's scheduled, the Executive Officer will promulgate any special areas of interest to be examined during that inspection cycle (this provision will allow the command to evaluate any particular area of the ship's operations and thus efficiently prepare for forthcoming inspections or special evolutions).

d. Once the above scheduling is complete, it is incumbent upon the division officer, his or her chain of command, and the designated inspecting individuals to automatically prepare for the conduct of the assessment.

e. The Executive Officer, or her or his designated representative, will maintain a file (enclosure (2)) of such notes as are necessary to ensure that problems and/or the guidance of the prior inspection will be reviewed during the current inspection. The current and previous assessments will be retained.

4. *Informality and Effectiveness.* It is very important to recognize that, with the exception of the zone inspection of the space, which is to be thoroughly cleaned and formally presented, and the 3M inspection, which is to rigorously apply applicable inspection checklists, these inspections are the most effective when kept informal and used as "working" quality reviews. This review procedure is designed to smoothly integrate with the daily management of each work center. The guidelines of this instruction and the enclosure (1) agenda are thus to be used with flexibility and with common sense liberally applied. To that end, suggestions for improvement of the process are always welcome.

J. CAPTAIN

Distribution: (SHIPINST 5216.1)

List I (Case A)

CO'S QUARTERLY DIVISION INSPECTION AGENDA

DIVISION: _____   DIVISION OFFICER: _____

INSPECTION DATE: _____

1 to 4 days prior to the formal review the following areas will be reviewed.

3M	PQS
PQS	PQS
TNG	Training
M&B	Messing and Berthing
ADP	ADP Review
DC	Damage Control
SUP	Supply
VM	Valve Maintenance
SEC	Security
MED	Medical
HAZ	Hazmat
GPETE	Test Equipment
SAF	Safety
RET	Retention
ADMIN	Administration
NS	Noise Survey
QA	Quality Assurance

On the day of review (normally $3\frac{1}{2}$ hours max, in the morning):

0745   CO Personnel Inspection (uniform to be determined)

0805   Party assemble in CO's Cabin

0810   Party review inspection plans/assignments. Comex (division to provide flashlight, clean rags and lead party on preplanned route). COG CPO/DO will be present.

TBD   Party concludes zone inspection. Begin conference in the Wardroom. The XO, DH, and senior W/C POs join at this point.

Enclosure (1)

CONFERENCE AGENDA

_____ PMS
_____ PQS
_____ TRAINING
_____ M & B
_____ ADP
_____ DAMAGE CONTROL
_____ SUPPLY
_____ VALVE MAINTENANCE
_____ SECURITY
_____ MEDICAL
_____ HAZMAT
_____ GPETE
_____ SAFETY
_____ RETENTION
_____ ADMIN
_____ QA
_____ NOISE SURVEY
_____ MATERIAL
_____ PERSONNEL APPEARANCE
_____ MANAGEMENT EFFECTIVENESS
_____ CO'S GENERAL APPRAISAL
_____ NEGOTIATED ADJUSTMENT OF DIVISIONAL PLAN

DIVISIONAL QUALITY PROGRAM

DIVISION: _____   DIVO: _____   DATE: _____

Event	Action Personnel	Results
Personnel Inspection	CO	
Zone Inspection	CO	

3M/PMS	CO/3MC
Training	XO/TRAINING OFFICER
M&B	XO
ADP	ADP COORDINATOR
DC	DCA
SUPPLY	SUPPLY DEPT.
VALVE MAINTENANCE	AUX OFFICER
SECURITY	SECURITY MANAGER
QA	ENGINEER
MEDICAL	MEDICAL
HAZMAT	HAZMAT COORDINATOR
GPETE	EMO
SAFETY	SAFETY OFFICER
RETENTION	NC
ADMIN	YN/PN
NOISE SURVEY	ASWO

Index

The **Naval Institute Press** is the book-publishing arm of the U.S. Naval Institute, a private, nonprofit society for sea service professionals and others who share an interest in naval and maritime affairs. Established in 1873 at the U.S. Naval Academy in Annapolis, Maryland, where its offices remain, today the Naval Institute has more than 100,000 members worldwide.

Members of the Naval Institute receive the influential monthly magazine *Proceedings* and discounts on fine nautical prints, ship and aircraft photos, and subscriptions to the bimonthly *Naval History* magazine. They also have access to the transcripts of the Institute's Oral History Program and get discounted admission to any of the Institute-sponsored seminars offered around the country.

The Naval Institute's book-publishing program, begun in 1898 with basic guides to naval practices, has broadened its scope in recent years to include books of more general interest. Now the Naval Institute Press publishes more than seventy titles each year, ranging from how-to books on boating and navigation to battle histories, biographies, ship and aircraft guides, and novels. Institute members receive discounts on the Press's nearly 400 books in print.

Full-time students are eligible for special half-price membership rates. Life memberships are also available.

For a free catalog describing Naval Institute Press books currently available, and for further information about U.S. Naval Institute membership, please write to:

Membership & Communications Department
U.S. Naval Institute
118 Maryland Avenue
Annapolis, Maryland 21402-5035

Or call, toll-free, (800) 233-USNI.